W9-ADX-029

BETRAYAL IN THE PHILIPPINES

BETRAYAL IN THE PHILIPPINES

By

HERNANDO J. ABAYA

With an introduction by
Harold L. Ickes

New York
A · A · WYN, Inc.
1 9 4 6

Printed in the United States of America
American Book–Stratford Press, Inc., New York

To my Friends
of the
FREE PHILIPPINES
RESISTANCE UNIT

Introduction

On last July 4, there was held in Manila one of the truly historic ceremonies of all times: the granting of independence to the Philippine Republic. It was the sort of act that makes one proud to be an American, this voluntary giving up of a territory and the granting to it of complete sovereignty. It was an occasion of great moment to us as a nation, as well as of incalculable concern to the thousands who observed it to determine the nature of the independence that we were granting. We gave the Philippines political freedom to enter the world family of nations, but did we give them internal political liberty? More important still, did we grant them economic freedom? Will the people of the Philippines find it necessary to fight for their civil rights, as did our ancestors, in order to give substance to the shell of freedom that we have bestowed?

In *Betrayal in the Philippines*, Hernando Abaya has given the reader many important facts that he should know. Other facts will doubtless evolve from subsequent events. The book will raise the question whether the freedom that we gave really redeemed our pledge to the Philippines, or whether, in effect, it is a mockery. It raises the question of our own "iron curtain," which has kept from us the realities of American political and economic machinations in the Philippines. It creates an awareness of the danger of continued official support in Washington of the demagogues and the grasping economic overlords in the Philippines whom, either knowingly or unknowingly, the United States has elevated to the control of this new nation, in disregard of every democratic principle.

The American intent was praiseworthy. Never did we falter in our determined effort to free the Filipino people from the Japanese invader. We had already proposed to give a loyal and fearless people independence of the American variety, democracy in the American image. We envisaged in our minds the right, under the Filipino flag, of every citizen of that country to enjoy freedom and equal opportunity under the law in the first Christian republic in the Far East. If these privileges were not inherent in the freedom and independence that we gave, then the United States has not carried out its intent. And if the United States is at fault, it is largely because our people were either uninformed, or misinformed in vital particulars regarding circumstances and events in the Philippines.

The collaborationists who held office under the Japanese during their occupation and who would have ruled the Philippines in the event of a Japanese victory are in power there now despite an overwhelming American military success. These men who are in power are there with the knowledge, and at least the passive consent, of American civil and military representatives.

As Secretary of the Interior of the United States, I was charged with certain responsibilities with respect to the Philippine Islands. After the fall of Bataan, the powers of the American High Commissioner to the Philippines were transferred to me by a special mandate of President Roosevelt. When the frail President Quezon came to Washington to establish his government-in-exile, I worked with him, as I did later with his patriotic and loyal successor, President Osmeña. I made the problems of the Philippines my problems. I shared President Osmeña's happiness when America had recaptured the Islands.

General MacArthur immediately requested the return of President Osmeña, with the stipulation that he was to go back alone, without an American High Commissioner. I firmly counseled Osmeña against this, knowing that he would need the help of someone who could make official representations directly to the President and have them received with respect. But the desire to be with his people overwhelmed him and Osmeña returned, on MacArthur's terms. In doing so, he defeated himself for re-election as President of the Philippines. When he later returned to the United States to consult his physician, I did not have to be told that my predictions had materialized. MacArthur thwarted and dominated Osmeña from the first, often by indirection, but always according to his own inclinations.

MacArthur promptly set free the collaborationist Roxas and proceeded to cover his collaborationist activities with a thick coat of whitewash. Without benefit of civil investigation into Roxas' relationship with the Japanese, he "liberated" him from detention with the other members of the puppet government. This official blessing did not go unnoticed.

Subsequently, President Truman appointed Paul V. McNutt as High Commissioner, a capacity in which he had served before the war. Since Mr. McNutt had served well as High Commissioner previously, when there was peace in the Philippines and he comported himself as the representative of his government, I did not oppose the appointment. I became disturbed later, however, when the High Commissioner, too, indicated that he was in Roxas' corner. Once he even defended Roxas' collaborationist activities, insisting that he had known Roxas intimately, that Roxas was both a gentleman and a friend and definitely not a collaborationist. After all, said McNutt, "collaboration is a matter of the heart." Of course, it goes without saying that unless a man's heart were in it he could not be a collaborationist. This must have been true of Norway's Quisling and the other European traitors who, after legal conviction, went before firing squads instead of being made chiefs of state.

Osmeña, having returned to the Philippines, selected a cabinet from which he had endeavored to exclude collaborationists. MacArthur's haste to reinstitute civil government in the Islands meant that all collaborationist senators would have to be permitted to assume their offices, or there would not be a sufficient number to conduct legislative business. Roxas dominated this senate and naturally he and his fellow collaborationists refused to confirm the Osmeña cabinet, with the result that Osmeña was forced, if he was to have any cabinet at all, to choose one satisfactory to Roxas and his henchmen.

In keeping with the policy laid down by President Truman and the even stronger demand of his predecessor, President Roosevelt, Osmeña set up the People's Court to try collaborationist suspects. The Attorney General of the United States sent an investigator to the Philippines to look into the situation. After a careful study, this man, Mr. Walter Hutchinson, filed a detailed report which has since lain buried in the files of the Justice Department. Its recommendations were never carried out, or even made public. And, while President Truman stepped with determination on the soft pedal, High Commissioner McNutt announced to the world that economic relief would be given to the Philippines, irrespective of who should be elected president. This was justly interpreted as an official smile in the direction of Roxas. Neither did this go unobserved by those most deeply concerned.

Agitate the kaleidoscope that is the political situation in the Philippines as you will and certain central figures will appear: Roxas, the collaborationist, in the uniform of a Brigadier General of the United States Army, but a supporter of the Philippine puppet government's declaration of war against the United States, and newly elected president; General MacArthur, Roxas' friend and apologist; Joaquin M. Elizalde, rich and economically hungry new Ambassador to the United States; Colonel Andres Soriano, Philippine tower of strength for Spain's General Franco and recipient of the Grand Cross of Naval Merit from Franco; High Commissioner Paul V. McNutt, Senator Millard E. Tydings, Congressman C. Jasper Bell, and others.

The integrity of men is to be measured by their conduct, not by their professions. Some of the acts of these men are revealed in this book and the careful reader will give them proper consideration.

And when he has turned the last page of this book, he will have little doubt that troubled days are coming in the Philippines and for the United States to which the Philippine Republic is bound both by sentiment and by indissoluble economic ties. In fact, as this is written, there already is serious unrest in the Philippines with armed soldiers at the point of guns insisting upon imposing both political and economic tyranny upon the people who, with the hope of liberty sustaining them, kept up the fight against the Japanese relentlessly while Roxas lived in safety and comfort under Japanese protection in Manila.

The Filipino people love freedom, the kind that they learned about at the knee of a kindly and friendly United States. They have wanted political and economic liberty. They will continue to insist upon it. They will struggle for it until it is theirs. Since we have failed to give it, they will seek it in their own way. And it would be a great crime against our own past and a cynical sacrifice of our professed ideals if we should permit ourselves to become an oppressor of a people in the Far Pacific who have sanctified their passion for freedom by fighting and dying for it.

HAROLD L. ICKES

FOREWORD

WHEN THE FIRST Japanese bombs fell in Manila in December 1941, I knew I had a job to do. Here was the biggest story I could cover in my career as a newspaperman. I took notes. Day after day, I kept a record of personalities, of events, of incidents, of bits of conversation, of an odd assortment of scraps of information about people, about our new masters. When night came, I always went out to listen on the bootleg radio, at this or that friend's house. Later on, I was to acquire my own; then it was a question of lying low and passing the news to the men who kept up the struggle while the quislings wined and dined with the enemy. Short-wave news kept my friends and myself going week after week throughout those dark three years.

Of course, there was underground work, but of that none of us talk now, because even the quislings claim they were guerrillas, our spiritual leaders no less. But that is beside the point. The Japanese came. Our quislings bowed low and welcomed them with open arms. The people held the torch of freedom high. They resisted silently, determinedly, heroically. The quislings, the men who had been the chosen leaders of the people they betrayed, sold out. Then the Americans returned and the quislings were the first to jump onto the bandwagon and welcome, with tears, the liberating forces they had damned for making the Philippines a battleground a second time. And today many of them are back in power again, making a determined bid to gain control of the state, to strangle the people politically and economically, and to keep them

chained to a feudalistic existence. Behind the quislings
are the forces of native and foreign reaction.

America has had its quislings, "those few timid, craven
and opportunistic helots who basely collaborated with the
cruel enemy who sought to enslave their people." This is
their story.

H. J. A.

CONTENTS

BETRAYAL IN THE PHILIPPINES

I BETRAYAL IN MALACAÑAN

December 11, 1941

FOUR DAYS AFTER Pearl Harbor a distinguished group
huddled outside the Malacañan Palace office of Quezon's
secretary, Jorge B. Vargas, later chairman of the puppet
Philippine Executive Commission. The siren had just
wailed an alert. Jap planes were overhead. Minutes
passed. Then came the faint, distant rumble of exploding
bombs. In the silence, the familiar voice of Jose P. Laurel,
president-to-be of the puppet Philippine Republic, challenged attention. "It seems we are really at the mercy of
the Japanese." His grin suggested a sneer. "We have no
chance." He said this with finality. Vargas gave Laurel a
quick look, then turned away and went into his office. The
group were silent. Then the all clear signal and they dispersed.

The Filipino puppets were smart; they went far with
the Japs. What they said on the record was bad enough;
what they said and did off the record worse. The sum total
of their work puts them in a class with the masters: Laval,
Pétain, *et al.*

Their line was this: We are neither pro-American nor
pro-Japanese. We are pro-Filipino. Sophistry, but they
kept monotonously repeating it. The line had a familiar
ring. Georges Bonnet, architect of French puppetry,
neatly phrased it in this way:

After all, why shouldn't there be German agents here
[France]? They represent the interests of their country.
We, on the other hand, represent the interests of France.
If that leads to our having something in common, that is
neither treason nor anything else except *patriotic action!*

The Filipino puppets said they were acting under instructions from Manuel L. Quezon, who had died at
Saranac Lake, New York, August 1, 1944. President Quezon, accompanied by his family and his war cabinet,
including Sergio Osmeña and Manuel Roxas, liaison officer
attached to General MacArthur's staff, left Manila for
Corregidor on Christmas Eve, 1941. The fall of Manila
was imminent.

There was apprehension when Quezon left. Franklin D.
Roosevelt's pledge, broadcast to the Filipino people on
December 28, 1941, failed to dispel the heavy feeling of
hopelessness and despair.

I give to the people of the Philippines [said the Presi-
dent] my solemn pledge that *their freedom will be
redeemed* [1] and their independence established and protected. The entire resources, in men and in material, of
the United States stand behind that pledge. It is not for
me or for the people of this country to tell you where your
duty lies. We are engaged in a great and common cause.
I count on every Philippine man, woman, and child to do
his duty. We will do ours.

Our freedom would be *redeemed!* This meant the battle
of the Philippines was already lost. The Filipinos could
only hope and pray, even as the enemy was methodically
consolidating his conquest, that the day of redemption
would come soon!

From Corregidor, Quezon wrote a note to Vargas, De-

[1] Italics supplied

cember 30, 1941, in which he gave his reactions to Roosevelt's message:

Jorge, after listening to the President's proclamation I have felt a tremendous sense of relief. I must confess that I have had days of anguish, such as I have never had in my life. When I saw our people standing by America to a man, and then saw our cities bombed and our defenseless men, women and children actually murdered from the air, I was distressed beyond description, and *almost* wondered whether I have been right in asking my people to sacrifice their lives and their all. But this proclamation of the President has shown me that I was right, not only because my stand was in line with my sworn duty, but because by this policy I have *secured* and *forever insured* the freedom, independence and well-being of the Filipino people. I do not care what hereafter happens to me, or even my family. We are all ready to be sacrificed, because we know our sacrifice will not be in vain. The Filipino people are saved!

Vargas received two other letters from President Quezon from Corregidor after this, one dated January 1, 1942, sending New Year greetings to Vargas and Jose Yulo and the other asking Vargas to see that his horses were well taken care of. Yulo was elected senator in 1941 and was Chief Justice of the Supreme Court under the puppet regime.

The tunnel life in Corregidor was too much for President Quezon's health and he decided to go to one of the southern islands and await developments. On the night of February 20 he and his party left Corregidor by submarine, stopping at Iloilo before proceeding to Negros and later to Mindanao. Vargas got word from Quezon that he would be in Negros until March 12. Some time in April, the presidential party flew by bomber to Australia and from there proceeded to San Francisco and thence to Washington.

Over KGEI, from San Francisco, Quezon broadcast a message to the Filipino people May 9:

> Our nation will not for long remain in bondage. The American forces will redeem their pledge. Led by their able general, they will rescue the Philippines. Stand firm for your freedom is not lost. The United States through its great President, Franklin D. Roosevelt, has pledged not only her armed might but also the total redemption of our land. I am here to work for the fulfillment of that pledge within the earliest possible time.

In President Quezon's party were his wife and three children, Vice-President Osmeña, Major General Basilio Valdes, Secretary of National Defense, Colonel Andres Soriano, Secretary of Finance, and Colonel Manuel Nieto.

Two members of the original party who went to Corregidor on Christmas Eve were left behind. One was Manuel Roxas, who remained on the "Rock" to act as the representative of the commonwealth there; the other was Chief Justice Jose Abad Santos, left in Cebu by his own wish, as acting head of the commonwealth government in the unoccupied areas.

The people conceded these men good faith.

To Quezon, on February 28, the men he left behind sent this wire:

> IN VIEW OF THE ENORMOUS TOLL IN LIVES AND PROPERTY NOW EXACTED OF OUR PEOPLE AND BECAUSE OF THE IMMI-NENCE OF FURTHER UNTOLD SUFFERING AMONG THE ENTIRE POPULATION AND AS IT IS EVIDENT THAT FURTHER RESISTANCE IN THE PHILIPPINES WILL BE FUTILE BECAUSE OF THE PRESENT SUPREMACY OF JAPAN IN THE FAR EAST, WE BELIEVE THAT THE TIME HAS COME FOR YOU TO CONSIDER THE ADVISABILITY

OF TAKING THE NECESSARY STEPS TO BRING ABOUT THE IMME-
DIATE CESSATION OF HOSTILITIES IN THE PHILIPPINES STOP IN
VIEW THEREOF WE ARE ALSO SENDING THE FOLLOWING TELE-
GRAM TO PRESIDENT ROOSEVELT:

WE THE UNDERSIGNED LEADING OFFICIALS OF THE NEWLY
ESTABLISHED CIVIL ADMINISTRATION OF THE PHILIPPINES BEG
LEAVE TO EXPRESS OUR DESIRE FOR THE RE-ESTABLISHMENT
OF PEACE IN THE COUNTRY AND EARNESTLY REQUEST YOU TO
CONSIDER THE ADVISABILITY OF ORDERING THE IMMEDIATE
CESSATION OF HOSTILITIES IN THE PHILIPPINES STOP WE BE-
LIEVE THAT IN VIEW OF THE TREND OF EVENTS FURTHER RE-
SISTANCE IN THE PHILIPPINES WILL MEAN MORE DESTRUCTION
OF LIVES NOT ONLY OF SOLDIERS BUT ALSO OF CIVILIAN NON-
COMBATANTS LIVING IN AND AROUND THE FIELDS OF BATTLE
STOP WE ARE CO-OPERATING WITH THE JAPANESE FORCES IN
THE RE-ESTABLISHMENT OF CIVIL GOVERNMENT ON THE
PROMISE BY THE JAPANESE GOVERNMENT TO GRANT THE FILI-
PINO PEOPLE THEIR INDEPENDENCE WITH HONOR STOP WE
HAVE TAKEN THIS STEP WITH THE AIM IN VIEW OF INSURING
AND REALIZING OUR ASPIRATION FOR OUR EARLY INDEPEND-
ENCE.

The telegrams to Roosevelt and Quezon were signed
by Jorge B. Vargas, Jose P. Laurel, Benigno S. Aquino,
Quintin Parades, Jose Yulo, Rafael R. Alunan, Teofilo
Sison, Claro M. Recto, and Antonio de las Alas.

And even as they were drafting this sell-out to the
enemy, the rumble of guns could be heard from Bataan,
grim reminder that Filipinos and Americans were still
bitterly fighting against the enemy, shedding their blood
to uphold Filipino honor.

While still "Somewhere in the Philippines," Quezon had
broadcast an appeal to his people:

I urge all Filipinos to be of good cheer, to have faith in
the patriotism and valor of our soldiers in the battlefield,

but, above all, to trust America and our great President,
Franklin D. Roosevelt. The United Nations will win this
war. America is too strong and too powerful to be van-
quished in this conflict. I know she will not fail us.

And from Corregidor, "The Voice of Freedom" warned:

It is inevitable that we may have to yield to the Japanese in the occupied areas, but it is inexcusable for some
of us to go out of our way to lick the boots of the hated
invader. You are not children. You know the gravity of
your crime against our cause. It is sufficient for us to say
that when we render judgment, we shall be as stern and
ruthless as you have been traitorous and disloyal. Our soldiers in Corregidor and Bataan will be the ones to mete
punishment.

The puppets merely shrugged. They said they were
ordered by Quezon to play ball with the invader.

Bataan fell on April 9, 1942. The fate of Corregidor was
sealed. The mighty Rock bowed to the enemy on May 6th.

Organized resistance ceased elsewhere in the Philippines shortly afterward. The Jap was the new master and
the puppets proceeded to receive him in proper style.
After all, he might not be as rude as he was pictured to be.
He might even condescend to clink cocktail glasses with
them. Perhaps they might be allowed to keep *some* of
their privileges. At any rate, they had nothing to lose.

Besides, the enemy was offering "freedom."

On January 17, 1942, the Jap-sponsored *Manila Tribune*
screamed:

TOJO PROMISES FREEDOM IN 1943!

Vargas asked newsmen that day how the public reacted
to Tojo's promise and, getting little encouragement, spoke
his mind: "To me, it matters little. Let independence come
in any form! We will co-operate!"

Malacañan continued to dance to the music. "The Harmony Boys" toed the line. Collaboration became the theme song of bureaucracy and privilege.

From Corregidor, the Voice of Freedom reminded the people on February 2, 1942:

> Japan has broken every promise she has made. How can she keep her promise of giving the Philippines independence when even now Japanese are overrunning our country, which she claims she will liberate?

From Washington, President Roosevelt broadcast to the Filipino people:

> Japan has brought only misery and slavery to countries whose independence she has guaranteed. You have seen it happen in Korea, Manchuria, China. The only independence she knows and can give is the independence of death. She will use every weapon and every trick to accomplish her aims.
>
> Just as you, brave people of the Philippines, have fought valiantly against the enemy, so now you must steel yourself against Japanese deception. I repeat my solemn pledge to you. Your freedom will be redeemed and your independence will be established and protected. The entire resources, in men and material, of the United States stand behind that pledge.

Writing for Domei in the *Osaka Mainichi* on the anniversary of the outbreak of "The Greater East Asia War" on December 8, 1943, Jorge Vargas reminisced:

> Responsible as I was for the safety of the lives and property of the citizens of Manila, I faced the impending entrance of the Japanese Imperial Forces with uneasiness and trepidation because American propaganda had led us

to expect abuses and excesses from the army of occupation, and we felt that the USAFFE had abandoned us to
a cruel and bitter fate.

I believe that my high esteem for the Japanese, which I
entertained long before the war, was completely justified
by the irreproachable conduct of the Imperial Japanese
Forces which entered the city of Manila during the first
days of January. My belief in Japanese nobility and honor
has been further strengthened by the benign policies
which have been followed subsequently. As I have said
time and again, the Imperial Japanese Forces came to us,
not as enemies, but as a liberating army of fellow Orientals.

The puppets played their parts with abandon. They got
along with their Jap masters so well that, on July 1, 1943,
Vargas could remind Jitaro Kihara, Jap adviser and liaison
man at Malacañan, of bonuses for the quisling cabinet.
Kihara sent this "strictly confidential" memo to Vargas:

> In accordance with your request the other day, I had a
> talk with Colonel Utonomiya [director of general affairs,
> Japanese Military Administration] about half-year bonuses
> for Commissioners. He will consult with Military Admin-
> istration.

Here were the patriots, getting all the privileges due
their rank, including an ample supply of prime commodities at controlled prices delivered at their back doors, those
men who professed to work only for the best interests of
the people, stooping so low as to ask for bonuses for themselves, forgetting the small man and thinking only of self.

In the Japanese city of Nara, the puppet Laurel was
interviewed on September 7, 1945, by a Filipino war correspondent, shortly before he was arrested by the United
States Army Counter Intelligence Corps. He justified his

collaboration on the ground that he was working under "a power of attorney" from Quezon.

Three days before this, Jose Abad Santos, Jr., related to a correspondent in Tokyo the circumstances of his father's execution by the Japanese on May 7, 1942, because of his refusal to collaborate.

Jose Abad Santos, Chief Justice of the Philippine Supreme Court, was given the choice by President Quezon of going with him to Australia or staying in the Philippines. Abad Santos preferred to stay and the president appointed him acting head of the commonwealth government in the Philippines.

The Japs captured Abad Santos and his son in Cebu. He was ordered to turn over to them his papers and instructions from President Quezon as the price for his life. He refused.

"I would be a traitor to my country if I did that," he said.

The Japs took Abad Santos to Malabang, in Mindanao. They told him they would shoot him for his refusal to collaborate. The jurist's son, who was with him in the cell, broke into uncontrolled weeping, but the jurist calmed him and smilingly said:

"This is a rare chance, Pepito. Not everyone is given the opportunity to die for his country."

Jose Abad Santos, the man Quezon left to run the Philippine government in the unoccupied areas in 1942, paid with his life because he refused to submit to the Jap invader.

He had Quezon's instructions. He remained steadfastly loyal to his country. He refused to collaborate. The Japs shot him.

"President Quezon," said Sergio Osmeña on August 2, 1945, the first anniversary of his death, "would have preferred death to service under the hated enemy."

The *Nippon Times* of January 13, 1945, in an editorial entitled FILIPINO PATRIOTISM declared:

> The voluntary action taken by these Filipinos to collaborate with the Japanese forces in the Philippines is, indeed, a damning refutation of the claims of the United States that she has come at last to "free" the Philippines. It has become manifest that the true liberator of their country is Japan and that there can be no real independence under the United States.

It is evident the puppets didn't fool their Jap masters.

Laurel and Vargas: Their Joint Responsibility in the People's Betrayal

In late 1945, Roy Howard reported that the late Manuel L. Quezon told him at Miami in March 1944, that the men he left behind were *loyal* and were acting *under instructions* from him.

The collaborationist *Manila Post*, on December 4, 1945, took up the Howard "revelation" with a banner headline: QUEZON ABSOLVES "PUPPETS."

Two days later, Joaquin M. Elizalde, ex-Philippine Resident Commissioner in Washington, said to Manila Rotarians that Quezon had always told him that he had faith in the leaders that stayed behind and that he was confident they would do their best to carry on the government.

Taking the joint testimonies of Howard and Elizalde on the loyalty of the puppets as a yardstick, let us consider the roles of Jorge B. Vargas, Quezon's secretary, and Jose P. Laurel, Quezon's adviser, who respectively headed the Jap-sponsored Philippine Executive Commission and, after "independence with honor," the Philippine "Republic."

Laurel's collaboration with the Japs was no mere flirta-

tion. Japan was Laurel's first love. He had always admired
the Japs. He sent a son to a Jap military school. This son,
Jose Laurel III, was a USAFFE captain and in December
1941 was assigned to the Mauban sector (where the Japs
made large-scale landings). He was "captured" by the
Japs. Shortly after the occupation of Manila on January 2,
however, he turned up on the society page of the *Manila
Tribune* as a bridegroom.

After his inauguration as puppet president in October
1943, Laurel sent another son to Japan as a Filipino *pen-
sionado*. In the same group, incidentally, were two sons of
Vargas and the sons and kin of other puppets. To the practical Japs, this was a demonstration of good faith.

The student of history will understand the roles of Vargas and Laurel better if he considers their actions not as
separate subjective acts done on the impulse of the moment, but as a series of correlated acts with one objective
in mind: to remain in the good graces of the Japs by keeping the "misguided" at bay, while satisfying the people's
minimum demands and, of course, what was to them most
important, holding onto and enjoying their privileges.

On July 15, 1943, the Jap Military Administration sent
an order to TVT newspapers (the big Alejandro Roces
chain before the war) to "play down Vargas" and to "play
up Laurel."

This was not without repercussions. Tojo was visiting
Manila a second time when Vargas wanted to give him a
present. Kihara, Vargas' Rasputin, said no. "It's Laurel's
turn *now*." (Kihara was on intimate terms with Laurel
and his family.) At the same time, he started poking into
Vargas' private life and otherwise made it patently clear
that Vargas was out and Laurel was in.

Still, Vargas carried on. He was solicitous of Laurel's

health. Laurel, on the other hand, had only contempt for
Vargas. In a talk with Jap and Filipino newspapermen on
July 15, 1943, he said: "Vargas cannot handle the situa-
tion. If I were given the chance to head the government,
I would place all who opposed me *under the machine
gun.*"

Both Laurel and Vargas went out of their way to serve
the Jap cause of peace with the bayonet. The other puppets, it must be noted, shared this common obsession with
peace and order *at any price.* "Pacification" became their
slogan. The occupied areas were divided into "pacification" areas and the various cabinet members and other
ranking officials were assigned respective "zones."

Returning from a pacification tour which took him to
Negros and Panay Islands, in the company of Jose Yulo,
Vargas told reporters on April 8, 1943: "Capiz [a province
on Panay Island and a center of resistance] is totally hopeless. Not a single official was in office. Provincial and
municipal officials have been taken by guerrillas."

Asked about Tomas Confesor, resistance governor of
Panay and Romblon who defied the Japs and the puppet
regime, Vargas replied: "He is hopeless. Nobody can make
him give up. We will go and get him!"

Under date of April 18, 1943, Vargas wrote to Yulo,
whom he had left behind in Negros on a pacification as-
signment. He stressed the need for keeping "order" and
revealed that he had suggested to General Wati (pronounced Wachi), Jap military administrator, that the
Iloilo constabulary be armed to go after Confesor. The
Japs could do garrison work, Vargas said; the constabulary
could "clean up" the province.

On this trip, Vargas took with him ₱7,000,000 ($3,500,-
000) in Philippine currency, to buy off emergency notes
issued by the Quezon government through the authorized
leaders of the resistance. The amount thus "retrieved" was

insignificant. Reporting to Jap General Tanaka, who "inspected" Malacañan on October 5, 1943, Vargas said:

The possession of these [emergency] notes has a very great psychological effect on their holders and induces them to wish that the Government that authorized their issue should come back. Firmly believing that the present order has come to stay and desiring to remove wishful thinking from the minds of the Filipinos who may still long for the return of the former regime, I am making an exhaustive investigation of the total amount that has been issued and will submit suggestions for dealing with this problem. Possibly, as a measure of relief, those notes that were legally issued and are in the possession of people for services rendered or articles sold may be redeemed by the Central Administrative Organization with reasonable discount, even if we have to secure funds by floating bonds, or by borrowing from the Imperial Japanese Government.

Significantly, this report said, regarding the Filipino flag:

With the surrender of the Fil-American forces in the Philippines, actual warfare was terminated. Fortunately, Japan has never considered the Filipino people as her enemy. I trust that the Military Administration will now give generous consideration of the revocation of the order temporarily prohibiting the use of the Filipino flag. The restoration of this flag would enhance the faith of the Filipino people in Japan and the Imperial Japanese forces and will no doubt make them eternally grateful. *The very sight of this flag alone would inspire them with greater determination, not only to co-operate in the maintenance of peace and order in this country, but also to fight side by side with the Imperial Japanese Forces in the sacred mission of eradicating all Western influences from the Greater East Asia Co-Prosperity Sphere, including those in India and Australia.*[2]

Touching on "illegal activities of USAFFE remnants," Vargas wrote:

A considerable number of remnants of the USAFFE in the provinces who have not taken advantage of the generous act of the Military Administration of giving them an opportunity to enjoy the status of released prisoners of war are still engaged in pernicious activities. This problem can be solved by the military authorities in two ways, either by sending sufficient troops to control the situation in the troubled provinces, or by authorizing the Executive Commission to organize, fully equip, and utilize the Constabulary for this purpose. Fortunately, we have a Commissioner of the Interior [Aquino] who is determined to put an end to all forms of lawlessness and upon whom we can depend for the successful execution of this plan if the Commission is given the necessary authority.

Laurel matched Vargas' ardor. On August 5, 1943, he told Jap and Filipino newsmen in his first interview as chairman of the Preparatory Committee on Philippine Independence [3] (he was still Commissioner of the Interior): "The constabulary will be reorganized and strengthened to compel obedience of unruly elements. The force will be increased as needed to maintain order. *If necessary, the Nippon forces will be requested to extend assistance dur-*

[2] Italics supplied
[3] Members of the Preparatory Committee were Ramon Avancena, Jorge B. Vargas, Teofilo Sison, Claro M. Recto, Jose Yulo, Miguel Unson, Vicente Madrigal, Pedro Sabido, Emiliano T. Tirona, Benigno S. Aquino, Rafael R. Alunan, Antonio de las Alas, Quintin Paredes, Melecio Arranz, Camilo Osias, Manuel C. Briones, Manuel Roxas, Emilio Aguinaldo, Aloya Alonto (Sultan Sa Ramain)

ing the transition period." This interview was published in the *Manila Tribune*.

At the first meeting of the Preparatory Committee on Philippine Independence (which drafted the constitution of the puppet "republic") in his suite at the Philippine General Hospital, where he was recovering from serious wounds from a guerrilla's gun, Laurel announced he was for giving the executive more power. He wanted an "authoritarian" government, a "constitutional dictatorship."

This was the obsession of Laurel the constitutional lawyer, considered one of the most brilliant. Early in 1941, when President Quezon was given extensive authority under the Emergency Powers Act, Laurel, then an associate justice of the Philippine Supreme Court, upheld the act, saying the National Assembly, in granting wide powers to the executive, intended to create a "constitutional dictatorship" in keeping with the trend in the rest of the world, with "totalitarianism gradually supplanting democracy." He told students at the College of Law of the government-financed University of the Philippines that he would accept "a benevolent dictatorship." And, significantly, he cited Japan as an example of "constitutional and benevolent dictatorship."

In point of fact, the constitution of Laurel's puppet "republic" is a rehash of the Japanese constitution and in its drafting Laurel had the unrestrained assistance of two of the seven minds that framed the Constitution of the Philippine Commonwealth: Manuel A. Roxas, Minister without Portfolio, and Claro M. Recto, Laurel's Foreign Minister.

Vargas urged that the "Sakdal" or "Ganap" Party be outlawed in accordance with a military order banning all political groups and authorizing only one government party, the Kalibapi.

Laurel, on the other hand, used this traitorous Sakdal

group as the nucleus of the republic-blessed "Makapili,"[4] whose fanatical members fought with the Japs against the Americans and guerrillas and joined the Jap savages in an orgy of pillage and killing and rape in many sectors of Luzon following the landings of American liberation forces.

Laurel's actions were thoroughly inconsistent, but both stemmed from and were motivated by the same urge: to please the masters.

The Making of a Puppet President

Vargas had had his chance, Kihara told him. He had outlived his usefulness. The Japs had found a new leader for the Filipinos. Laurel's turn had come.

"I am doing what I conscientiously believe is for the best of our people," he told admirers some time in August 1943, while preparations were being rushed for his "election" and his inauguration as "President of the Philippine Republic."

"When I go down to my grave, I can face my Maker and say, 'Lord, I have done my best for my country.'"

And he continued: "My prayers are that the Americans don't come back. If they do, God save us, for our people will again be divided. For us of this generation, the aspiration to make our country great has already disappeared."

On August 11, 1943, hero-worshiping women leaders of the Kalibapi called on Laurel. He addressed them: "It will take two more years to put down Germany; it will take another three years to beat Japan, that is, five years. In the meantime, we must keep peace and order to fore-

[4] The renegade "Sakdalista" or "Ganap" Party of Benigno Ramos, which figured in an abortive uprising in 1931. Ramos was a rabid pro-Jap

stall pestilence and famine. We *must* liquidate all guerrillas."

The women were thrilled. At last the Philippines had a leader! One nation, one leader, one flag!

On September 5, the framers of the puppet constitution affixed their signatures at a rehearsed public ceremony. Two days later the constitution was ratified by the "people," acting through a special Kalibapi convention.

It was then the turn of the puppet National Assembly to accept the constitution in the name of the people. But first, the delegates had to be "elected." The Kalibapi did the trick in no time and on September 25 the newly "elected" National Assembly met and chose Benigno S. Aquino speaker.

The same day, Laurel was "elected" President of the Philippine Republic.

The new leader was interviewed.

REPORTER: What were your feelings upon being elected President of the Republic of the Philippines?

LAUREL: Not having aspired to the position at any time, I was filled with both pride and humility.

The interview appeared in the *Manila Tribune*, September 29, the same day the top puppets, Laurel, Vargas, and Aquino, left for Tokyo, presumably to make final arrangements for the proclamation of "independence with honor."

Before his "election," Laurel sent his son, Jose III, to survey Malacañan Palace to see how the Laurel brood could be spread out into its twenty-four rooms.

Laurel returned from Tokyo after ten days. On October 14, the puppet "republic" was proclaimed and he was inaugurated president. The Filipino flag waved alone from the legislative building. But all over the city the Rising Sun was very much in evidence.

We were given back our flag, but only after we had been deprived of every means of defending it. For five weeks before the inauguration of the "republic," Jap Military Police scoured the city for all firearms and deadly weapons such as "rifles, revolvers, air rifles, toy guns, bullets or ammunition, hand grenades, gas masks, sabers, bolos, *balisongs* [double-edge knives], daggers, bows and arrows, and any other arms which may be the subject of 'misunderstanding.'"

Not even toy guns to defend our flag!

But to trusted hands the carbines and the Thompsons and the hand grenades were being distributed.

Following his inauguration, Laurel threw Malacañan open to "*my people.*" There was the usual round of entertainments. At a luncheon on October 16, he told a known noncollaborator: "The real cake is coming. In the meantime, there is no harm in being satisfied with the cookies. When the Americans come back, I'll hand over the government to them." (Unfortunately, the Japs had him in a cave in Baguio at the time of the Leyte landings!)

From the same mouth came:

I for myself do not want the Americans to come back. One need not be a military strategist to realize that there is no likelihood for America to reconquer the Philippines. Because I like my country to be free, I do not like America to come·back.[5]

On October 30, Laurel, accompanied by his Foreign Minister, Claro M. Recto, and Minister Quintin Paredes of Public Works, left for Tokyo to receive well-deserved decorations from the Son of Heaven. Laurelites and puppet apologists circulated rumors then that the Japs were not satisfied with Laurel for hedging on the question of a war declaration and on conscription.

Actually, their hero was at war, against the guerrillas whom he swore to liquidate. And he had conscripted Fili-

[5] *Manila Tribune,* August 6, 1943

pino labor in the service of the Jap Army he admired so much. By June 1944, he had succeeded, through his Labor Recruiting Agency, in supplying 250,000 laborers to the Jap forces for such "public works" as airfields, runways, and port facilities.

The first months of 1944 saw Laurel wrestling with the problem of food. On January 2, he summoned absentee landowners of Central Luzon to Malacañan and told them: "We have to get rice. If necessary, we must compel the planters to sell to the BIBA [the government-owned Jap-run rice corporation]. We will strengthen the constabulary to keep peace and order and if the constabulary can't do it, *I will ask the Japanese Army to help me.*"

The people planted, but it was the Nips who reaped their harvest. The BIBA was a creation of Laurel to use the Filipinos to corner the rice supply for the Japs.

At this time, Laurel must have been assailed by doubts of his own ability to make the people see the situation the way he saw it. He blew hot and cold, threatened and pleaded for co-operation to keep "peace and order" and bring back "normalcy."

"I am not a puppet," he intoned on December 8, 1943. "This is real independence. I and my government are not working for selfish ends."

On January 9, 1944, he issued a manifesto to the Filipino people:

> This government would be driven to the necessity of utilizing its available armed forces to bring them to reason. Posterity will doubtless pass judgment on my acts, but I will venture to say right now that it will point its accusing finger to those of our countrymen who, blinded by false promises, have refused to understand the true situation and to do their part even when their co-operation was most needed.

Three days before this Laurel had told intimates at Malacañan: "If necessary, we have to sacrifice one third of our people in order to save the other two thirds." It was for this reason that he called on the Nipponese Army on January 25, the end of the amnesty period for all guerrillas to surrender, to open an all-out drive against "disturbers of peace," the guerrillas. Ignoring the amnesty pledge, the Japs had herded guerrillas who trusted Laurel's word to the dungeons of Fort Santiago.

"Zonification" was a ruthless reprisal measure which the Japs took against guerrilla activities. During the months preceding the inauguration of the "republic" people around Manila were concentrated in churches, convents, etc.; then the men were separated from the women and children. The men were passed one by one for identification for underground activities and those thus identified were tortured. Nobody was exempt. Nobody will ever know how many perished.

Here was this hero of the hour setting his new masters against his own people. Laurel compelled subservience to a brutalizing regime that respected no rights but its own, that must exploit and destroy since it could thrive only in chaos.

On April 8, 1944, Manuel Roxas accepted the chairmanship of Laurel's Economic Planning Board. Laurel had at last found a scapegoat for the food problem.

On the afternoon of April 12 Laurel played a foursome at golf at Malacañan Park. With him were General Kuroda, Commander in Chief of the Jap Army in the Philippines; Admiral Oka, Commander in Chief of the Jap Navy in the Philippine Islands; and Ambassador Murata. That night there was a dinner at Malacañan with the same Japs. The week before the new Jap chief of staff, Lieutenant General Harachi Isayama, called on Laurel.

On April 16, 1944, Laurel, in a radio announcement,

offered forty thousand Filipino laborers to assist his Jap friends in building Philippine defenses.

Before his appointment as chairman of the Economic Planning Board, Roxas played golf at the municipal links. Could it have been that, as liberation drew nearer, he wanted to clinch popular support and squelch whatever chances his prospective rivals might have had?

At this time, the price of rice was soaring. The black marketeers, getting their supply from the bodegas of absentee landlords of Central Luzon, held fast to their stocks. Laurel appealed to the people to give up their daily rice rations of 120 grams.

The next day, through the *Manila Tribune*, the "public-spirited" leaders voluntarily relinquished their 120 grams of rice daily. Near the head of the list were Aquino and Camilo Osias. The *Tribune* did not say, however, that the Laurel ministers were getting more rice than they needed direct from the Primco (the distributing agency for prime commodities).

On May 21, Laurel started to hoard rice and sugar on the ground floor of the Palace.

On July 7, 1944, Laurel issued a statement apparently to prepare the public mind for a declaration of war: "No right-thinking Filipino should allow the reconquest of the Philippines. We must bear in mind our commitments as an ally of Japan."

What these commitments were, the people could only guess. A treaty of alliance was discussed by Laurel, Vargas, and Aquino when they flew to Tokyo on September 30, 1943, but the people did not know of the existence of such a pact of alliance until October 19 when Domei published its version.

It was a shock for the people, who heard the late President Quezon's broadcast on October 15, to learn that a military pact of alliance had been made.

Events were moving fast. On July 21, the *Manila Tribune* screamed: TOJO CABINET RESIGNS IN BLOC.

Laurel and his cabinet were preparing to flee to Baguio. Two days before, Laurel gave cabinet colleagues a special ration of sugar, coffee, and cigars. He told his cabinet at the last meeting on July 20 that he would stick to his "demand" that there be no forced evacuation of Manila. But he was prepared to flee just in case . . . The behavior pattern is here exposed.

The buy-and-sell gentry were liquidating their assets from sales of war materials, the big landlords were going up to Baguio, where they expected "peace and order" because the leader Laurel would be there. But they found no sanctuary at Baguio.

From Station BLC 6 came the warning voice of J. Weldon Jones, onetime Acting United States High Commissioner to the Philippines: "The Americans are coming back, make no mistake about it. And make no mistake about this, when the collaborators are *removed from office* . . ."

In May, 1945, the headlines told a different story:

LAUREL FLEES TO TOKYO

PATRIOTS ASK DEATH
PENALTY FOR PÉTAIN

MUSSOLINI EXECUTED
BY ITALIAN PATRIOTS

Collaborators on the Carpet

Among active participants in the betrayal of the Filipinos, certain names stand out. One is Benigno S. Aquino, speaker of the puppet National Assembly; another Claro M. Recto, Laurel's Foreign Minister.

In March 1939 Aquino visited Davao. He was Secretary of Agriculture at the time. At a farewell banquet given by Representative Cesar Sotto, to which the Jap Consul was invited, Aquino came out for "equal opportunities" in Davao for Filipinos and aliens (Japs). "We are Orientals," he said. He praised the Japs for what "they are doing in the Philippines" and urged Filipinos to "emulate" them.

Orientalism became Aquino's obsession. Japan's early victories turned his head. He never recovered. Given to "frankness," he talked his head off, venting his spleen on the corruptive influences of "degenerate occidentalism." As early as February 25, 1942, he cast his lot with the Japs, volunteering to start on a propaganda tour in Legaspi. The Japs gave him a plane to Legaspi, where he publicly came out for all-out collaboration.

Vargas, uneasy, told newsmen: "I can't understand why he acts this way. His actions border on servility."

Aquino had told a Malacañan employee on February 17, 1942: "I don't know what is wrong with these Americans. I was talking with Nishima [one of his first Jap friends] and he says MacArthur was great in 1914, but now he is just no good. The Japanese can launch attacks any time, but MacArthur doesn't seem to know what to do. These Japanese certainly know their business. Imagine what they have accomplished in such a short time." Then, after a pause, impatiently: "What is wrong with the Americans? When are they coming?"

The rest is history. Aquino could not hold his tongue. He talked his way up to the Kalibapi director-generalship, the National Assembly speakership; he talked Hirohito into giving him two decorations. His public utterances became the constant nightmare of his fellow puppets. There was talk of liquidation. They tried to tone him down.

Aquino defined his position:

It is possible that some would say that since the war
has not been ended, our attitude would constitute treason
to America. If such be the philosophy advanced by some
people, I would not hesitate to say that I do not care if I
were called a traitor to America.[6]

Aquino had no patience with the "misguided" elements
and he went after them. On May 20, 1942, he had written
Vargas pointing to the "need of calling the attention of the
Japanese" to the constant danger to which peaceful tenants in Central Luzon were exposed due to the activities
of the "bad elements, otherwise known as the USAFFE"
and suggesting that a force of Jap soldiers be "distributed
evenly" in Central Luzon.

On September 30, 1942, Aquino sent a seven-page memorandum to His Excellency the Commander in Chief of
the Imperial Japanese Forces, recommending purchase of
arms and ammunitions (from a five-million-peso proposed
bond issue) not only to equip the constabulary but also
"to diminish the activities of the lawless [guerrilla] elements. The way we can combat this campaign [America's
promise of full indemnity for war losses] is by informing
the people of the true state of affairs and *by specially con-
vincing them that in no way can America win this war.*"

Such statements always gave his colleagues a chill. The
people's temper was rising. But that did not dampen
Benigno's ardor: the people would be proved wrong in
the end.

In Tokyo on April 24, 1944, Aquino again spoke. "Quezon," he said, "is a 'puppet'; final victory will be Japan's."

That was not all. On April 25, 1944, the *Manila Tribune*
quoted him as saying the Anglo-Americans were suffering
from "spiritual anemia," were "rotten to the core." After

[6] *Manila Tribune*, February 28, 1943

two years "not an inch of territory" had been recovered.
Invasion of the Philippines was "an impossible enterprise."
On June 18, 1944, back on native soil, he told the truth
for the first time. Said he in Tarlac: "If America should
attempt to come back, she would first rain us with bombs,
shell us with cannon balls, and fight for every inch of
ground." And he concluded dramatically: "Anyone who
wishes America to return thus wishes the death of his own
people and the destruction of his own country," forgetting
that one destroys to build anew.

On June 18, 1944, Claro M. Recto wrote a sixteen-page
letter to General Wati, Jap Military Administrator. The
letter is pure propaganda, but in the combined ringing
prose of Recto and Salvador P. Lopez (Recto's ghost-
writer) it elicited genuine praise from well-intentioned
Filipinos for his (Recto's) courage, risking his life and fortune by working with the Japs and, now, taking them to
task in his letter for unwittingly abusing the "sensitive
Filipino." The letter, through the expert machinations of
Recto's political stooges, reached many a home. Eventually, the Jap MPs got on the trail and rudely confronted
Recto with the poser: "Did you write this letter?" Recto
disowned authorship. The letter, it turned out, reached
everyone but the addressee, General Wati.

Recto was twice decorated by the Jap Emperor for well-
intentioned utterances like this:

> "The freedom promised by America was inspired by
> motives of self-interest and self-aggrandizement on the
> part of the Americans rather than by a genuine desire to
> see a subject people free."

And for *unsolicited* press handouts like this, on the "fall"
of Imphal (prepared by Lopez who got a tip from his
friends in Domei on the "imminent fall" of the city):

"None can better appreciate the rejoicing which this
event must bring to the people of India than those who
have themselves known the torments of being oppressed
and exploited by an alien power." (This was sent April 17,
1944, when the Nips were reported twelve kilometers
from Imphal.)

Laurel also sent a message to Domei on the "fall."
On October 11, 1944, I dropped in at Malacañan.
Recto's secretary hailed me, declared the "Minister" would
be glad to see me, and, arm around me, led me in. The
Minister inquired about the war situation. Still the wishful
thinker, he said he believed the Americans would land
in Mindanao and make it the major base for the drive to
the Chinese mainland. America would not make Luzon a
battleground twice.

Recto was the military strategist of the puppet cabinet.
He tried to juggle American and Jap claims to get a more
rational picture of the war situation, like, for instance, the
"fall of Imphal."

Recto also made good use of his oratory to boost the
pacification drive in Laguna, Batangas, and Tayabas early
in 1944. "The recent rice shortage as well as the present
hardships suffered by the people," he told a San Pablo
crowd, "are due mainly to the activities of the guerrillas,
who hinder food production." [7]

As it had Aquino, the Kalibapi got into the blood of
Camilo Osias, Minister of Education in the Laurel Cabinet. At the first Y.M.C.A. get-together in Manila to honor
Y men in the government like Osias and Barza, Osias came
the last, gave the Kalibapi salute, bowed slightly in all
directions. "There," he said, deeply satisfied, "that dis-
penses with all hand-shaking. It's inefficient, unhygienic,
foreign. I recommend the Kalibapi salute, gentlemen."

[7] *Manila Tribune*, January 22, 1944

Camilo's first order upon taking over the educational portfolio, under the "revitalized" puppet cabinet in August, 1944, was to prescribe the Kalibapi salute as a "must" for instructors and students alike in all schools and colleges, public and private.

For all his reputed political shrewdness, the late beloved President Quezon was wrong about Leon Guinto, later puppet mayor of Manila, as he was wrong about other political stooges. Guinto was an all-out Quezon man, a real yes man. His political credo under the Japs was: "It is the imperative duty of all Filipinos in the government to be *loyal to the Japanese Military Administration to which we owe our appointments.*"

Filipinos could stomach only so much of Guinto. In a common pun in Tagalog: Leon Guinto: You are no longer gold (*ginto*) but brass (*tanso*); you are not a lion (*leon*) but a cat (*pusa*)!

Born in Fraud and Deceit

Vargas had his chance. Laurel also had his.

When Laurel defied the world to withhold recognition of the puppet republic, President Roosevelt said:

On the fourteenth of this month a puppet government was set up in the Philippine Islands with Jose P. Laurel as "president." Jorge Vargas and Benigno Aquino are closely associated with Laurel. *The first act of this new puppet regime was to sign a military alliance with Japan. The second act was a hypocritical appeal for American sympathy which was made in fraud and deceit and was designed to confuse and mislead the Filipino people.*

I wish to make it clear that neither the former collaborationist "Philippine Executive Commission" nor the present "Philippine Republic" has the recognition or sympathy of the Government of the United States. *No act of either*

body is now or ever will be considered lawful or binding
by this Government.

The only Philippine government is that established by
the people of the Philippines under the authorization of
the Congress of the United States: the Government of the
Commonwealth of the Philippine Islands. At my request,
the principal executive officers of the commonwealth were
transferred in 1942 from Corregidor to Washington.

Further, it is our expressed policy that all the resources
of the United States shall be employed to drive the treach-
erous Japanese from the Philippine Islands, to restore as
quickly as possible orderly and free democratic processes
of government in the Islands, and to establish there a
truly independent Philippine nation.

Our sympathy goes out to those who remain loyal to the
United States and the Commonwealth, to that great majority of the Filipino people who have not been deceived
by the promises of the enemy and who look forward to the
day when the scheming, perfidious Japanese shall have
been driven from the Philippines. The day will come.[8]

[8] From the *Department of State Bulletin,* Vol. IX, No 226, October
23, 1943

II QUEZON DIES; THE PUPPETS PRAY

Death, Fasting, and Feasting

AUGUST 2, 1944, news bulletin: "President Quezon of the Philippines died this morning August 1 at Saranac Lake, New York. Sergio Osmeña has succeeded to the presidency."

This was a jolt to the quislings. Only the day before Laurel III had been telling Malacañan friends that Quezon had just made a broadcast praising his father's "marvelous" work here. *And the earth trembled as Quezon's underlings felt the ground break from under them!*

The story went around that the very bright and farvisioned wives of cabinet members and other worthy heroes of the day had been paying social calls on Mrs. Osmeña.

The old ways coming back? The "misguided" had a tremendous job on their hands.

On August 4, Laurel issued a statement on Quezon's death. Said he: "It is hard to believe that he could have given the so-called independence [Laurel's is the genuine one, naturally] law recently passed by Congress the seal of his approval."

On August 6 Laurel had mass said at Malacañan Chapel for the "inner circle": cabinet and Council of State members and their families. The puppets prayed not so much for Quezon's soul as for their own souls, for now more than ever they shared a common fate.

The cabinet even talked of political succession after the war, the prospects of each leader: Laurel, Aquino, Recto, and the rest of the puppet *canaille*.

Now that Quezon was dead, where did Roxas stand? He must now realize the blunder he made when he accepted the EPB appointment and had to make that dishonest statement blaming the guerrillas for the shortage of rice. Had he remained on the sidelines, for a few more months, what an enviable position his would have been, with Quezon out of the picture! But, as it was, he had identified himself with the puppets.

On August 12, Laurel met Murata, General Takahashi, and General Iishi to discuss the defense of Manila and promised to declare martial law when the first bomb fell. War declaration next? Laurel apologists claim their hero would resign first. At least, there is the example of Songhkram, Occupation Premier of Siam . . .

Our bureaucrats went by the slogan "Make hay while the sun shines." But their sun was setting.

In July 1944 Laurel started to brag that he would rather quit than declare war, so the Japs asked General Artemio Ricarte[1] and his gang if they had the men. Yes, of course, said Ricarte. Now Laurel, suffering from a serious case of leader complex, believed a declaration of war would be the "lesser evil" in the expectation that he could, or might, wangle concessions for "my people" and "save" them from undue hardship.

Highly placed Jap officers asked Socialist Pedro Abad Santos: "What do you think of the present leaders?" Abad Santos replied: "These politicos are smart. They fooled the

---

[1] Filipino revolutionary leader, who returned with the Japs from voluntary exile in Japan. Died in liberation campaign

Americans. They fooled and have been fooling the people. And now they are fooling you!"

Late in August Laurel began "revitalizing" the cabinet. Roxas was given "ministerial rank." What was Roxas after? Perhaps to be the "protector" of the puppets? His tearful appeal for "rice donors" finally yielded this fruit (among others): Manuel Urquico, *one* sack; Arsenio Urquico del Rosario, five sacks; Cecilio de Leon (a Roxas kin), two sacks. Many landlords amassed fortunes selling rice to our Jap guests at fantastic prices. Here indeed is the answer to Laurel's perennial cry of *work, sacrifice!* While the poor went hungry, those who had gave away *one* sack out of thousands. *Rice at two thousand pesos a* cavan *and still shooting up!*

On August 26 Antonio de las Alas said: "As long as we run the show, you can expect nothing untoward to happen. We will do our utmost to 'protect' you. If we are *forced* to declare war, then it will be against our will."

Our leaders were really serving us. Strange how the leader complex works on feeble minds. Always, when the tide has turned, the scoundrels seek the easy way out. The horizon had cleared; the rats were cracking their heads, turning over in their minds watertight alibis. "We did our best. We did everything in 'good faith.'"

On September 7 Leon Guinto instructed: "No hostile acts against the Republic and the Imperial Japanese Army and Navy will be tolerated. I weigh my words when I solemnly declare that the consequence of such hostile acts will be fatal!" What about hostile acts *against* the commonwealth? *Against* the Filipino people?

Laurel said: "The welfare of the people is the entire concern of the republic."

On August 16, 1943, Laurel, the Secretary of the Interior, submitted this "partial list" of prime commodities for his family (of eighteen members) for one month: lard,

3 cans; soap, 100 bars; rice, 10 sacks; corn, 4 sacks; salt, 2 sacks; matches, 20 packs of 12, and other items. This list, a formidable one considering that the people lived on rations of 120 grams of rice daily (one plateful), was nothing compared with what Laurel enjoyed when he took over Malacañan.

And consider this menu to suit the insatiable puppet cabinet's taste:

COCKTAIL   *Canapés*

GRAPE FRUIT COCKTAIL

GIANT

FISH SINIGANG

TENDERLOIN STEAK

AND CALF'S LIVER

MUSHROOM SAUCE   SPINACH

ROAST TURKEY

CRANBERRY SAUCE   GIBLET GRAVY

STRING BEANS

CHAMPAGNE

AVOCADO SALAD

Atis

ICE CREAM

BIRTHDAY CAKE

COFFEE   CIGARS

This was at luncheon given by Vargas honoring Chief Justice Yulo on the eve of his birthday. A smiliar treat was given each cabinet member on his birthday. Vargas started this tradition; Laurel kept it up.

This certainly is worth struggling for and dying for!

On September 27 Laurel revealed that the declaration of war against America and Great Britain was with the "unanimous consent" of the cabinet and the Council of State.

Hoarded rice confiscated by the government had been

stored in the Department of Finance building. On October
2 the Japs took over the building and with it the rice.

Laurel, two days later: "I give my solemn word that
every grain of rice taken by the government will be given
to the people. I cannot allow it to pass into other hands."

Between two and three A.M., the same day, the republic,
in the person of Jap soldiers, entered Placido Mapa's resi-
dence, got forty sacks of rice; forty-three of forty-four
sacks from Senen Gabaldon; seven of eight sacks from
Meneleo Carlos. The Sons of Heaven descended on peaceful citizens' homes and ran away with their food.

Recto pleaded on October 7: "Let's have abiding trust
and faith in Laurel."

They would have had us pin our hopes, our faith, on one
man and this man a fascist puppet, whose main theme
was: "You help me, I help you, we help one another. We
sink or swim together, in misery or in health: the people
in misery, the puppets in health."

On October 8 Laurel received General Yamashita in
Malacañan. The conqueror of Singapore was here to defend the Philippines.

A week later Laurel and fellow puppets were decorated
by their emperor for work well done.

Curtains on Laurel's Republic!

Cabinet and Council of State were in an emergency
closed-door meeting on October 23. Aquino and Roxas
conferred with Laurel. Every time Laurel's clerk entered,
the two stopped talking. What was going on? Meeting at
noon. The atmosphere was very much like that at Quezon's Marikina home three years ago (December 1941)
when the *castila* (Quezon) "abandoned" them. Men of
little faith, a pathetic look of helplessness and bewilder-
ment written on their faces. The Yanks had landed in

Leyte. The props were knocked from under them. Theirs
was not a happy lot. Roxas' role, it seemed, was to calm
them.

Over in Leyte two weeks later Osmeña created a board
of inquiry to try "those whose loyalty to the United States
and the Commonwealth Government is *under question.*"
No mention of treason. The politicos were up to their old
tricks . . .

Said Vicente Madrigal, prewar shipping magnate and
newspaper publisher: "Romulo is in Leyte. I am taking
care of his family. I can sell some more to the Japanese!"

The next day, November 7, Roxas conferred confiden-
tially with Laurel for forty-five minutes.

Over in Leyte, MacArthur and Osmeña talked of "rewards" to those who have served the Philippine cause.
People who fight for their freedom don't think of rewards.
And so we had the case of an American guerrilla whom
the Voice of Freedom made much of, a navy man named
St. John. He spent two and a half years with the guerrillas
in Leyte under their care and protection. Braggingly, he
was "everything to the natives but God himself"; he performed everything except marriage contracts. And this
hero was going back to "the dear old U.S.A. to eat bread
and butter." To him this war of liberation meant only that.
And MacArthur and Osmeña talked of rewards!

One got into Fort Santiago and nothing was heard until
he was released, a cripple or a corpse. That was Jap justice. Romulo shouted from the housetops that there would
be "no rough tactics" here as in Europe. Our American
friends, the writers, talked of simple-minded "natives." In
Bataan and Corregidor, was it the "natives" who fought?
What was this line if not the old one of racial prejudice?
MacArthur, Osmeña, Sutherland, and Romulo looked very
warlike wading ashore at Leyte, Old Glory waving from
a coconut tree.

On November 11 Roxas and Aquino played golf with Laurel at Malacañan Park. While in Leyte, Osmeña talked of return to the "old order," "no bloodshed," "justice for everyone," "specific, not merely overt acts of collaboration."

Osmeña played the same tune as Laurel, talking of "peace and order." Romulo, in America, broadcast that they were "taking over where we left off." All over Europe the quislings were being shelved while here, in the only Christian democracy in the Orient, the returning heroes, nursing political ambitions, were courting the puppets. Could they have been thinking of compromise with these puppets for another sell-out of the people?

For *Free Philippines* I wrote a warning to Puppet Laurel and his fellow quislings:

The break in the East has come at last! Darkness is lifting. The hour of our liberation has struck! America has kept faith with us; she has redeemed her word. Once again, Filipinos and Americans are fighting side by side on Philippine soil—heart and mind fired by that indomitable spirit that made Bataan immortal.

You did not think this was possible—not so soon—you men of little faith. You never dreamed that some day the unconquerable forces of liberation would sweep across the vast Pacific and land on our shores to help free our people just as other enslaved peoples have been liberated from the crushing weight of Fascist rule and exploitation. Instead, the enemy found you weak and self-seeking politicians and bureaucrats too willing, even eager, to play the Judas role, the role Pétain and Laval played to perfection.

To your credit, you too played it well, so well that you thought you had the people fooled. Professing to serve the people, the same people whose interests you never hesitate to betray whenever they conflict with your own, you kowtowed to the new master, waited for his orders, and blindly and unblushingly did his every bidding. Vociferously you shout earnest protestations of your honesty of purpose and good faith. And just as noisily you trumpet the borrowed precepts of a new world order in which justice is unknown and the bayonet alone dictates the peace.

You are contemptuous of "recalcitrant" patriots whom you choose to call "brigands" and "misguided" because you are incapable of the fine sense of loyalty and patriotism that propels to heroic action and sacrifice. Look around you. The people go about in rags, starving and diseased. The enemy continues to loot, murder and rape, stripping the people of their humblest possessions and snatching the much needed food from the hungry mouths of the old and young alike. Truth and justice, the freedoms we cherish, every little thing we call decent, are trampled under his murderous boot.

But the *rigodón* is over. The curtain falls on your farcial republic. The sovereign people now take the stage. Why do you draw back in alarm? Have you suddenly become afraid of the people whose welfare you so jealously claim to protect? You have reason to be afraid. Did you not sell out to the hated enemy? Did you not barter your people's dignity, honor and liberty? All for your own selfish ends?

The people are not stupid. You cannot compromise with treason and disloyalty. They now see through your transparent mask of hypocrisy and deceit. You have deservedly earned for yourselves only the undying hatred of a people betrayed. They demand that the ends of justice be served.

You played for high stakes as other quislings elsewhere have done. And you have lost.

And then came the Makapili. Laurel bestowed the cloak of authority on the arrogant, traitorous Ganaps and thereby sealed his own fate. He had sown the seeds of internecine conflict and would reap a bountiful harvest. Even as this new "patriotic" organization was being presented noisily to the people, to preserve "peace and order," and collaborate "positively" with the Jap masters, those "guardian angels" of Asia were perpetrating the bloody slaughter of innocent, helpless men in Polo and Obando, Bulacan, the first large-scale Jap reprisals, comparable with the atrocities following the American landings.

The Makapili aim was to destroy. Into vengeful hands were given weapons to destroy innocent lives.

Said Pio Duran (Makapili Vice Supreme Head and new Home Affairs Vice Minister), in the *Manila Tribune:* "They [the guerrillas] have gone far enough, they shall go no further."

And so were the traitorous Ganaps armed to bring "peace and order" to our unhappy country. In San Pedro, Laguna, the price for each guerrilla caught and executed was one sack of rice. In Santa Cruz, Makapilis demanded passes for meat and other foodstuffs. No salary was promised these "patriotic" soldiers. Hence an open incentive for looting.

It took an American, William Winter, KGEI commentator, to denounce the puppets. Said Winter on December 14: "They will claim they have been forced; but the people know the answer. The traitors must pay!"

On the 19th there was a special cabinet meeting with Roxas attending. Laurel to Yulo, who arrived late: "We are just talking about going to Baguio, Joe." Laurel III had already departed that morning.

Laurel to Malacañan employees: "I want to 'save' Manila and convince the Japanese to clear out and make Manila an 'open city,'" forgetting that it takes three to make an open city.

Jap women and children continued to be evacuated.

Yamashita made Baguio his headquarters. The cabinet
met again. Roxas regularly attended the meetings; he also
joined his colleagues Thursdays and Sundays to see Jap
movies in the palace, was an almost daily caller on Laurel.
Was this the man who had MacArthur's "password"?

On the 21st Laurel and his cabinet left for Baguio under
Yamashita's protecting wings.

Yamashita had tea with Laurel on December 18.

A year before, on January 6, 1943, Laurel told DANAS
(neighborhood associations) officials: "Give me time to do
and serve the best interests of the Filipino people. Don't
judge the government by one single instance nor by one
mere fleeting glimpse of the whole superstructure. I am
not God!"

A year later the man who would "serve the best interests
of the Filipino people" was roosting in Baguio under the
protection of Nip guns.

Jose Paez, who joined the Laurel cabinet in August
1944 as Minister of Public Works and Communications, is
quoted as saying: "Why didn't I hold off longer?"

Could Laurel's professed good faith be considered miti-
gating? The question of subjective good faith serves no
useful purpose. He who is in the wrong must pay.

The day of retribution had come. The quislings must
pay!

III MacArthur Returns and Liberates a Puppet

Roxas in the Jap Scheme of Things

A STORY went the rounds shortly after the liberation of
Manila that General of the Army Douglas MacArthur had
given instructions to the United States Sixth Army com-
manders to send out their best operatives and locate his
Bataan aide, Manuel Roxas, a brigadier general in the
USAFFE. Roxas must be rescued at all cost.

The story was an obvious fabrication, or so resistance
fighters thought at the time.

General MacArthur wired on November 28, 1944:

> WHEN OUR MILITARY FORCES HAVE LANDED IN LUZON, IT
> SHALL BE MY FIRM PURPOSE TO RUN TO EARTH EVERY DIS-
> LOYAL FILIPINO WHO HAS DEBASED HIS COUNTRY'S CAUSE SO
> AS TO IMPEDE THE SERVICES OF USAFFE OFFICERS OR MEN
> WHO HAVE CONTINUED TO RESIST. SUCH ACTIONS CONSTRUE
> DIRECT AID TO THE ENEMY IN HIS WAR AGAINST THE UNITED
> STATES OF AMERICA AND THE PHILIPPINE COMMONWEALTH.

But the story persisted. Then on April 18, 1945, Manila's
liberation press, controlled largely by men tainted with
collaboration, blared in its boldest type:

ROXAS IS LIBERATED

The story was disturbing to resistance fighters. The
army-controlled *Free Philippines,* published by the OWI,

carried the story under a three-column headline, with this subhead:

ROXAS IS AMONG LIBERATED,
4 CABINET AIDES CAUGHT

The item read:

General MacArthur announced today that American liberation forces, battering at the gates of Baguio, have rescued more than 7000 civilians including Brigadier General Manuel Roxas, former speaker of the Philippine Assembly, and captured four members of the collaborationist cabinet.

The puppet officials who fell into American hands were Jose Yulo, Antonio de las Alas, Teofilo Sison, and Quintin Paredes.

"They will be confined for the duration of the war as a matter of military security," General MacArthur said, "and then turned over to the government of the Philippines for trial."

Roxas was a member of the same quisling cabinet as Minister without Portfolio, but here he was "liberated" by General MacArthur and four of his colleagues "captured" and ordered to be confined for the duration of the war for reasons of "military security." Roxas was promptly restored to his military rank and assigned to G-2, USAFFE headquarters.

Interviewed upon his "liberation" by an Associated Press man at his home, Roxas was quoted as saying that Laurel's puppet government acted most of the time "under duress."[1] But Roxas happened to be identified with that puppetry.

The puppets worked to "save" Roxas when he was in a concentration camp in Bukidnon, Mindanao. There was a report that he had been court-martialed and sentenced to

[1] *Manila Post*, April 19, 1945

death. However, the Jap commander, General Masaharu
Homma, interceded. Vargas told reporters of the Jap-
controlled press on August 18, 1942, that he, Isaac Barza,[2]
who became his chief adviser, and Imamura,[3] top Jap
civilian adviser at the military administration, had pleaded
with Homma to spare Roxas for he would be "a valuable
man." The other puppets, like Benigno S. Aquino, also
claimed they were working for his release.

Roxas returned to Manila from concentration a "sick"
man. This was in March 1943. He feigned sickness. Anyway, he had a good excuse. He kept to his home. Here was
a hero, the people thought. The top puppets served the
Jap masters well and fattened at the trough. The Japs
tried hard to get Roxas to collaborate, especially to help
them pacify the "misguided" elements. Roxas would not
budge. He could have been in Vargas' place, or in Laurel's, but he managed to persuade the Japs to lay off. He
was a sick man. And the puppets did not encourage the
Japs. Roxas would have stolen their thunder.

On April 8, 1943, upon his return from a pacification
tour through Negros and Panay, Vargas confided to the
press that the situation in the southern islands, especially
Capiz, Roxas' home province, was chaotic and they would
need a man like Roxas to restore "peace and order."

"We need Roxas there," Vargas said.

"Suppose he refuses to go?" a reporter asked.

"He can't refuse," replied Vargas. "The military will
order him to join the pacification. But the commissioners
and I are in doubt whether to take him. Will he steal the
show?"

"I think he will steal the show," said the reporter.

Vargas smiled. "In that case . . ."

---

[2] Deceased; was prewar business partner of Arsenio Luz, Laurel's official spokesman
[3] Prewar lumber man and merchant

The puppets thought that the competition would be too great.

Roxas kept to his home. Laurel could, and did, visit him, as did also his political friends like Alunan, Aquino, Recto, Osias, Sabido, and General Francisco,[4] who all held key positions in the puppet regime. Throughout the period of his illness, Roxas remained very popular with the people because of his abstention from the cause of the Jap emperor.

Roxas did not come into the picture until the birth of the puppet republic late in 1943. He definitely rode on the crest of popular favor then. The mere mention of his name in public evoked popular acclaim. It was because of this popularity that the Japs insisted that his name be included in the Preparatory Committee on Philippine Independence. This was created to lay the groundwork for the "Philippine Republic." Roxas hedged; he finally yielded after he had several talks with Laurel. The PCPI began to meet regularly with Laurel.

Of his part in framing the constitution for the puppet republic at this time, Roxas claims: "I wanted to prevent a dictatorial government which would give the Japanese even more power."[5]

In contrast to this statement are the facts. The puppet constitution, as prepared, written, and signed by Roxas, was modeled after the fascist constitution of Japan. All the power in the government was centralized in the president. Legislative powers were vested in the puppet national assembly, half of whose members were to be appointed by provincial governors, who in turn were to be appointed by the president, with the Japs' approval of course, thus giving the president full control of that body.

---

[4] General Guillermo Francisco built up the puppet constabulary, spearheaded the "pacification" drive against resistance groups
[5] *Time*, June 11, 1945

In a public ceremony "The Founding Fathers" of the puppet republic affixed their signatures to the constitution. Roxas signed and posed with his fellow drafters. The quisling republic was born on October 14, 1943.

Roxas disappeared from the scene again, but only for a time. Laurel's "republic" began to founder. The people clamored for rice, which was being diverted into the hands of the Japs by such enterprising individuals as Sergio Osmeña, Jr.

At this critical period came an announcement from Malacañan Palace that Roxas had accepted the chairmanship of Laurel's Economic Planning Board, had become the food czar.

The "republic" survived the crisis. Roxas had, by becoming the food dictator, bolstered the prestige of Laurel's republic which, had it fallen, would have made the task of controlling the Filipinos immeasurably more difficult for the Japs.

At least two weeks before the formal announcement of his appointment, Malacañan had hinted that Roxas would be named economic dictator. Those who still trusted Roxas were skeptical. The rumor persisted, however, and finally came the official announcement. Just prior to the announcement Roxas made his first friendly public appearance with Laurel.

Roxas took his new job seriously. He appealed to the people to help the government solve the rice problem. He placed the blame on the guerrillas for obstructing the flow of rice into Manila (and into the Jap depots) and for "disrupting" the food program of the Japs.

The first thing Roxas did on taking over the BIBA (*Bigasan ng Bayan,* the National Rice and Corn Corporation) as EPB chairman was to allow the partial "free entry" of rice into Manila with license. The Japs then held all the supply in Manila but needed more. By means of the license requirement, they were able to keep track of all rice entering from the provinces.

The Roxas plan to enable Manilans to get some of their rice from their farms in the provinces became the solution to the Japs' rice problem and they lost no time in pressing their advantage. It was at this time that hundred-peso "Mickey Mouse" notes were issued. Stocked with bundles of this worthless currency, the Japs went on a buying spree.

In the meantime, the price of rice continued to shoot up. Black marketeers had a Roman holiday as the price of rice per sack (about 120 pounds) jumped a hundred pesos a day. Central Luzon's absentee landlords hogged much of the windfall and were able to bring in a supply to Manila. This supply eventually was channeled to the Jap depots and Jap raiding parties made a systematic roundup of rice warehouses in Manila and in the near-by provinces.

The Japs took drastic measures to curb the rising unrest. On May 18, 1944, the Imperial Japanese Army warned:

> The army's policy is to deal rigorously with those atrocities [guerrillas were raiding Jap food depots in daring attacks in Central Luzon] in accordance with military law, to liquidate the sinister groups that disturb peace and order.

It was evident that Roxas had played into the hands of the Japs. His culpability in this instance cannot be explained away. Fully aware that the Japs desperately required rice for their armies and that the puppet government could not prevent the use of the rice for this purpose, Roxas nevertheless assured the people on his word that every grain of rice they "gave to the government would be used to feed a hungry Filipino."[6]

[6] *Manila Tribune,* July 22, 1944

On August 25, 1944, Laurel gave Roxas the rank of Minister without Portfolio, as chairman of the Economic Planning Board. Rice, at this time, was quoted at two thousand pesos a sack, compared with four hundred pesos hardly a month before.

Roxas claimed after his "liberation" that he did not attend any meetings of the Laurel cabinet. This assertion is refuted by his actions.

On October 23, 1944, Roxas, unannounced, conferred with Laurel in Malacañan for the entire morning. At noon the same day he attended the joint emergency luncheon meeting of the Council of State and Cabinet called by Laurel. This was three days after the American landings on Leyte.

Throughout this period, Roxas' extreme friendliness with Laurel, Aquino, and the other top puppets was not the action of a man *forced* to participate in the puppet regime. On November 11, 1944, he played golf with Laurel and Aquino. The next day, Jose Yulo joined the group.

Socially as well as politically, therefore, Roxas was inextricably linked with the leading Filipino puppets.

On November 7, Roxas conferred for about an hour with Laurel. The occasion was the announcement made by President Osmeña from Leyte that a board of inquiry was to be created to pass on collaborators.

On November 30 the Japs abandoned all pretense of noninterference with the rice supply. Laurel dissolved the BIBA, the chairman of which was Roxas, and created in its place the RICOA (Rice and Corn Association). The object of this agency was to assure that the supply of rice continued to reach the Japs. Roxas made no protest, issued no threat of resignation from the Economic Planning Board.

Rice had reached ₱7500 a sack. The people were in an ugly mood.

On December 19, Laurel called another special cabinet meeting. Roxas was present. The following day another meeting was called. This time Roxas not only attended but led in the discussion. (This was after the new American landings on Mindoro.)

During this period, just prior to the departure of the cabinet for Baguio, Roxas conferred with Laurel almost daily. Twice weekly he visited Malacañan to witness Jap movies and discuss affairs of state.

On December 21 Laurel and his cabinet left in the morning for Baguio under heavy escort, for protection against the "misguided" who were active all along the road to the Philippine mountain capital. Roxas went along with his family while Recto and Aquino stayed behind, following later.

By December 28 rice had reached twelve thousand pesos a sack and was still going up, the signal achievement of Laurel's RICOA!

Hunger stalked the streets of Manila.

A Filipino officer is the authority for the following story of Roxas' surrender to the Japs:

After the fall of Bataan and Corregidor, Roxas called a meeting of his staff in Mindanao. The staff decided to continue resistance. Roxas carried the decision to the Jap garrison. He never returned, but sent a message to his staff to surrender.

In the letter he addressed to USAFFE officers, Roxas urged them to give up their arms. "Upon my request," said Roxas, "the Japanese military commander has given you another opportunity to do so [to give up their arms] before he sends Japanese forces to kill you in the hills. Your presence in the hills is causing grave concern and is greatly delaying the return of the people to their normal occupations." Roxas warned that unless the people returned to their homes soon there would be "an acute shortage of food among our people" and he concluded his appeal: "As a man who has shared your sufferings, I urge you to obey your Commander's [Roxas'] orders and present yourselves immediately to the nearest Japanese post.[7]

Most of his men gave themselves up. Quite a number, however, took to the hills. Following this, Roxas was offered release, but he refused, saying he would leave only after all the men below his rank had been freed.

That was a good line.

Late in April 1945, a week after his "liberation" by General MacArthur's forces, Roxas figured again in the talk in collaborationist circles in Manila. He had admitted to General MacArthur, so the story went, that it was he who told Laurel to declare war, for otherwise Laurel would have had to step out. And then where would the poor Filipino people have been?

MacArthur and Osmeña Work at Cross-purposes

Sergio Osmeña was in Washington when Douglas MacArthur announced the "liberation" of his onetime friend and aide Manuel Roxas, this man who was puppet Laurel's closest adviser and colleague.

With one stroke, General MacArthur thus threw out of gear the clear-cut policy laid down by Franklin D. Roosevelt and the United States Congress with respect to the Philippines after liberation.

This was the policy:

> It is contemplated that as soon as conditions warrant, civil government will be set up under constitutional officers. It will be their duty forthwith to take emergency measures to alleviate the hardships of the Philippine people, and to prepare the Commonwealth to receive the independence which we have promised. The latter includes two tasks of great importance: *Those who have*

[7] From a letter released by Tomas Cabili, former Secretary of National Defense. Published in Manila newspapers on February 27, 1946

*collaborated with the enemy must be removed from au-
thority and influence over the political and economic life
of the country, and the democratic form of government
guaranteed in the Constitution of the Philippines must be
restored for the benefit of the people of the Islands.*[8]

The political confusion that this action of General Mac-
Arthur precipitated in Manila verged on the chaotic. But
the repercussions in Washington were even more serious.

With Roxas when he was "liberated" were Jose Yulo,
Rafael Alunan, Quintin Paredes, and Teofilo Sison, his colleagues in the Laurel puppet cabinet. These men were
shipped to the Iwahig penal colony on Palawan Island.
Roxas promptly slid into a uniform as a one-star general
and was assigned to G-2, USAFFE headquarters. In this
same office was his and MacArthur's mutual friend, Colonel Andres Soriano, who became a naturalized American
citizen on October 4, 1945.

In Washington, Osmeña quietly read between the lines
of MacArthur's communiqué, underscoring Roxas' "rescue"
and his fellow puppets' "capture" by MacArthur's forces.
He was perturbed. He had come to Washington precisely
to sound out feeling at Capitol Hill on the issue of collaboration and here was MacArthur drawing the line on
puppetry, liberating one top puppet and capturing the
rest.

MacArthur's obvious liking for Roxas and his generous
tolerance of Roxas' political activities even while he remained in uniform assigned to USAFFE headquarters
merely fanned Osmeña's belief that the general was batting for Roxas. Nevertheless, Osmeña cabled a friend in
Manila saying he was "happy" over the "liberation" of his
onetime protegé Roxas.

MacArthur's action must have surprised Washington.

[8] Italics supplied

Osmeña was not surprised. He had misgivings and they were not unfounded.

The "liberation" of the puppet Roxas was not an isolated act. It was the implementation of a corollary policy first enunciated by MacArthur immediately after the landings in Leyte. In his first proclamation on Philippine soil, issued on October 23, 1944, MacArthur announced the re-establishment of the Philippine Commonwealth and the end of Laurel's "republic organized under enemy duress."

"I do hereby announce my purpose," the proclamation read, "progressively to restore and extend to the people of the Philippines the sacred right of government by constitutional process as rapidly as the several occupied areas are liberated and the military situation will otherwise permit."

MacArthur and Osmeña did not see eye to eye on the progressive steps that should be taken to restore the right of government constitutional process. One basic point of contention was whether to convene the Philippine Congress. Osmeña decided not to call Congress to a session. Many of its members had served in the puppet National Assembly and had accepted other positions in the puppet regimes and there was therefore the question of its legality to consider.

Of the twenty-four elected senators, two were deceased and seven were arrested and confined for security reasons and later turned over to the Commonwealth by the United States Army Counter-Intelligence Corps as collaborators. Of the fifteen that subsequently held office, seven accepted positions under the Vargas and Laurel puppet regimes, most of them serving in the Council of State. The rest, eight of them, stayed on the side. The seven arrested included the most influential of Nacionalista leaders: Recto, Paredes, de las Alas, Yulo, Proceso Sebastian, Vicente Madrigal, and Emiliano T. Tirona.

The House of Representatives had ninety-eight members. Taking out the members deceased, or arrested by the CIC, the house had a membership of seventy-three that held office in the reconstituted Commonwealth Congress. Of the ninety-eight, twenty served in the puppet National Assembly and eleven others in other official capacities under the Japs. The CIC arrested seven.

If the collaborators were to be removed, there would be no quorum in the senate.

MacArthur, however, had other plans. He believed that the organization of the Philippine Congress was the logical step in the restoration of the right of government under constitutional process. He acted on the basis of this belief.

From his headquarters came a directive which classified those who collaborated with the enemy according to their rank and the positions they held. In this classification, the members of the Philippine Congress were placed *below* the level of provincial governors. It was not explained why this distinction was made, but it was clear that in the opinion of the military high command members of the legislature who served the Japs were less "tainted" with collaboration than the provincial governors.

It is against the backdrop of this policy that the significance of the MacArthur communiqué on the "liberation" of Roxas must be viewed. The political atmosphere at the time of Roxas' "liberation" was surcharged. It became obvious, immediately after his "liberation," that the forces of reaction, which were closely identified with the Japanese during the occupation, were out to wrest the government from Osmeña. The Americans had come back sooner than they dared hope possible. Collaborators must be punished. There was Roosevelt's injunction that those who had collaborated must be *removed* from authority over the life of the country.

With the "liberation" of Roxas the collaborators knew

their fears were unfounded. MacArthur had clamped the members of Laurel's cabinet in jail. But he had made an exception of Roxas. This was all that they were waiting for. Here at last they had their "strong man," to steer the prostrate country back to normalcy.

The home of Roxas in Manila became the mecca of collaborationist politicos, who called to pay their respects to the acclaimed "Redeemer."

Roxas buckled down to plot the collaborationist strategy. He took everything in his stride, currying favor from all elements. He sought contact with leaders of all political groups, promising generous rewards. He was for everything and for everybody. He was for both independence and its postponement, depending upon whom he was talking to.

In May 1945 he invited the adviser of the Hukbalahap, Vicente Lava, to his house. He told Lava he had always been for independence, but that he believed freedom should not be given *earlier* than July 4, 1946. Before his talk with Lava, three men of opulence had called to pledge their support to Roxas and postponement: Eugenio Lopez, sugar and air-transport man from Iloilo, Manuel Elizalde, No. 2 boss of the powerful Elizalde interests, and Ramon J. Fernandez, one of three top Filipino shipping owners.

Talk of re-examination of independence stirred Manila. From Roxas boosters came reports that postponement was being discussed as an issue in the election. The collaborationist press of Manila started to drum up re-examination sentiment because of the "dangers" that faced the Philippines.

President Osmeña was apparently tipped off on goings on in the Roxas camp. On May 3, 1945, he issued a statement in Washington announcing that he was running for re-election. He reiterated his stand that independence was a "settled issue." By coming out for re-election and for independence, the president neatly put Roxas on the defensive, for no Filipino could come out for postponement or re-examination of independence and expect to be elected to public office.

Nevertheless, Roxas toyed with the idea of re-examination, but was careful not to commit himself in public.

Late in June Roxas sent for Amado V. Hernandez, editor of the Tagalog edition of the OWI's *Free Philippines,* to offer him a job as editor of a Tagalog daily to boost Roxas for president. "Shall we include independence as one of the issues?" asked Hernandez. "No," replied Roxas. "We will talk about that *after* the election." Hernandez left, saying he would consider the offer.

Just before Christmas J. "Mike" Elizalde had as dinner guests some of McNutt's staff men and Roxas.

A McNutt staff man asked Roxas: "Why don't you come out for re-examination?"

"I will," Roxas replied, "*after* the election."

Failure of a Mission: Tydings Leaves

The political scene was in ferment when President Osmeña returned in May. The presidential fight was in the offing. The collaborationists had entrenched themselves in Congress, the legislative body that Osmeña did not want reconstituted because of the presence of many "whose loyalty is under question." The Nacionalista leaders were divided between "traitors" and "superpatriots."

Osmeña knew that bickerings had been going on within his party. But he was unprepared to handle the situation upon his return. He had opposed calling Congress into session. While he was in Washington, members of Congress, led by Jose Zulueta, who was later to be elected speaker, burned the wires urging him to call the legislature into session. Osmeña was noncommittal.

There was little that he could do. He had to face the disturbing facts.

Senator Millard Tydings, coauthor of the Philippine Independence Act (Tydings-McDuffie Act), came with President Osmeña at the head of a United States Congressional mission to survey Philippine war damage before recommending legislation for rehabilitation. He saw the facts and left post-haste for Washington on the fifth day of a projected four-week survey.

The story made the headlines. But the story behind the headlines was never told. Drew Pearson revealed only a little in his column after the return of the mission.

The Maryland senator stated publicly when he arrived in Manila that he expected to remain about a month. He planned to make a thorough survey of the Philippine picture.

But after Tydings conferred with MacArthur [Pearson wrote] he suddenly told his commission that they would not need to remain more than a few days. Before the week was up they departed.

While Tydings kept mum as to what MacArthur told him, which caused such an abrupt reversal of plans, he did tell some of his advisers about MacArthur's remarks regarding another Senatorial mission. Tydings had informed MacArthur that another group of Senators were coming to the Philippines later in the summer.

MacArthur looked sour when Tydings broke this news and remarked: "Well, if they want to come, I suppose I can't stop them."

General MacArthur had reasons for discouraging missions, for the Philippine political situation was in a sorry mess. The collaborationists were on the offensive. And they had the general to thank for it! Did he not "liberate" Roxas, their acclaimed "man of the hour"?

Osmeña took the rap for the rumpus over the collaboration issue. "If he had had the guts in Washington," declared Eugenio Perez, Roxas' spokesman in the House of
Representatives, "none of our leaders would be in Iwahig[9]
today."

Philippine politics are notoriously petty. Politicos who
were witness to the Osmeña-Roxas meeting at Nichols
Field in May, could not erase from their minds the belief
that Osmeña and Roxas would patch up their differences,
because the Army, or rather MacArthur, wanted it that
way. There was open talk now of reconciliation, revival
even, of the Os-Rox leadership that challenged Quezon in
1934. Emilio la Paz,[10] a Fort Santiago hero, put it this way:
"General MacArthur greeted Osmeña and Tydings as they
came out of the plane at Nichols Field, walked some dis-
tance with them until they spotted Roxas. The general
stepped aside, grasped Roxas' right hand, and, taking Osmeña's right hand, made them shake hands, remarking:
'Shake, boys; it's a deal.' And the general walked between
them, an arm around each man's waist."

Notoriously lacking in backbone, molded under Quezon's lashing whip into a meek yes brood, the Nacionalistas
now sang the same tune: Forget all for the sake of party
unity, for national unity, for more power to the *one* party.

Tydings arrived in Manila on Wednesday, May 23. An
office was set up for him and his mission at USAFFE headquarters. In an interview with the press May 25, he said
he would try to see as much of the war damage as his time
would allow. He would go out of Manila to the provinces
and to the southern islands, Cebu, Panay, Negros. The
destruction in Manila, he said, was something unbelievable.

Thursday and Friday, Tydings spent receiving callers
and in the afternoon driving around in Manila and en-

[9] Government penal colony on Palawan Island
[10] Representative from Rizal; in Fort Santiago seven months

virons. Friday noon, Osmena had MacArthur for lunch at
the Palace; in the afternoon Osmeña accompanied Tydings
to the mission's USAFFE office, where the senator gave a
press interview in which, among other things, the question
of independence "possibly in December" (1945) was
brought up. In the evening, Osmeña gave a state dinner
for the Tydings mission.

On Saturday, something definitely was afoot. There was
talk of the mission leaving "any day." Tydings and Mac-
Arthur were at loggerheads? Why was Tydings leaving
right away? What could have happened to make him
change his plans? Could the Osmeña-Roxas feud have had
anything to do with it?

On the morning of May 26th J. Amado Araneta, sugar
man and a political backer of Roxas, dropped in at the
Roxas home and was told the "good news." Tydings was
"disgusted" with Osmeña, Roxas told Araneta, and would
leave definitely on Tuesday the twenty-ninth.

On the day Araneta called, Saturday, Roxas gave his
men the go-ahead signal to launch his candidacy. Roxas
supporters hinted their leader would step out of his army
uniform "within a week."

Incidentally, two days before, Roxas had an hour's conference with Osmeña at Malacañan. In this conference,
Osmeña offered Roxas the job of Philippine Resident Commissioner in Washington. Roxas laughed it off and bluntly
told Osmeña he wanted the presidency and no other job.

On Monday, May 28, Osmeña had a conference with
MacArthur. In the evening, he was host at dinner to the
Tydings mission. Also present was General MacArthur.
MacArthur spent his time talking with small-fry Filipino
legislators. Early the next morning the Tydings mission
left.

Roxas was quick to capitalize on the sudden leave-
taking of the Tydings mission. His supporters declared

Tydings left because he was disgusted with Osmeña.
This was a good line, calculated to fan the temper of
the public. But it was not the real reason. Roxas knew
what really happened. He knew in advance Tydings
would leave. He knew what MacArthur *told* Tydings. It
was this:

The situation in the Philippines demanded action. The
Osmeña administration was slow and incapable of meeting
the situation. What the Philippines needed was strong
leadership under a man of action, a "strong man." It was
impossible to start things going without calling the Philippine Congress to a session.

Osmeña knew this too. He was disturbed. He told a
friend what had been preying on his mind.

"I have done it before," Osmeña told his friend. "I'll
do it again today when there is a greater need for unity
than ever. Let Roxas run. I will give way to him!"

The pressure was tremendous. And Sergio Osmeña,
aging and ailing, was retreating.

IV COLLABORATORS RETURN TO POWER TOO

Rule by Nacionalista Oligarchs: Roxas Wields the Gavel

IN 1907 YOUNG SERGIO OSMEÑA, then twenty-eight, dynamic speaker of the first National Assembly, founded the Nacionalista Party, the party of national liberation. It became the people's party. Every other political group died out. Only one party, the Democrata, rose to challenge the Nacionalista, but even in its heyday during the Wood administration the Democrata opposition was at best a threat to the party in power.

By 1941 the Nacionalista Party, grown old and soft, had become the omnipotent party of reaction. The party steam roller made a clean sweep of the elections.[1] Under Manuel Quezon's iron heel cabinet men and legislators had become puppets.

When the Japs came Nacionalista bigwigs left behind by Quezon and Osmeña cast aside all pretense of nationalism and chose collaboration with the masters. Philippine democracy was diseased. The three years of Jap oppression clearly exposed the moral bankruptcy of Nacionalista leadership. The result was the betrayal of the Filipino people, of the cause of freedom, of justice, of human dignity.

By the simple expedient of Sergio Osmeña's return from

[1] The twenty-four senators and ninety-five of the ninety-eight representatives were Nacionalistas

the land of the dollar and the GI the Nacionalista Party was again in the saddle, because Quezon's successor as party boss found that after three years of absence from the Philippine scene he had to invoke party loyalty if he were to retain a political machine to back up his program. It was a far cry from 1907. The Nacionalista Party, the party that sold out to the Japs, was being rammed down the people's throat.

On June 2, 1945, Roxas had an off-the-record chat with a group of newspapermen. What he said in this interview was revealing, for he set down the pattern of his strategy in his bid for power. His line was simple and logical.

Washington policy was that constitutional processes of orderly government should be restored in the Philippines as soon as the country was liberated and law and order established. Government is a continuing process. The years of Jap oppression were merely an "interruption," a "transition" in this process; so that the Filipinos should really start where they left off three years ago. All government officials and employees who were in the services at the outbreak of the war should continue in office until otherwise removed for cause by law.

On June 6, 1945, the pro-Roxas *Manila Post* screamed: ROXAS DRIVE IS ON. This was hot political news. Behind the headline was this fact: Roxas had cleared all possible hurdles and was confident nothing then stood between him and the presidency and he was out to get it even if he had to force Osmeña's hand.

Osmeña called Congress to a special session on June 9.

The opening session was Roxas' big show. Before an audience that packed the hall, he staked his reputation on a total whitewash of collaborators. Every man who held a job under the Japs, he said, not only remained loyal but resisted the enemy.

The galleries broke down in hysterical cheering.

As Roxas took his seat amidst the din, up rose Romblon's political boss, Leonardo Festin, an active supporter of resistance, to inquire why Roxas had deliberately omitted the name of Jose Abad Santos, Quezon's courageous Secretary of Justice, who died a hero's death in Mindanao [Roxas had sung the praises of resistance-movement heroes like Ellsworth (General Vicente Lim), Nakar, Thorpe, Cushing, Vinzons, Ablan, and others]. But why was he silent on one of the most courageous Filipino patriots, Festin demanded. He supplied the answer: Because Abad Santos chose death to keep the honor of his country untarnished; because he refused to collaborate. The galleries broke into spontaneous ovation; Festin's colleagues gave him a big hand. But Roxas maintained silence.

Out of the welter of campus oratory and noisy pro-Roxas stomping in the opening session, these facts became apparent:

The Nacionalista oligarchs, by steam-roller tactics, again held the reins of government. Roxas definitely was running the show, with Osmeña an unwilling compromiser.

Congress was in the grip of collaborationists, taking orders from Roxas.

The Philippine official hierarchy following the liberation of Manila was definitely collaborationist. And Osmeña must share a heavy responsibility for this.

With both houses of Congress looking to him for their cue before deciding on anything, Roxas held the balance of power between the legislative and executive department, with the judiciary, whose independence is a fundamental constitutional guarantee, reduced to a mere pawn in the hocus-pocus. (As president of the senate, Roxas was ex-officio chairman of the powerful Commission on Appointments composed of twelve senators and twelve representatives. All presidential appointees had to be Okayed by this body, which bore the inevitable Roxas stamp since both houses were dominated by the collaborationist clique.)

Roxas drew strength politically not so much on his own personality, though Osmeña was "ineffective" compared to him, as on Osmeña's own lack of spunk, not to mention an inept cabinet which bungled his policies by conflicting and ill-advised statements, particularly on the delicate issue of collaboration. Osmeña's primary concern had been party harmony. This meant that all appointments had to be acceptable to Congress and must perforce be made only after previous consultation with and approval by congressional leaders, specifically by Congress Boss Roxas.

Thus, the executive under Osmeña had taken a defensive position, in marked contrast to the dominant position the executive enjoyed in prewar days when Manuel L. Quezon had everything and everybody under his thumb.

The Osmeña post-liberation cabinet was third-rate. He had two staunch supporters in Tomas Confesor and Tomas Cabili, active leaders in the resistance movement in Panay and Mindanao respectively. Confesor was named to the top cabinet post, the Interior, and Cabili to National Defense. The two committed the Osmeña administration, during Osmeña's second trip to Washington in April and May 1945, to a strong, uncompromising policy against collaborators. Osmeña repudiated Confesor and Cabili, on pressure from the collaborationist groups, and the two former guerrilla leaders were packed off to Washington to serve as members of the Philippine Rehabilitation Commission. Cabili later represented the Philippines at the United Nations Monetary Conference in London in January 1946, while Confesor was sent at about the same time to Tokyo as Philippine representative to the Allied War Reparations Commission.

Osmeña selected another guerrilla leader, Alfredo Mon-

telibano, underground governor of Negros, to succeed
Cabili and, concurrently, Confesor, in dual capacity as
Secretary of National Defense and Secretary of the Interior. Montelibano was not a happy choice. An ambitious
man, he was later to betray Osmeña's trust.

The other cabinet appointees of Osmeña were no less
ill-advised. The Secretary of Commerce and Agriculture,
Vicente Singson Encarnacion, placed the Osmeña administration on the spot as a result of the scandalous sale of
1,500,000 yards of clothing materials from the government-
owned National Development Company to Chinese merchants and black-market sharks, to the prejudice of the
majority of Manila citizens rendered homeless and practically destitute by the destruction of the city. Singson
served under the Japs as a member of Laurel's Economic
Planning Board (of which Roxas was the chairman) and
as a director of Roxas' BIBA. He is a conservative of the
old school. He was the only member of the Osmeña cabinet who served under the Japs. His appointment to the
cabinet was a clear concession by Osmeña to Roxas and
set the precedent in the filling of key government positions.

Another leader of the resistance in the cabinet was
Marcelo Adduru, Secretary of Labor. Dr. Jose Locsin, of
Health and Public Welfare, was a Negros sugar man, with
a belief in social-security legislation as a major step in a
planned economy. Locsin's honesty and integrity and his
earnest concern for the common man marked him as the
most progressive of the Osmeña cabinet appointees.

For Information and Public Instruction, Osmeña had
Maximo Kalaw, also an unpopular choice, whom he had
to shelve and send to Washington as member of the Philippine Rehabilitation Commission dumping ground of
political "miscreants." In his place Osmeña named an old
friend, Francisco Benitez.

For Public Works and Communications, he had Sotero Cabahug, an efficient administrator. Secretary of Justice was Ramon Quisumbing. Jaime Hernandez, Secretary of Finance, was the only member of Osmeña's war cabinet who still carried on.

Of the eleven members of the Philippines Supreme Court, five served under the puppet regimes. The Chief Justice, Manuel V. Moran, carried on under both Vargas and Laurel. Four others who remained in the judiciary under the Japs were Ramon Ozaeta, Cesar Bengzon, Manuel Briones, and Ricardo Paras.

The other justices were Delfin Jaranilla, a conservative of the old school; Mariano H. de Joya, and Felicisimo Feria, conservatives; Guillermo Pablo and Emilio Hilado, who came from the landowning class of Pampanga and Negros respectively; and Gregorio Perfecto, for many years congressman from Manila. None of these six served under the Japs, but each maintained only the most passive resistance.

Two first appointees of Osmeña to the Supreme Court were Francisco Delgado, a delegate to the United Nations Conference in San Francisco, and Jose Espiritu, dean of the College of Law of the University of the Philippines. The two declined rather than give the collaborationist-controlled Commission on Appointments the chance to block their taking office.

The actuations of the Commission on Appointments, which was headed by Roxas as chairman and composed of twelve senators appointed by him and twelve representatives appointed by Speaker Zulueta, a Roxas man, heavily underscored the Roxas strategy of undermining and gradually wresting control of the government by a brazen resort to political blackmail.

Consider the cabinet appointees. They did not have to be submitted to the Congressional Commission on Appointments, which was under Roxas' thumb. Osmeña submitted them anyway. Realizing that two, and possibly three, would be blackballed (Confesor, Cabili, and Kalaw), he kicked out the first two, his most outspoken champions, by naming them to the Philippine Rehabilitation Commission in Washington. He would not risk a clash with Congress over the two undaunted Tomases and yet he knew that an adverse action on their appointments would merely brand Congress as collaborationist. This may have been good strategy, but was bad for party unity. So Osmeña drew back timidly.

Roxas, lusting for power, had made of his rubber-stamp Commission on Appointments a monster which now stalked the sedate halls of Malacañan Palace, giving the Old Man (Osmeña) the chills. Roxas was after Osmeña's scalp. He was flagging the Commission on Appointments with a vengeance. On July 10 the commission okayed Jose Locsin and Alfredo Montelibano for Health and Public Welfare and National Defense, respectively. Both represented Negros sugar interests. In prewar days, both were pro-Roxas, but had now pledged loyalty to Osmeña. Balked temporarily were Vicente Singson Encarnacion and Sotero Cabahug for Agriculture and Commerce and Public Works and Communication respectively. Singson Encarnacion was a puppet, but an Osmeña man, an "old crony." Cabahug was Osmeña's bet in Cebu politics. That was why Osmeña-phobe Mariano J. Cuenco went gunning for Cabahug in the July 10th session of the commission.

The commission was deliberately withholding action on Osmeña's first eight Supreme Court appointees, but would approve at its next meeting the last three, Moran, Ozaeta, and Paras, who served under the Japs. Roxas contended that the Supreme Court never dabbled in collaboration.

The Commission on Appointments had most prospective Osmeña appointees bulldozed. Many appointees found it

necessary to seek Roxas' "advice" before even considering
appointment by Osmeña.

The commission was following a clear-cut collaborationist line. In the meeting on July 12, it laid down an all-out
collaborationist policy. With indecent haste it approved
the appointments of ex-Vargas and Laurel appointees
Moran, as Chief Justice, and Ozaeta and Paras, as Associate Justices of the Supreme Court. On the eight other
justices who did not serve under the puppets action was
withheld and a Manila daily reported: "New [collabora-
tionist] justices are under consideration." The commission
explained: Moran's is a new appointment; Ozaeta's and
Paras' are mere confirmations of their 1941 appointments.
Returned to Malacañan were appointments of Jose Lopez
Vito, Francisco Enage, and Vicente de Vera to the Electoral Commission. Confirmation was not necessary, the
Commission on Appointments said.

Roxas was for maintaining the 1941 status quo. We
could forget the past three years under the Japs. We could
simply take up where we left off. The commission's action
on the above appointments tacitly recognized the transi-
tory nature of the Jap occupation and at the same time
acknowledged no mistakes, no disruption, in the governmental processes under the Japs. This was the meaning of
Roxas' exhortations that the constitution should be upheld.
All his demands for the recall of elective officials, civil-
service men, and members of the judiciary who were in
the service in December 1941 stemmed from this source.

MacArthur Cracks the Whip in the Name of Unity

The political hocus-pocus continued. On July 1, 1945,
Congress made handsome Douglas MacArthur, friend of
Roxas, an honorary Filipino citizen.

Taking the cue from his astute advisers on Philippine affairs, General MacArthur had taken unto himself the job of peacemaker. In the luxurious study of sedate Malacañan Palace, where Quezon's puckish ghost still languished and taunted brother Filipinos, MacArthur, Osmeña, and Roxas spent many hours parleying, with Quezon's successor often in the minority.

On June 27, Roxas and his Zulueta talked, threatened to cause trouble if Osmeña didn't come across. The Commission on Appointments was to meet that afternoon and the Old Man had better be realistic, or else . . .

Out of that conference something like this formula was reached: Henceforth, the executive and legislative branches were to work in close harmony; the executive was to be purged of anti-Roxas "undesirables" and the legislative was to reciprocate by railroading administration measures.

Up for appointment were Roxas choices Colonel Salvador Reyes and Lieutenant Colonel Amado Martelino, both with collaboration records, as Chief of Staff and Deputy Chief of Staff, respectively, of the Philippine Army.

But here the Os-Rox harmony deal backfired. Osmeña's congressional props, Senator Carlos Garcia and Representative Leonardo Festin, demanded that the Old Man keep his word and appoint Colonel Luis Ramos, Adjutant General, Philippine Army, as Chief of Staff. Osmeña hesitated, then withdrew the ready-made Reyes and Martelino appointments.

All this had happened. Roxas-hating anti-puppets in Congress like Garcia, Festin, and de la Paz, stung by Osmeña's flirting with the "enemy," were out to save the Old Man in spite of himself. A strong move was in the offing to organize a left-wing Nacionalista Party which would fight for Osmeña. In January 1946 the Nacionalistas finally split into the Osmeña "loyalist" wing and the Roxas "rebel" wing, with the rebels who called themselves "liberals" taking the majority of the puppets.

The struggle for power within the Nacionalista ranks was on.

On July 3, 1945, Drew Pearson asserted that General MacArthur had advised Senator Tydings to return to Washington, because of the political situation in the Philippines.

In the *Manila Post*, July 5, 1945, MacArthur denied the Pearson statement, saying: "Conjectures involving President Osmeña and Senator Roxas are unfounded and made without the slightest appreciation of the true facts which exist here." He added: "These two high officials are apparently working in close harmony in the reconstruction of their country and both unquestionably enjoy the fullest esteem and respect, not only of their countrymen, but of all others in the Philippines. A distinct disservice is rendered them by attempts to stir up friction."

And what were our politicos harping about? The Osmeña-Roxas truce. A compromise with collaboration and puppetry. With treason and disloyalty. With truth and justice. With victory. With death.

Three years of bitter struggle, hard, dreadful years. History written with the blood of all. Of men whose faith in truth and justice is as unshakable as death itself. Of women whose love for their men is equal to any sacrifice. Of infants whose only crime was to be born under the Japs.

In our hearts and minds was profound gratitude to those who fell in the night of Jap oppression. Abad Santos, Lim, Thorpe, Vinzons, Nakar, Bautista, Roces, resistance leaders liquidated by the Japs. From failing hands, they snatched the torch of freedom, held it high.

But those men of steadfast faith would now be forgotten and the whole heroic Filipino resistance they inspired and directed would be betrayed, because the men of little faith, men with only the faintest notions of the meaning of liberty and patriotism, talked of compromise. They would foist on us a new breed of heroes, the puppets turned "patriots" because they too "fought": Roxas, Laurel, Vargas, Aquino, Osias, Madrigal, Sison, Guinto, Duran, Luz, Capinpin.

And so were the Filipino people being betrayed a second time by the same men who betrayed them to the Japs.

On July 9 General MacArthur made an emotional plea to Congress. "It is absolutely essential that you operate without undue friction," he said. "Petty jealousy, selfish ambition, and unnecessary misunderstanding must not be permitted to impede progress and rend your country."

Political observers at the session could not erase from their minds the half-embarrassed looks on Osmeña's and Roxas' faces as the big crowd that packed the hall cheered the general's plea for unity.

The Manila press played up the MacArthur unity plea the next day. Roxas' *Daily News* came out with its maiden issue, but it gave the MacArthur story only secondary billing. In double-decked headlines Roxas' news sheet scooped the town:

REPUBLIC MINISTERS
PLEAD FOR RELEASE

And no quotes around Laurel's "republic." From Iwahig, the government penal colony on Palawan Island, the puppets had written to General MacArthur and President Osmeña asking for release. They claimed no formal charges had been filed. They were being treated as criminals. "These political prisoners explain," said the *Daily News* naively, "that *at heart* they *never* liked the Japanese nor did they collaborate with them." They served only

because they did not want Ricarte, Ramos, and the renegade Sakdalistas to rule.[2] The Sakdalistas ruled nevertheless, as Makapilis, but they did it over the puppets'
protests. And they were anxious to meet the Americans;
they "braved the dangers of crossing the Japanese lines"
to do so.

MacArthur's appeal was received with jubilation by
members of Congress tainted with collaboration. A compromise between Osmeña and Roxas would mean one
thing, the side-tracking of the issue of collaboration.
Without such an issue—for independence was a settled
question—their re-election could be assured and that alone
mattered.

Zulueta and other congressional leaders had taken Mac-
Arthur's injunction to preserve national unity to mean an
Osmeña-Roxas *rapprochement.* Zulueta even claimed privately that his proposal for indefinite postponement of the
election (originally set for November 1945) had been
inspired by a "hint" from MacArthur himself that the
election should not be held as long as a large number of
unlicensed arms and ammunition remained unaccounted
for. It would be "up to General MacArthur," Zulueta told
the press, to proclaim that conditions of "peace and order"
were such as to justify the holding of an election.

Malacañan and Congress were trying to put their heads
together to preserve "national unity," which meant Nacionalista party unity. The shrill cries of Roxas, it was
suggested in some congressional circles, were merely calculated to browbeat Osmeña into giving concessions. So
far, Roxas had succeeded in pushing him to the wall. But
for the first time in his long political career the Old Man
was standing pat on his decision to run for a public office
instead of leaving it up to the people, or to the party.

[2] Both Ricarte and Ramos were reported killed in the liberation campaign on Luzon Island

He was for re-election. The question of party unity was definitely up Roxas' alley and his alone.

On the night of July 18, 1945, Osmeña gave a dinner at Malacañan Palace in honor of his friend Don Andres Soriano, friend of Roxas, friend of Franco.

The Redeemed "Generalissimo" Talks

Bohol's Carlos Garcia told a surprised senate on June 21, 1945, that the time had come to weed out collaborators. His remedy: The fifteen senators were to draw lots to eliminate the third (eight senators) supposed to serve only two years. This would leave only seven senators, therefore *no* senate. "It would be for the best," Garcia told his colleagues.

The night before, into an easygoing lower house, Cebu's Pedro Lopez [3] hurled a bomb. Taking advantage of the one-hour privilege, Lopez took the floor to read a speech. He was shouted down. He had branded Roxas a "Jap puppet."

. . . All thinking Americans [Lopez reminded his listeners] would be asking themselves this question: Why should we be fools to impose upon ourselves more heavy taxes if only to rehabilitate the Filipinos who are perpetuating in office and power those who had acted as high-ranking puppets and collaborators for the Japs?

The pro-Roxas *Manila Post* screamed:

ROXAS BRANDED
JAPANESE PUPPET

and reported that Roxas would answer the charge.

For two and a half hours at noon of the twenty-first, Roxas recited the saga of his heroic over-all stewardship

[3] Both Garcia and Lopez were in the resistance

of the Philippine resistance movement. Tears welled in his eyes.

> I can say with pride [he intoned challengingly] that no
> ·man, in uniform or without a uniform, has fought on more
> fronts than I have. I invite contradictions.
>
> As a soldier I had to obey. I could have been released
> in ten days but I refused to collaborate. I spent seven
> months in a prison camp.
>
> I was offered the chairmanship of the Executive Com-
> mission first. I refused. I was offered the presidency of
> the republic. I refused.

Calling accusations against him "absurd," Roxas cited witnesses, living and dead, read letters as "conclusive evidence."

"Modesty aside," shouted General Manuel Roxas, "Manuel Roxas was *the* leader, THE LEADER, of the resistance movement in the Philippines!"

He quoted from "unsolicited" letters signed by guerrilla leaders.

About his rendezvous with Quezon, Roxas tearfully related. "President Quezon did not want to leave. He wanted to suffer and die with his people. But he was persuaded by General MacArthur that it was unwise to risk his life, for he was the leader and the symbol of the Filipino liberation movement. Quezon, with tears in his eyes, left with a broken heart only because he believed his presence in the United States would accelerate the sending of aid to the Philippines. *President Quezon would have spoken as I am speaking now;* unfortunately, Quezon is dead."

Quezon, according to Roxas, tried to dissuade him from his decision to stay behind until the last minute. Roxas replied: "I will, if you order me. But if I do, I am afraid the soldiers in Bataan would be disillusioned. Their morale would slacken if we all leave." And that was, Manuel Roxas added, "General MacArthur's opinion too." Said Quezon: "You are right. Go to Bataan and tell them I am leaving to get more reinforcements." (Curtain!)

Before Quezon left Corregidor, Roxas declared, he dictated an executive order naming "Manuel Roxas as the legitimate successor to the Presidency" when Quezon and Osmeña were no more. This, Heir Apparent Roxas said, was cabled to President Roosevelt.

From Bukidnon (Mindanao), Quezon wired Corregidor, to quote Roxas, that IT IS HIGH TIME FOR ROXAS TO COME TO AUSTRALIA. HE IS TOO VALUABLE A MAN TO RISK. OUR COUNTRY NEEDS HIM. AFTER THE WAR, THE SAFETY OF OUR COUNTRY CAN ONLY BE IN HIS HANDS. Roxas told his enthralled listeners he would try to produce the original of this wire, which he quoted to the letter, adding he was "absolutely certain" he quoted "the exact text." He never produced the wire.

Roxas flew to del Monte, Bukidnon, in a "small unarmed plane" to convince Manuel Quezon that Manuel II's place was here just as much as Manuel I's was in Washington. Manuel I left unconvinced, but promised to send a plane "even if I have to buy it out of my pocket" because "I will need you in America." Manuel II tearfully parried: "Mr. President, your presence there would be enough and more." "I wanted to continue fighting. I did my share," rasped Roxas. "Over Mindoro," related Roxas, "my plane was met by two Japanese zeros. My pilot's face told me we were finished. Our plane could make only ninety miles an hour, the zero over 350 miles. In a split second I decided. I whispered into my pilot's ear. We skimmed the swirling waters only ten to twenty feet and dodged the zeros."

On collaboration, Roxas said: "What is collaboration? There are *no* puppets and collaborationists in this house.

I am against every collaborator. I would be the first to bring them to justice. But the mere fact of service under the Japanese is not conclusive evidence of collaboration! *Not a single senator can justly be accused of collaboration!"* The senate broke into applause.

On July 12, 1945, the *Star Reporter* blared:

Osmeña Dead Politically, Can Be Licked by Romulo, Says Roxas

Osmeña looked upon Roxas as a father would on a prodigal son. An intimate friend quoted him: "I pity Roxas. He is a capable man. We can use him. But, if he runs against me and he loses, I will destroy him!" This was Osmeña. He could not forget a friend, whatever his faults. A sinner could go to him and atone for his sins and he would forgive. But if you bucked him . . .

V POLICIES AND POLITICS

The Indecisions and Omissions of Osmeña

ON NOVEMBER 23, 1944, Osmeña broadcast his first message to the Filipino people after liberation. The message came to be known as Osmeña's "government of law" speech, which defined the official policy of the Osmeña administration on collaboration.

He classified collaborators in three categories: Those prompted by a desire to protect the people, those actuated by fear of enemy reprisals, and those motivated by disloyalty to our government and cause.

He cautioned his countrymen against allowing "acts of personal revenge and misguided zeal to cast a reflection on our civilization and ability to maintain an orderly government," adding rhetorically: "Ours is a government of law; the splendor of its majesty must never be dimmed in our land."

Out of the three categories of collaborators, Osmeña generously opened two loopholes. The speech did not define any policy on collaboration. It opened the way for the distortion of the basic issue because it laid stress on the motive of an act, rather than on the act itself. Patriotism very often is the last refuge of a scoundrel.

Osmeña's subsequent fumbling with the collaboration issue was the best refutation of the policy as enunciated in his government-of-law speech.

One of Osmeña's purposes in making a second visit to Washington in May 1945 was to get an official statement on collaboration. There was the Roosevelt policy, but he wanted a commitment from Truman.

The day after Osmeña's return, May 24, Roxas called to ask him what he meant by collaboration. Osmeña, said Roxas later, "passed the buck" to Truman who was, said Osmeña according to Roxas, not himself clear on collaboration.

Osmeña later said: "President Truman reiterated at his last conference with me President Roosevelt's strong position against collaborationist elements, a stand the new president would firmly adhere to. President Truman stressed particularly the case against collaborators in the Philippine Army. For these men it meant 'a change of uniform' and a betrayal of their oath to the United States and the commonwealth."

In private talks, Osmeña gave hints that he would be "very liberal" in dealing with collaborationists. To a good friend, he said in confidence on July 29 that after all one could not blame many officials and employees for continuing in office under the Japs. They had no other means of livelihood. In the case of the army, Osmeña was of the belief that those who accepted civilian jobs, for instance, should be judged "differently."

It was not surprising therefore that he should appoint to his cabinet Roxas' colleague in the Jap-sponsored BIBA, Vicente Singson Encarnacion. With this precedent, the way was cleared for collaborationist elements to jockey for key positions in the government.

On July 9, Osmeña announced the appointment of three men who served under the puppet regime to the Supreme Court: Moran, Ozaeta, and Paras. This was the new line.

If the Singson Encarnacion appointment was a "concession," the appointment of Moran, Ozaeta, and Paras could

only mean a definite change in the Osmeña line. Osmeña
had always hedged whenever he was confronted with the
collaboration issue. Now, he did not draw the line. This
latest wooing of collaborationists weakened Osmeña's position to the same extent that it strengthened Roxas' hand.
Henceforth, every collaborationist or pro-puppet, whether
he *meant* well or not, could boast, without batting an eyelash: "I too fought. I now claim my just reward!"

Malacañan apologists could find no explanation for
Osmeña's change of front other than to suppose that the
appointment of the three magistrates had Washington's
O.K. But it was known Osmeña had definite instructions
from Truman regarding the collaboration issue. The fact is
that Osmeña seems to have made up his mind to let things
drift.

On April 19, 1945, he was scheduled to confer with
President Roosevelt on collaboration. Roosevelt died on
the twelfth. On the nineteenth, Truman kept his predecessor's appointment with Osmeña, but he could only
reiterate F. D. R.'s stand on collaboration "without quali-
fying it." Osmeña arranged to see Secretary Stimson. An
interview was set, but on that day Germany surrendered
and Osmeña could only snatch a few words of greeting
with Stimson. Before leaving Washington, he arranged for
his representative, Dr. Hayden, to take up the issue with
Stimson. In San Francisco to catch the first available
plane for home, for he had a rush summons from Mac-
Arthur, Osmeña wired Hayden to ask what progress had
been made. Hayden had yet to see Stimson; then death
took Dr. Hayden.[1]

So the Old Man returned unsure of himself and as inarticulate about collaboration as he was before he left.

[1] Joseph Ralston Hayden, on General MacArthur's staff as civilian
adviser on Philippine affairs, died in the United States on May 19, 1945,
while on a short visit preparatory to returning to Manila as Osmeña's
adviser

And from Malacañan came the hint that more collaborationists were up for important appointments.

There was, however, one thing Osmeña did not tell his friends. It was this: President Truman told him in their last conference that the Philippines would not get any rehabilitation money unless all known collaborators were kept out of office.

Reminiscences of a Sphinx

On the night of July 27, 1945, the Sphinx of Malacañan talked.[2]

More than a month before the executive council of the Democratic Alliance [3] sought a conference with Osmeña. He received the DA bigwigs cordially, reminisced for fifteen minutes, called it a day; the DA men filed out of the palace disgusted.

A few days before the twenty-seventh Osmeña's Hannegan, Eulogio Rodriguez, Sr., told the DA leaders the Old Man would like to have them for dinner to talk things over. On the appointed evening the DA executives were treated to a sumptuous dinner. Usually cynical and hard to impress, they went home after a three and a half hours' chat with Osmeña with a mixed feeling of surprise and admiration.

Just before the DA executives took their seats at the dinner table, Rodriguez gave DA Chairman Jesús Barrera a nudge, told him to pump the Old Man hard and not mince words. Barrera passed the word around.

The DA got a rise out of the Sphinx.

On collaboration: Osmeña had been closely following his government-of-law speech in Leyte in filling vacancies. Some collaborators had been appointed. Some appoint-

[2] In Philippine politics, Osmeña is known as "The Sphinx"
[3] See Chapter XIII

ments like that of Vicente Singson Encarnacion had boomeranged. Osmeña frankly admitted he did not know all the facts in the case, but he stressed the fact that, henceforth, he would appoint only those who had previously been cleared. As for those he had appointed who held jobs under the Japs, he would welcome charges against them. Should the charges be substantiated, these appointees would be booted out.

On *rapprochement* with Roxas: This was still a possibility, but definitely the move must come from Roxas. Osmeña was confident of re-election. He was concerned over party unity and Roxas might, or could, remain in the party only by taking No. 2 spot.

But, the DA reminded him, this would mean the collaboration issue would be sidetracked, since Roxas was for the total whitewash of puppets and collaborators.

The Sphinx smiled, but said nothing. And he reminisced.

In regard to his chances of re-election Osmeña had no misgivings. He knew he might lose in Manila, but he was sure the provinces would give him a majority. And this is where the Democratic Alliance came in. Affiliated with the DA was the Hukbalahap, which had a strong hold on the peasantry of Central Luzon. Every politician, from Quezon down, had tried to win over the peasantry, for their vote was the decisive factor there. Osmeña's job dispenser Rodriguez, shrewd and practical, offered the backing of the Nacionalista party machine if the DA would support Osmeña. The DA executive council almost bit. Osmeña still was not clear on collaboration and the DA was uncompromisingly against collaborators.

"Why is McNutt here?"[4] Frankly, said the Sphinx, "I know as much as you do." "Do you think he will press re-

[4] See Chapter X: Mr. McNutt and Re-examination

examination?" "I don't think so. Re-examination is out of
the question now. McNutt knows the line."

"Why was Elizalde kicked out of the cabinet in Washington?"[5] There was much talk about Elizalde's fascist
activities and Osmeña did not want to embarrass the commonwealth. Elizalde was rabidly pro-Roxas.

"Suppose charges were brought against a puppet, say,
Claro M. Recto. Would Osmeña ask the United States
Army for his release, so he could be tried?" This, said the
Sphinx, would be interfering with military affairs. The
puppets simply have to wait until the Japs give up.

"Why did you oust Tomas Confesor and Tomas Cabili
when these two men were your stanchest champions?"
The Sphinx beamed. Confesor, especially, had committed
his administration to an uncompromising anti-collabora-
tionist policy. This had confused people and caused the
government some harm and embarrassment. And he was
trying to undo what the undaunted Tomases had done.

"Had he picked his vice-presidential mate?" Again that
enigmatic smile.

That night's conference, said DA key men, was merely
an "indoctrination" conference with Osmeña as the guinea
pig. It really was the other way around. The DA's biggest
poser now was whether to support Osmeña against Roxas
or run independently in the April election.[6]

Did MacArthur Clear Roxas?

The "liberation" of Manuel Roxas was accomplished by
a routine communiqué from General MacArthur's headquarters, which left his intention to supposition and con-
jecture.

[5] Joaquin M. Elizalde was Quezon's Resident Commissioner in Washington up to the time of Quezon's death in August 1944
[6] See Chapter XIII: The Progressives Join Forces with Osmeña

This communiqué became in Roxas' hand a double-edged weapon. General MacArthur had become, in the eyes of many Filipinos, an idol. His word was gospel truth. When he announced in a communiqué the "liberation" of Roxas, he in effect signed Roxas' clearance papers.

Roxas' position on his own "liberation" is best expressed by his *Daily News* in an editorial, titled Roxas Is Cleared, on August 2, 1945. Roxas, said the *News,* is

> no more a collaborator than either President Osmeña, who ran away to the United States, which he should not have done for the head of the Commonwealth had decided to do that, or Confesor himself who was so scared all he did was to be in hiding. The decision *clearing* General Roxas was rendered, so to speak, by no other than General of the Army Douglas MacArthur who approved the petition to revert Brigadier General Roxas to inactive service.

Again, on August 26, 1945, the *Daily News* ran a defense of Roxas:

> We wish to inform the Filipino people that the case of General Roxas, if there has been any touching on collaboration, has long been disposed of and that *the General has already been cleared by no less an Army authority than General of the Army Douglas MacArthur.*[7] General Roxas was recognized as the leader of the underground, or guerrillas, in the Philippines during the Japanese occupation.

First, General MacArthur "liberated" Roxas. Next, he called him to active military duty and assigned him to his headquarters. This tacitly "cleared" Roxas. Then, on Roxas' request, MacArthur reverted him to inactive status so he could lay the groundwork for his bid for power.

[7] Italics supplied

Free Philippines carried the story of Roxas' reversion to inactive status in a two-column box on the front page.

With Roxas "cleared" it was easy to infer that the other members of the Laurel cabinet would also be cleared. "Those now detained in Iwahig for military necessity," wrote Roxas in his *Daily News* in August, "will in a day or so be turned over to our government, presumably to stand trial for presumed collaboration with the enemy."

He added:

The charge could not be more serious or drastic, and the men involved—many of them—could not be more prominent or distinguished. By their natural talents in statecraft, by their long and rounded experience in public affairs, they were admittedly the *logical* leaders who *had* to take over the reins of government in the harsh and onerous circumstances then obtaining, when the President and the Vice-President of the Commonwealth had to leave the homeland and had to stay away and afar during enemy occupation.

Did those men collaborate with the enemy during their incumbency; that is, did they voluntarily give aid, comfort and sustenance to the enemy?

The most eloquent answer, of course, was Roxas' own "liberation."

With indecent haste, the pro-Jap collaborators were being "returned" to the position of power they enjoyed before the war. In Roxas' *Daily News* on August 19 the Generalissimo was quoted as saying that General Mac-Arthur "personally had assured him" that the senator puppets then in Iwahig were to be released just as soon as the Japs got around to signing the formal surrender terms. And from his friend Senator Arranz came the bright idea of including in the senate drawing of lots (to deter-

mine the terms of office of the present members) the
names of those senators.

General MacArthur's actuations in Roxas' behalf cast
doubts as to his intentions. And his reticence and, worse
still, his occasional statements through his official spokesman merely fanned the suspicions, groundless or not, that
he had his nose in the Philippine political muddle.

In an article in the *Nation,* by Freda Kirchwey, Mac-
Arthur was charged with imposing a "dictatorship" over
the Philippines.

> Never were the Philippines more completely cut off
> from the world. They are MacArthur's private sphere of
> influence. We have not heard how limited are President
> Osmeña's actual powers, or how careful MacArthur's con-
> trol has been to protect him from his Left Wing sup-
> porters by throwing them into prison.

This was a sharp charge, but it drew a weak denial from
MacArthur's spokesman. The reply was revealing:

> Such a story is pure poppycock. The Commonwealth
> Government is in complete control of civil affairs in the
> Philippine Islands, and the military forces are exercising
> absolutely no political interference. They are aiding in
> every possible way in the reconstruction of the Islands but
> are not involved in the slightest degree in the political
> situation. The great mass of the guerrilla forces have been
> incorporated into the United States Army. Only collabora-
> tionists with the Japanese, whose freedom might menace
> military operations, are held in custody by the Military
> as a measure of military security. They do not number,
> out of the entire population of 17 million, more than 2,500.
> All elements in the Islands are completely united in
> their support of the Commander in Chief who assiduously
> abstains from political encroachments. There are *no* left

wing or right wing elements in the Philippines. All are united on basic issues. The only political rivalries are based on the personalities of candidates. No place which has suffered from enemy occupation has been so rapidly freed from military influences and permitted to establish democratic processes. There is absolutely no political censorship being imposed. The Islands are being constantly visited by committees of the American Congress and other governmental agencies who are completely cognizant of conditions and have reported in approval of what they have seen.

But a *New York Post* editorial of September 20, 1945 (*Manila Post* September 22), spoke of the "Quisling Leader Roxas [who] is running for President while Partisan Commander Luis Taruc is in jail".[8]

Roxas promptly issued a denial and in his defense brought out the MacArthur angle. "I have never been a collaborator," he said. "I was not captured by the American forces. I escaped from Japanese-held territory and after crossing the firing lines [with seven thousand others] I joined the American forces to report for duty. *General MacArthur immediately allowed me to serve in his headquarters.*"

Said Tomas Confesor, then Filipino member of the Far Eastern Advisory Council, on February 19, 1946: "Even the Japs in Tokyo are now pro-American."

The net result of MacArthur's policy, or rather of the confusion resulting from the implications of his well-considered acts, was disillusionment and despair on the part of the men who resisted. One resistance fighter wrote in the *Philippine Press* on August 30, 1945:

Very few talk about him now. He is forgotten and un-

[8] Released a few days after a big demonstration by peasants in Manila on September 23, 1945

honored, he is dead. He clung to his principles to the very
end, he chose death to dishonor, so that even his own
executioners, impressed by so much courage, admitted
they faltered for a moment in the execution of their
orders.

He kept the spirit of the people alive during those dark
days. For several weeks, he operated an underground
radio station in the very heart of Manila. At 12 o'clock
sharp, he would go on the air and urge the people to keep
faith in the force of liberty. The enemy finally caught him,
tortured and killed him. He was told he could save his life
if he would broadcast and take back all he said. He defi-
antly answered: "You can kill my body but not my spirit."

Today nothing is said about him. And those who called
him a "misguided element" are being hailed as martyrs.
Those who traded with the men who killed him are being
held up as heroes or heroines before a bewildered nation.
He is now nothing but a silly, impractical fool, a young
hothead, a dreamer.

Carlos Malonso, "The Voice of Juan de la Cruz," and
all the others that died like him are nothing but suckers.

They're suckers because while they kept faith with us
we have not kept faith with them.

A Jap Militarist Bats for the Quislings

Late in August 1945 MacArthur flew to Tokyo to begin
the "democratization" of Japan. With the war correspondents chosen to cover the general and his occupation
troops were four Filipinos, one of them Felixberto G.
Bustos, biographer of MacArthur's friend and ex-aide
Manuel Roxas.

Bustos had a mission to perform: to seek out Hirohito's
Filipino puppets and interview them and make them toe
the line by giving them the right cue.

The cue was this. On September 6, 1945, Roxas' *Daily
News* came out with a front-page editorial: Collaboration
Is Nothing but a Myth in the Philippines." Taking the
statements of United States High Commissioner McNutt
and Senator Tydings that every Filipino remained loyal at
their face value, the *News* asked:

> Is it not a fact that nearly all the so-called puppet offi-
> cials of the Executive Commission first and later the Re-
> public were in constant contact with guerrilla elements
> and many of them were in fact guerrilla leaders?
> Is it not a fact that many in the buy-and-sell trade
> during that infamous period contributed much to the un-
> derground movement?

Roxas' shrill mouthpiece answered its own questions:

> Yes, not one of us was a collaborator. Every one of us
> who were left behind acted to help the Filipinos them-
> selves survive until America could come back. Why will
> there be punishment for a crime that was not committed?
> Or punishment for the service rendered for the good of
> the Filipino people alone when the enemy was here.

A day after this editorial, from the Japanese city of
Nara, Roxas' buddy Laurel "confidingly" echoed the *Daily
News* line to Roxas' biographer Bustos. Shrieked the *News*
on September 8, 1945: COLLABORATION FAKED—LAUREL.
This was followed the next day by another Bustos exclu-
sive interview which the *News* banner-headlined: AM
RESPONSIBLE ALONE—LAUREL. The same day Bustos inter-
viewed Laurel he also talked with other prize Filipino
puppets, Benigno S. Aquino and Camilo Osias. Said
Aquino: "No one in our country could doubt my patriot-
ism and sincerity of purpose." (At about the same time in
Norway the traitor Quisling was saying: "I am Quisling

the patriot.") Said Osias: "I have converted it [the Kali-bapi] into an association of, for, and by the Filipinos." (He did not add: "under the Japs.")

The C.B.S., which employed Bustos, gave him a bonus for his journalistic feat in locating Laurel and springing the scoop, but what the other war correspondents did not know was that Bustos had to get to Laurel first, and quickly, to deliver a message from Roxas. It was no strange coincidence that the Filipino puppets in Manila and in Tokyo were talking the same line.

NOTE: United States Army Intelligence got wise to the Bustos mission and on his return to Manila from Tokyo late in September 1945 he was grilled. He admitted he carried a verbal message from Roxas to Laurel and Laurel's reply, also verbal. Roxas assured Laurel everything was being done in Manila to vindicate the puppets' names and to see that they got "justice." Laurel expressed his gratitude through Bustos.

The first interviews which the top Filipino puppets in Tokyo gave following the surrender of Japan and prior to their arrest by the United States Army CIC, were very revealing.

Interviewed by the United Press on August 3, 1945, in Tokyo, Jorge B. Vargas confessed he was worried and wondered what General MacArthur "thinks of my acts."

September 1 Vargas seemed no longer worried. "My conscience is clear," he told Filipino war correspondents. And he could talk again, as he did under the Japs, of "a solidly united Philippines." He gave out this statement:

I have only one poignant regret, and that is that our great patriot and leader [Quezon] who, together with Osmeña, Yulo and Roxas, laid the foundation of the Commonwealth in preparation of the coming Republic [Laurel's quisling one is of course now conveniently forgotten] has not been given the opportunity and satisfaction of seeing his monumental work come to fruition.

But let us not fail to profit from his great vision.[9]

Reason for this new confidence, apparently, was the gratuitous whitewash of Filipino puppets by the Jap General Masaharu Homma, of the infamous Bataan Death March, who was reported, under a Yokohama date line of September 1 (*Manila Chronicle* September 3, 1945), as saying the puppets "could not have done otherwise."

Homma, reported the *Chronicle* correspondent, who himself worked with the Japs, "doubted that any administration could be formed in the Philippines at that time which did not include former Quezon cabinet men."

It was Homma who said on August 4, 1942:

When soon after we entered Manila, you offered to cooperate with the Japanese Forces, I know that you did so at the risk of your lives. The Bataan campaign was only beginning and both the Americans and the Filipinos were fighting furiously, because of the promise made by the President of the United States that reinforcements were to come. Nevertheless, it was very brave of you gentlemen to have extended your collaboration [*sic!*]. I do not know what would have happened to you gentlemen if reinforcements had come. This fact is important and makes me all the more appreciative of the courageous stand you took and your willingness to extend to me your co-operation. No one can foretell exactly when the war will end. Whatever may happen, I have confidence that you gentlemen will continue serving *loyally* and *faithfully*. I have no doubt that with the devotion which you have shown, much good will come from *collaboration*.

It appeared clear that there was a concerted attempt to whitewash the pro-Jap collaborators in Japan and in this

[9] *Manila Chronicle,* September 3, 1945

way prepare the ground for the total whitewash of all collaborators in Manila, in prison and outside, without any
charges being filed against them. There was evident "con-
tinuity" when Vargas talked (even when Japs were still
fighting in many sectors of the Philippines despite the
surrender) of Osmeña, Yulo, and Roxas having laid the
foundation of the commonwealth in preparation for the
coming republic. And, what was significant, Filipino war
correspondents, including a paid biographer of Roxas and
a former staff member of Domei, were up in Tokyo to tell
the Filipinos how the puppets felt.

Why the United States Army permitted Filipino war
correspondents with a background of collaboration with
the Japs to cover the Tokyo occupation is another of those
things that must be considered "top secret" because they
are sometimes not easily explained.

Their arrest came as a shock to the puppets. Interviewed by a United Press man following his arrest in
Tokyo, Vargas said: "I am glad that the war's over, but
the war's not over for me."[10]

In Manila, the arrest was viewed with apprehension in
collaborationist circles. Members of the Philippine Congress were disturbed by a press statement in Tokyo from
General MacArthur's Chief of Counter-Intelligence, Brigadier General E. R. Thorpe, on September 12: "There will
be no hurry in sending Vargas, Laurel and other Filipino
puppet officials to Manila. They wanted to come, didn't
they? Well, they can stay here for a little while more." [11]

Sarcastically the CIC chief added: "They'd be better
fed in jail than outside. We'll let them look around for
their food for a while. In Manila, I found collaborators
fattening up in prison, while many of the loyal elements
starved outside."

[10] *Philippine Press*, September 14, 1945
[11] *Philippine Press*, September 14, 1945

When news of Laurel and Vargas was received in Manila late in August 1945, the *Manila Comet* shrieked:

LAUREL, VARGAS ALIVE

And the collaborationist-edited *Manila Post* screamed:

AWAIT ARRIVAL OF LAUREL, VARGAS

The prize puppets were being awaited by a "grateful nation" which they had "saved" through collaboration.

The Promise that Failed: Surrender on the Missouri

I have it down in my diary. "And of course," said Franklin D. Roosevelt, "the Philippine government will have its rightful place in the conferences which will follow the defeat of Japan."

This was on August 13, 1943, when Roosevelt reiterated his solemn pledge to the "heroic people of the Philippines" that their freedom would be redeemed.

Defeat came to Japan in the second week of August 1945. In Manila talk was that the surrender terms would be signed in the capital of the Philippines. It was logical. It would give a flourish to a drama in which the Philippines had played a heroic part.

But it was not in the books.

On August 30 MacArthur's C-54 *Bataan* landed on Atsugi Airfield, two hours from Tokyo. The terms of formal surrender were signed on board the *Missouri* on September 2. Every nation in the Pacific was represented at the ceremony and had a seat of honor among the conquerors, except the Philippines, "a nation fit to be respected as the equal of any on earth," which "won all" in "trial and disaster."

"Your country," said MacArthur with emotion on February 29, 1945, when the commonwealth government was re-established at a simple ceremony in Malacañan, "is again at liberty to pursue its destiny to an honored position in the family of free nations; your capital city, cruelly punished though it be, has regained its rightful place: Citadel of Democracy in the East."

That statement today has a strangely mocking ring.

VI Osmeña Is Told to Clean House

Sabotage of the People's Court

ON SEPTEMBER 1, 1945, press censorship was lifted in the Philippines. With it, the political fog began to clear.

Significantly, with MacArthur "out of the way," Osmeña started to take a firmer stand on political problems raised by the occupation, particularly on the decisive issue of collaboration.

Since the time of Roxas' "liberation" by MacArthur, Osmeña had been laboring under a self-imposed restraint; his belief that MacArthur was for Roxas and would not be averse to seeing him elected to the presidency. This feeling of restraint had worked to his disadvantage. His Sphinxlike silence, his seeming indifference to day-to-day problems, his obvious "blundering" and "fumbling" on the collaboration issue, caused many a supporter and sympathizer, who had looked up to him for leadership, to shy away in disgust. And the scandals that came in the wake of his reinstatement of corrupt public officials meant more prestige lost. The Roxas forces were quick to make political capital out of government corruption.

"Collaboration is NOT for the people to decide," Roxas declared. "That is the work of the People's Court."

The story of the People's Court, particularly the determined attempts of the collaborationists in Congress to emasculate it and the stellar role Roxas played in it, left little doubt about Roxas' position on collaboration.

When Congress was convened for its second special session on August 14, two bills were filed, one by Senator Elpidio Quirino and the other by Congressman Francisco Ortega. The bills sought the creation of a People's Court. Quirino's idea was to have as prosecuting attorneys only men from the Judge Advocate General's Service, Philippine Army, who were, with the exception of three minor assistants, all collaborators. Ortega wanted a court of politicos, in addition to Supreme Court Chief Justice Manuel V. Moran, who served on the bench under the Japs, and Roxas himself.

Both Quirino and Ortega were Roxas men. Everywhere in the world collaborators have been tried by noncollaborators, in the majority of cases resistance fighters and leaders. In the Philippines, only collaborators could try collaborators.

On August 24, Osmeña showed for the first time an eagerness to act with firmness on collaboration by sending to Congress for favorable action a bill creating a special collegiate court to try collaborationists. Osmeña proposed that the court be composed of judges of first instance *not* identified with collaboration, either politically or economically, and that the prosecution be handled by a staff of prosecutors, also noncollaborators, headed by the Solicitor General.

The Roxas-flagged senate tried to beat Osmeña to the draw. On August 27, the senate passed the Quirino bill on second reading and sent it to the house. Reporting the approval the next day, Roxas' *Daily News* said: *"The senators who are among the prisoners may be allowed to attend the session of the senate next week before the closing of the present special session."*[1]

[1] Seven puppet senators were then held by the United States Army CIC

Osmeña ordered administration supporters in the house to buck the Quirino bill, which, as revised, sought the trial of collaborators by a court composed of noncollaborators. The bill, however, had an escape clause which was intended obviously to whitewash most of the big collaborators. It would limit the "collaborators" only to those held by the CIC, the presumption being that those not otherwise held were free and could not be tried for having collaborated with the Japs. Roxas was out, because he was not held by the CIC. So also are the several thousand collaborators whose cases the CIC, handicapped by lack of personnel and time, could not handle.

On June 21, 1945, Quirino told the senate: "There are no so-called collaborators in this body." And he pleaded: "Let us follow our constitution in trying to eliminate the so-called collaborators. But, I say, do not delay justice by confining them [the puppet senators] in prison."

At this time, Osmeña was determined to see his own plan for a collegiate court go through. The senate was trying to drive a hard bargain to get a "compromise" People's Court bill passed. Osmeña supporters, however, would not budge.

The Roxas forces let the whole thing ride. Then, on September 3, a systematic drive to cripple the court began. Contrary to all legislative procedures, three senators, Roxas, Quirino, and Arranz, attended the lower-house session and were instrumental in pushing through an "improved" version of the original Osmeña bill by a close vote of twenty-six for and twenty-three against.

The whole procedure followed in railroading the substitute bill was irregular and questionable. The house committee on judiciary, in whose name the bill was submitted by a Roxas man, Floor Leader Perez, did not know of the existence of the new measure until Perez presented it in the committee's name.

The substitute bill thus passed was the Osmeña administration's original bill minus its teeth.

Under the original bill, members of the bar with the necessary qualifications could be named judges of the People's Court and special prosecutors to assist the Solicitor General. The substitute bill entirely left out bar practitioners from both the court and the prosecutors' staff. The intention, of course, was as obvious as it was sinister.

Roxas was so sure the People's Court bill would be approved in its mangled form that on September 6 he sent out emissaries to canvass special prosecutors in the Judge Advocate General's Service, Philippine Army, and in the Judge Advocate Service of recognized guerrilla units. His intention was that he himself would "process" these prosecutors.

Roxas was sure Osmeña would sign the bill. In fact, his *Daily News* said so and speculated that Osmeña would organize the people in ten days. Osmeña, however, would not be rushed.

In addition to the provisions in the substitute bill limiting the choice of judges and special prosecutors, one section had Department of Justice officials, who drafted the original measure, worried. This was Section 2, which read in part:

> The People's Court shall have jurisdiction to try and decide all cases of crimes against national security [originally this was "treason and other crimes against national security"] committed between December 8, 1941 [originally September 1, 1939], and filed within six months [two years in the original bill] from the passage of this Act.

Under this provision, confirmed and outspoken Japanophiles like Pio Duran, Artemio Ricarte, and Benigno Ramos might not be tried for acts of disloyalty committed *before* December 8, 1941. Bad faith might not be im-

puted to such men as Jose P. Laurel and other learned
"Orientalists" who, before Pearl Harbor, showed inclinations in favor of Japanese hegemony over the Far East
and all Orientals. To this extent the prosecutor was to be
restrained. At the same time, the substitute bill, which was
underwritten by expert Roxas legal minds, would rush the
prosecutors, allowing them only six months after the passage of the bill within which to file charges against the
5600 odd political prisoners detained by the CIC and several thousands more. Department of Justice officials asked
for at least two years, but the collaborationist clique would
not budge on six months.

Solicitor General Lorenzo M. Tanada, an uncompromising resistance leader, was so disgusted that he told
friends on September 6 he would resign if the bill were
approved.

He said:

> We need men who can sit in that tribunal [People's
> Court] who are truly of the people, not judges of first
> instance who, although they did not serve in the Execu-
> tive Commission and the puppet Philippine Republic,
> nevertheless owed favors to influential officials before the
> war broke out; men who, in one way or another, were ap-
> pointed or recommended by Laurel, Jose Yulo, Teofilo
> Sison, Quintin Parades, Claro M. Recto and company.

> What will happen? We will have accused looking up to
> judges with a lurking look or smile that can say: "You're
> trying me! I appointed or recommended you to a similar
> post once in the past!" We will have a case of judges who
> can not really look down on the accused.

Then came the Ickes blast. The Ickes directive coin-
cided with the resumption of the consideration of the
People's Court bill passed by Congress in an emasculated

form. Osmeña promptly returned it with a recommendation that his original plan for a strong People's Court be
considered.

The house, led by the Festin-De la Paz-Primicias bloc
restored the Osmeña plan to virtually its original form,
but with the choice of judges and prosecutors still limited,
and pushed it through. The senate had to submit.

The People's Court was finally approved by both houses
at the close of the second special session on September
17, 1945.

Mr. Ickes Issues a Directive

On September 9, 1945, Osmeña observed his sixty-
seventh birthday. To the well-wishers that filed into Malacañan to greet him and to wish him long life, he stressed
the compelling need for a collective effort to put the
Philippines back on her feet. The fundamental principle
that must guide Filipinos, he said, is "that we must retain the confidence which America has always shown
toward us."

From Washington, Harold L. Ickes, United States Secretary of the Interior, broadcast America's greetings to the
commonwealth president. Mr. Ickes said he knew President Osmeña well enough "to realize that today he is
looking not backward but forward to the months and
years in which the Filipinos must cope with the great
problems of healing the wounds of war, building anew
the magnificent cities of the Commonwealth, restoring its
farms and industries, and unifying the spirit of its great
people."

In characteristic vein, Mr. Ickes gave some indication
of how the Filipinos could retain the "confidence" Osmeña
spoke of when he expressed his faith that the Filipinos

"will finally, coldly and relentlessly cast out those few
timid, craven and opportunistic helots who basely collaborated with the cruel enemy who sought to enslave their
people."

The statement was a preview of what was to come.
Collaborationist circles were perturbed over the Ickes
statement but their mouthpiece, the *Daily News,* was sur-
prisingly noncommittal. Something definitely was in the
air.

There was marked apprehension in Congress. Only two
days before, Truman had announced the appointment of
Paul V. McNutt as United States High Commissioner to
the Philippines. Congressmen were puzzled. When Osmeña returned from Washington for the first time, in February 1945, he said informally that he had convinced Truman a High Commissioner would not be necessary here
in the short period before independence. Now, however,
without fanfare, Mr. McNutt was coming to take up an
old job. Why?

Mr. Ickes' statement was well timed. He put in a good
word for Osmeña just about the time the commonwealth
president was getting ready to show Roxas and the administration baiters in Congress he could say No. Back to
Congress Osmeña sent the People's Court bill, as doctored
by Roxas, Quirino, and Arranz, with the request that his
original plan be approved.

Two days later, on September 11, came the Ickes directive on the open wire, uncoded. Said Ickes to Osmeña:

BOTH OFFICIAL AND PRESS REPORTS INDICATE THAT A
SUBSTANTIAL NUMBER OF PERSONS WHO ADHERED TO THE
ENEMY AND GAVE HIM AID AND COMFORT THROUGH THEIR
SERVICE IN THE PUPPET GOVERNMENTS DURING INVASION ARE
NOW HOLDING IMPORTANT OFFICES IN VARIOUS BRANCHES OF
THE COMMONWEALTH GOVERNMENT INCLUDING THE JUDI-

CIARY. I AM INFORMED THAT YOU INTEND TO RELEASE
NUMEROUS PERSONS AGAINST WHOM EVIDENCE WAS COL-
LECTED BY THE UNITED STATES ARMY. YOUR ATTENTION IS
INVITED TO THE STATEMENT OF PRESIDENT ROOSEVELT ON
JUNE 29, 1944, THAT THOSE MUST BE REMOVED FROM AU-
THORITY AND INFLUENCE OVER THE POLITICAL AND ECONOMIC
LIFE OF THE COUNTRY. IT WAS INTENDED THAT THIS STATE-
MENT WOULD SERVE AS GUIDE TO THE POLICY OF THE COM-
MONWEALTH AND THAT THE COMMONWEALTH WOULD FIND
THE MEANS OF EFFECTIVELY INVESTIGATING CHARGES AND
SPEEDILY TRYING THE OFFENDERS BEFORE COURTS OR TRIBU-
NALS COMPOSED OF JUDGES OF UNQUESTIONED LOYALTY. I
DEEM IT ESSENTIAL THAT THIS TASK BE COMPLETED BEFORE
THE HOLDING OF THE NEXT COMMONWEALTH GENERAL ELEC-
TION AND I WOULD CALL THE ATTENTION OF YOUR GOVERN-
MENT TO THE PROBABLE RELUCTANCE WITH WHICH FUNDS
MAY BE APPROPRIATED FOR RELIEF, REHABILITATION AND
SUPPORT OF THE COMMONWEALTH GOVERNMENT IF IT BE-
COMES GENERALLY BELIEVED THAT THAT GOVERNMENT HAD
FAILED DILIGENTLY AND FIRMLY TO CONVICT AND PUNISH
THOSE GUILTY OF COLLABORATION.

Here was a political weapon. With it Osmeña could
have pushed the collaborationist clique that dominated
Congress to the wall. But Osmeña himself felt uneasy
over the directive. It was, he realized, a slap in his own
face, too.

Undecided what to do, he summonded Roxas and Zulueta and showed them the directive. He let two days
pass before he had it read before Congress. Nevertheless,
it caught the collaborationist clique off balance. From
Roxas' vice-presidential running mate, Elpidio Quirino,
came a proffer of peace, "a moratorium on electioneer-
ing," a thumping handclasp between Osmeña and Roxas

so that "they may work for badly needed funds for re-habilitation."

Roxas made no public statement. His *Daily News* ignored the story while all other Manila papers played it up in V-J type. But, writing in his column, "The Compass," in the *News*, Roxas termed the warning "insolent" and "so reminiscent, if not worse, of the abominable Japanese way." In subsequent issues, he continued to heap abuse on the "gullible Mr. Ickes" and to sing, at the same time, high praise to the "craven helots" who had collaborated.

On September 18, Roxas charged: "Mr. Ickes is unduly pressing with threatening vehemence the trial and punishment of the supposed collaborators."

In the same issue, a *News* staff man concluded a defense of Roxas, Laurel and Company in these words: "Therefore, to us, Laurel and those who worked with him (like Roxas) are not 'traitors and rats,' but heroes and patriots."

Significantly, the Ickes directive marked the changed role of Speaker Zulueta from that of a Roxas stooge to a spokesman of the Osmeña administration. Zulueta, an opportunist, knew then that he could hope to retain the speakership only by toeing the administration line.[2]

At the same time, the anticollaborationist feeling began to crystallize. The lifting of press censorship by the United States Army, the shrill Chinese baiting by the Roxas press, and the Ickes warning brought into sharp focus the collaboration issue, which Roxas and the collaborationist clique in Congress would dismiss as "nothing but a myth."

The impact of the directive was somewhat dampened by Osmeña's reply, which his advisers felt left the door open for more charges of "ineptitude" from Roxas.

[2] Zulueta changed colors again in January, 1946, following the Osmeña-Roxas split

Here is Osmeña's reply:

IN REPLY TO YOUR TELEGRAM OF SEPTEMBER ELEVEN I
DESIRE TO STATE THAT INFORMATION GIVEN YOU THAT I IN-
TEND TO RELEASE NUMEROUS PERSONS AGAINST WHOM EVI-
DENCE WAS COLLECTED BY THE U.S. ARMY IS ERRONEOUS STOP
PERSONS KEPT IN DETENTION BY COUNTER INTELLIGENCE
CORPS OF U.S. ARMY AND LATER DELIVERED TO THE COMMON-
WEALTH GOVERNMENT HAVE BEEN ORDERED DETAINED BY ME
EVEN BEYOND THE PERIOD OF SIX HOURS PERMITTED BY THE
CRIMINAL LAWS OF THE PHILIPPINES STOP A FEW OF THEM
HAVE BEEN TEMPORARILY RELEASED ON BAIL AS DETERMINED
BY THE DEPARTMENT OF JUSTICE PENDING PRESENTATION OF
CHARGES AGAINST THEM AND THEIR TRIAL BEFORE THE
COURTS STOP THE PHILIPPINE CONGRESS HAS ENACTED A LAW
CREATING A SPECIAL COURT TO TRY ALL PERSONS ACCUSED OF
COLLABORATION WITH THE ENEMY STOP THE JUDGES OF THIS
COURT WILL BE PERSONS WHO NEVER SERVED IN ANY CAPACITY
UNDER THE PUPPET GOVERNMENTS AND THE PROSECUTORS
ARE CHIEFLY RECRUITED FROM ARMY JUDGE ADVOCATES AND
GUERRILLA LEADERS STOP DOUBTLESS THE PROSECUTION OF
ALLEGED COLLABORATORS WILL BE DILIGENTLY CONDUCTED
AND THOSE FOUND GUILTY WILL BE PROMPTLY PUNISHED IN
ACCORDANCE WITH LAW.

WE HAVE NEVER KNOWINGLY REINSTATED ANY OFFICIAL
WHOM U.S. ARMY AUTHORITIES HAVE DETAINED FOR COLLAB-
ORATION STOP SEVERAL OFFICIALS AND EMPLOYEES WHO
CONTINUED IN THEIR POST DURING THE PUPPET REGIME BUT
COMMITTED NO HOSTILE ACTS AGAINST THE PHILIPPINE OR
AMERICAN GOVERNMENT HAVE BEEN REINSTATED BY ME IN
EXECUTIVE OR JUDICIAL BRANCHES AFTER THEY HAD BEEN
CLEARED BY THE COUNTER INTELLIGENCE CORPS OF THE U.S.
ARMY STOP I REINSTATED THEM ON THE BASIS OF THE VIEWS
I EXPRESSED IN A SPEECH I DELIVERED LAST NOVEMBER
SHORTLY AFTER THE LANDING OF AMERICAN FORCES IN LEYTE

AND AFTER CONSULTATION WITH ARMY AUTHORITIES STOP IN
CONFERENCES ON THE SUBJECT OF COLLABORATION HELD IN
WASHINGTON WITH SECRETARY OF WAR STIMSON FIRST BY ME
AND LATER BY SECRETARY HERNANDEZ THIS LEYTE SPEECH
WAS SUBSTANTIALLY APPROVED AS A PROPER BASIS OF ACTION
IN PURSUANCE OF THE POLICY ENUNCIATED BY PRESIDENT
ROOSEVELT ON THE SUBJECT.

Osmeña's reply was "puzzling." People felt that with
the Ickes directive he could act with determination. Given
the political atomic bomb, however, Osmeña was uncer-
tain of its effects and appeared reluctant to shift to the
offensive and force the collaborationists to the wall.

In his reply, he confessed he exceeded his authority by
detaining CIC-blocked nationals "even beyond the period
of six hours permitted by the criminal laws of the Philippines." This was ill-advised. His claim that he had reinstated some collaborationist officials "after they had been
cleared" by the CIC was half truth. The fact was that
these officials appeared in the CIC roster of blocked nationals but had not been cleared and were subject to
trial before the People's Court.

From Washington, in the meantime, came broad hints
that no rehabilitation money was forthcoming for the
Philippines unless "something is done soon" about collaboration. Osmeña therefore prepared for a trip to Capitol
Hill, as he was also perturbed over Truman's directive
delegating all his powers and authority to High Commissioner McNutt. Admittedly an expert at reading between
the lines, he nevertheless was anxious to hear from Truman
himself what certain sections of his executive order meant;
to what extent, for instance, could the American High
Commissioner act on the issue of collaboration?

At the same time, Osmeña continued to play around
with the idea of taking Roxas along with him on his

"economic mission" to Washington. Through an emissary, he asked Roxas to go with him and work for rehabilitation. Roxas was frankly suspicious of the Osmeña invitation and he asked his newspaper friends to sound out "people in the know" as to whether he stood to *gain* from the trip. Osmeña's offer was one way of putting Roxas on the spot.

"But, Don Sergio, you would be sending collaborators," administration man Emilio de la Paz, congressman from Rizal, told the President late in August. "Don't you think there would be strong reaction in Washington?"

Osmeña replied: "But if I should go, do you suppose they would be so openly critical of Roxas?"

Osmeña was in earnest about his offer to Roxas. He asked official Washington circles about the advisability of taking Roxas along on his projected trip to ask for relief. The reply was a positive no.

All this time, Roxas' *Daily News* was hitting a new high in its smear campaign against Osmeña. On September 26, the *News* rasped: "President Sergio Osmeña is the Chinese puppet leader in the Philippines."

The Osmeña offer to Roxas fizzled out and was forgotten in the wake of renewed political mongering among Nacionalista top brass.

Roxas motored out to the Muntinlupa prison to visit his former colleagues of the puppet Laurel republic and to see about arranging for their early release on bail. That was on September 18, the day he fumed in his *Daily News* column at Mr. Ickes for pressing "with undue vehemence" the trial of "supposed" collaborators.

Always the politico, Roxas did not forget to see two detained prisoners, Luis Taruc and Castro Alejandrino, youthful leaders of the Hukbalahap, who were being kept by the United States Army as "security risks." The two Huk leaders, Roxas had been told, had made quite an

impression among the political detainees, especially with
the big collaborators, and Roxas saw no point in not trying to befriend them.

He therefore called on them in their cells. The Huk
leaders were surprised. Without disguising his intentions,
Roxas asked Taruc for the support of the Hukbalahap in
the next election and, failing to get a reply beyond a
smile, offered to foot Taruc's bail, or to help him raise
one. Taruc declined politely.

It was Roxas' *Daily News* which demanded editorially,
on August 25, 1945, that the Hukbalahap, the same
group whose support he pretended to seek, be disarmed
and appealed to the United States Army to undertake a
relentless campaign to put down these "lawless elements."

At Jimmy's, a favorite night spot in Pasay, a suburb of
Manila, one evening on November 26, 1945, Edgar Snow
had as dinner guests three friends, Luis Taruc, Casto
Alejandrino, and V. Gokhale. They had a table on the
lawn.

Unseen by them at a table on the second floor of Jimmy's
were three notables: Lieutenant Commander Julius Edelstein, McNutt's press-relations man, Miss Pacita de los
Reyes, a good friend of Roxas and Aquino, and Roxas
himself.

Someone whispered to Edelstein: "Snow is around."

"I must see him," Edelstein said, excusing himself.

So to Snow's table went McNutt's press-relations man.
Introduction.

Remarked Huk leader Taruc: "So you are the guest of
General Roxas upstairs. Having a good time?"

Edelstein was evasive. "Oh, I just met him here. He
has other guests."

After Edelstein had left, Gokhale suggested to Taruc
that he see Roxas and return the call he paid Taruc at
Muntinlupa in September. "After all," urged Gokhale,

"you don't lose anything and it would be interesting to see him again."

So Taruc returned Roxas' call. Roxas was gracious.

Informed by Taruc that he wanted to see McNutt in three days, Roxas offered to help him out. "Why don't you come to my office before you see the High Commissioner?" Roxas asked. "I'll clear my desk for you. We can talk." Without batting an eyelash, Roxas told the peasant leader: "You know, I am more radical than you."

"By the way, Senator—" Taruc was disarming—"what about this talk of fusion between you and President Osmeña?

The Redeemer's face clouded, became rigid. "To hell with the fusion!"

With all the backing that President Osmeña was getting, however, he still continued to hedge and temporize. The Ickes directive left no doubt where Washington stood on collaboration. It was clear-cut. Collaboration must be dealt with firmly. But Osmeña felt he had to play politics and because he had committed himself, on insistent prodding from the Roxas camp, to the recall of all 1940 elective officials, he proceeded to reinstate them in office.

His political fences must be strengthened. And he acted accordingly. The broad lines of his strategy began to take shape. There were "decent" collaborators. That one must admit. Osmeña tried to win over the "decent" ones and leave the others to Roxas. Osmeña would take Yulo, Alunan, and Avancena and would leave Laurel, Aquino, and Osias to Roxas. Immediately following the announcement by the United States Army CIC that the detained collaborators would be turned over to the commonwealth (September 1945), Osmeña sent a list of detainees he wanted sprung out first. Roxas did likewise. Osmeña would draw the line on collaborationists. This, he felt, was easier to swallow than Roxas' collaboration-is-a-myth line. Especially after Mr. Ickes' dig at "those few timid, craven and opportunistic helots who basely collaborated."

The Democratic Alliance cabled a protest to Secretary Ickes on September 18, 1945:

THE FILIPINO PEOPLE ARE SINCERELY GRATIFIED BY YOUR FORTHRIGHT CLARIFICATION OF COLLABORATION ISSUE. YOUR KEEN APPRAISAL OF PHILIPPINE INTERNAL SITUATION IS VERY REASSURING IN VIEW OF PERNICIOUS ATTEMPT OF POWERFUL COLLABORATIONIST CLIQUE LED BY ROXAS TO SABOTAGE PLANS TO BRING COLLABORATORS TO SPEEDY TRIAL BEFORE PEOPLE'S COURT. SIGNIFICANTLY, OSMEÑA ADMINISTRATION SEEMS RELUCTANT OR UNWILLING TO FACE ISSUE SQUARELY. EVEN AFTER YOUR MESSAGE PRESIDENT OSMEÑA HAS APPOINTED TO SUPREME COURT MANUEL BRIONES AND CESAR BENGZON WHO SERVED UNDER PUPPET REGIME.

ROXAS BEHAVIOR DURING JAPANESE OCCUPATION CLEARLY MARKED HIM AS COLLABORATOR. HE AND THE OTHER PUPPETS NOT ONLY GAVE SUPPORT TO JAPANESE FORCES BUT ALSO ORGANIZED AND PRESSED PUPPET CONSTABULARY TO FIGHT THE GUERRILLAS IN NAME OF PEACE AND ORDER. WE HAVE EVIDENCE TO SUBSTANTIATE OUR CHARGES AGAINST HIM, FIRST AS SIGNER OF PUPPET CONSTITUTION, SECOND AS CHAIRMAN OF PUPPET ECONOMIC PLANNING BOARD AND NATIONAL RICE AND CORN CORPORATION, THIRD AS PRINCIPAL ADVISER TO LAUREL IN ALL IMPORTANT POLICIES INCLUDING DECLARATION OF WAR AGAINST UNITED STATES. HIS CONTINUANCE IN OFFICE WIELDING TREMENDOUS POWERS IS DISTURBING TO GUERRILLA GROUPS AND THE BROAD MASSES OF THE PEOPLE WHO HAD STEADFASTLY RESISTED THE ENEMY AND HAD SUFFERED AT HANDS OF JAPANESE FORCES AND PUPPET CONSTABULARY.

WE REQUEST YOUR CONTINUED INTEREST AND SUGGEST FURTHER SURVEY COLLABORATION SITUATION WITH A VIEW OF ENFORCING PRESIDENT ROOSEVELT'S DIRECTIVE.

The Alliance then laid plans for a public demonstra-

tion and a march to Malacañan to present the peasants'
"Bill of Rights" to Osmeña.

The Peasants March on Malacañan

The rain poured. But the hatless peasant, soaked to the
bones, sat complacently atop the rickety truck in the
crowded plaza, holding the dripping placard: GIVE ROXAS
BACK TO THE JAPS!

Into Plaza Guipit, Hyde Park of Manila's underprivi-
leged, on September 23, 1945, had trekked more than
twenty thousand peasants. The plaza was jammed. It
smelled of the earth. From Nueva Ecija came four thousand. From Pampanga, five thousand. From Bulacan, five
thousand. From Tarlac, two thousand. From Laguna, two
thousand. From Cavite and Rizal, more thousands. And
the city's labor ranks swelled the crowd to an estimated
thirty thousand.

The bulk of the peasants made the long trek on foot.
Those from Nueva Ecija, some two hundred kilometers
away, started at dawn three days before to arrive just in
time. Many sold their pigs and chickens to have enough
money to make the trip. They had not been to Manila
since Pearl Harbor. And they wanted their voice heard.
Bulacan farm hands rode standing in trucks. Six government schoolhouses sheltered the marchers the night before the demonstration and the night after. They came
with their food, rice and smoked fish and the inevitable
sardines, for most of them the only "luxury" since the
Americans came.

Soaking wet, the peasants and workers stood in the
rain for more than three hours at Plaza Guipit. The DA
speakers voiced their sentiments. The peasants gave them
lusty and repeated ovations. The place was red with flags
of the National Peasants' Union. In the maze of flags

and strongly worded placards, the discerning could not mistake two hammer-and-sickle banners, from the Manila Communist Party group.

The peasants knew what they wanted. Their placards spoke from the heart. ARREST COLLABORATORS AND PUT THEM IN JAIL. PUT TO DEATH ALL PUPPETS AND COLLABORATORS!

The common man was exasperated at the Osmeña administration's inaction. President Osmeña did not escape the injunction. WAKE UP, MR. PRESIDENT, CLEAN THE GOVERNMENT OF COLLABORATORS. STOP COLLABORATIONIST PARTICIPATION IN THE GOVERNMENT. PUT ANTI-JAP FIGHTERS IN OFFICE. WAGES TO MEET COST OF LIVING. SEEDS AND FARMS FOR FARMERS.

They looked on Congress with suspicion. SUSPEND THE TRAITOR-CONTROLLED CONGRESS. CREATE THE PEOPLE'S COURT FROM THE GENUINE RESISTANCE MOVEMENT. REHABILITATE THE PEOPLE, NOT THE FASCISTS.

On independence, Ickes, and sundry: GIVE US INDEPENDENCE, OR ONE Atomic Bomb! WE ARE FOR ICKES' "ATOMIC" TO THE PHILIPPINE CONGRESS. PRESIDENT TRUMAN, GRANT INDEPENDENCE NOW. COLLABORATORS HINDER THE REHABILITATION OF THE COUNTRY. CONFISCATE THE PROPERTIES OF COLLABORATORS.

The Democratic Alliance leaders spoke: Manuel Crudo, member of the DA executive council; Bayani Alcala, of the League of National Liberation; Lorenzo Zabala, president of the Commercial Employees' Association; Eduardo Alabastro, of the Blue Eagle Guerrillas; Pedro Castro, of the Communist Party; Mateo del Castillo, president of the National Peasants' Union; Mariano Balgos, acting head of the Hukbalahap, and J. Antonio Araneta, member of the DA executive council, who delivered the keynote speech.

The Chinese guerrillas, who fought side by side with

the peasants and workers against the Japs, were not invited. This was a political rally. Nevertheless they came and with a band. The president of the Philippine Chinese Anti-Jap and Anti-Traitors League (most active Chinese guerrilla group), asked to be heard. Said he in clear, measured English:

> We are with you against Roxas and Company, who were liberated by General MacArthur. Roxas and Company are against us Chinese. There is no difference in their method and those Hitler used against the Jews and other minorities. If we are not wanted here, we will leave. But, if you like us, and I know you do, for we fought a common enemy together, we will stay and help you in the reconstruction of your country. [Shouts of "Long live the Chinese!"]

A message from Huk Commander in Chief Luis Taruc, held by the CIC for security reasons and released on October 1, was read by Balgos, acting commander. Taruc appealed for continued vigilance against the "fascist vested interests" seeking to control the life of the country. He also sounded the call for greater unity among the peasants and workers "to help keep the peace."

At four-thirty the march to Malacañan got under way. Permit to parade had been denied, because traffic, said the American MP chief, would be clogged, but the peasants trooped to Malacañan on the sidewalks in columns of four. They trudged into the well-kept grounds of sedate Malacañan. All along the route, no more than six paces apart, jittery, white-helmeted Filipino MPs stood on guard, dressed for action, complete with trench knives, their steel helmets slung on their backs under their ponchos giving them the curious look of armed hunchbacks. Sternfaced, visibly nervous, they stood there, the muzzles of their carbines fairly brushing the soaked marchers.

From Alabang, Laguna, had come the MPs, ten truck-loads. Besides the MPs, Manila's police force turned out to the last man to "control traffic." On hand, too, to supervise traffic were Colonel J. P. Holland and Major Angel Tuazon, Manila's chief and assistant chief of police, respectively. Tuazon piped his whistle nervously and needlessly.

It was a spectacle. Driving from her Santa Mesa home to Malcañan, Mrs. Osmeña stopped by Mendiola, then drove down slowly on Aviles to the Palace. What she saw was too much for her. Sending for the commander of the Malacañan Guards, she stormed: "What is the meaning of this? Why are the guards all armed? And those MPs with their bayonets. The peasants are not our enemies. They are our own people."

The word was passed around. Put arms on sling. Clear away from the crowd; leave only enough men to maintain order. The First Lady was angry.

But outside the Palace gates, the businesslike, if jumpy, MPs kept at their battle stations.

From the west balcony of Malacañan, Osmeña emerged waving.

Speaking for the demonstrators, Araneta read the Democratic Alliance's demands, presented the peasants' petition to the president. The Alliance demanded that the government clamp down on prices and sell commodities to the people at cost; a minimum living wage of a dollar and a half; payment of three years' back salary to noncollaborators; condonation of peasants' debts and extension of easy-credit facilities to them; increase of the peasants' share in the harvest; immediate relief to families of victims of Jap atrocities and resistance heroes; a sweeping purge of puppets, crooks, racketeers, and political lame ducks from the government; immediate construction of temporary shelters for the thousands of homeless; im-

mediate release of resistance leaders like Luis Taruc and
Casto Alejandrino, top Huk commanders, who were "un-
justly arrested while exercising their legitimate constitutional rights." [3]

Moved by the demonstration, the president could not
restrain a tear. He edged to the microphone and delivered
a short speech in English:

> In this postwar era, when all chauvinistic aims must
> give way to collective responsibility, it would be fatal not
> to open our eyes to the realities emphasized by war. These
> realities are basically economic, and their main goal is the
> well-being and security of the common man. I have said it
> before and I say it again now that the citizens' Bill of Po-
> litical Rights is no longer enough; that there must be,
> besides, a Bill of Economic Rights. To formulate, adopt,
> and enforce this Bill of Economic Rights, we must stand
> and work together as a people one and indivisible.
>
> Our national economy and public finance are in a pre-
> carious condition. It is my duty to go again to the United
> States as soon as my pressing official work here will per-
> mit. [4]

The speech over, the president surveyed the crowd
again, then announced he would go down and shake
hands with everyone. There were rousing cheers.

Before coming down, he was met at the Palace stairs
by leaders of the various DA affiliates. One enthusiastic
peasant tugged at the president, asked nonchalantly: "Mr.
President, why did you not touch on collaboration?" Osmeña beamed, but did not say a word.

The handshaking was a tedious process. It was "heroic"
for the president to do it, reported one newspaper. The
authorized one thousand demonstrators who could enter

[3] Alejandrino was released three days later and Taruc October 1
[4] Osmeña left for the United States on September 26

the Palace grounds had swelled to some four thousand and each was eager to pump Don Sergio's hand. But the Old Man was game. Then someone announced that the peasants would be overtaken by darkness, so would they please let go of the president's hand, or words to that effect. They walked out of the Palace grounds. What had been a well-kept lawn had turned into a muddy, soggy field. In it the peasants had planted their placards.

GIVE ROXAS BACK TO THE JAPS! shrieked one.

MR. PRESIDENT, WAKE UP! CLEAN THE GOVERNMENT OF COLLABORATORS! demanded another.

The Philippine Congress Goes on a Witch Hunt

The peasants' march on historic Malacañan was not without repercussions. Two days after the demonstration an uneasy collaborationist Congress ordered an investigation of the "subversive" rally following a speech by an ex-special representative of the puppet Laurel, Prospero Sanidad, speaker pro tempore. One placard carried by the demonstrators left its sting on the legislators: SUSPEND THE TRAITOR-CONTROLLED CONGRESS.

The investigating committee, in many respects no different from the infamous Dies Committee to probe un-American activities in the United States, lost no time in getting down to work. Leaders of the Democratic Alliance were summoned. The committee was balked, however, when the Alliance challenged not only the right of the committee to conduct the probe but also the legality of the "traitor-controlled" Congress itself.

Through the newspapers, the Philippine Dies Committee hurled threats to arrest the Alliance officials who refused to testify. The threats were unheeded.

The congressional witch-hunters, however, were unruffled. Into the office of the chief prober the morning of

October 5, 1945, strode a burly American MP to inform him that two United States Army officers, a major and a lieutenant, were witness to the Democratic Alliance rally of September 23 and were volunteering what they knew to help the committee. The MP told the chief prober to expect the brass hats sometime that day.

Later in the morning, an American MP lieutenant presented himself to the chief investigator and was led to a closed room. For reasons of security, the accommodating lieutenant said, he would rather that his name be withheld. In fact, stenographers did not take down his name, but what he had to say was "hot stuff."

The officer described himself as a "Communist." Every one of the probers was awed. He told them he had been closely following the activities of "subversive" groups like the Communist Party and the Hukbalahap and he was convinced that they were preparing for a coup to overthrow the organized government by force.

The confessed "Communist" talked at some length, describing various "radical" groups and their "insidious" activities. He lumped together several resistance groups, mostly labor and peasant, as "communistic," including the Democratic Alliance, the Hukbalahap, the National Peasants' Union, the Committee on Labor Organization, the League for National Liberation, and other affiliates of the Alliance.[5]

These groups, this anonymous American officer told the Philippine "Dies Committee," had been carrying on a "systematic campaign" to undermine the Osmeña administration and to misrepresent facts to discredit elements (the collaborationists) that are "sincerely working for the public interest."

This was supposed to be the situation, according to

[5] See Chapter XIII: The Masses Find Their Voice

the American "Communist" in an officer's uniform. The
line was familiar, though rather crude and stupid.

But the Filipino "Dies men" were scared. The chairman
himself made no attempt to conceal his feelings. The
probe over and the "Communist" officer gone, the chief
prober rushed to the Speaker of the House and burst out:
"Mr. Speaker, this *is* serious. What are we going to do?"
He added, lamely: "You know, forewarned is forearmed."

The speaker, a good poker player, reacted indifferently.

The chief prober was in a state of high tension the
whole day. Another American officer, a major, was coming to implement the lieutenant's story. The prober waited
the whole afternoon. But the major who the MP said
was coming to volunteer what he knew did not show up.

At any rate, the scared "Dies men" had a complete
picture of the Huk threat and the "subversive" activities
of the Democratic Alliance from two other "sneak" witnesses. The probers declined to reveal their names for
"security reasons," but they admitted the witnesses were
"landowners from Tarlac and Pampanga."

The witch-hunters were naive enough to believe the
testimony of a landowner against his slave tenant, who
had discovered his own freedom and his own strength in
resistance against the Japs and would not relinquish them
now.

The investigation fizzled out eventually, but the constituted authorities did not rest. When the Democratic
Alliance applied for a permit to hold another public
meeting on October 14, 1945, to protest against the appropriation by Congress of ₱3,500,000 of relief money to
pay the three years' back salaries of its members, the chief
of police and provost marshal of Manila, Colonel J. P.
Holland, denied the permit.

At about the same time, the ban on free speech and
free assembly was being lifted in Japan. The Filipinos

had fought and resisted fascist enslavement for three hard years. But that day they were being muzzled.

The commonwealth government showed its deep appreciation by decorating Colonel Holland with the Meritorious Service Medal.

VII KEEPING THE IMPERIALIST PEACE: THE MP WAY

Law and Order at Any Cost

ON JANUARY 6, 1946, a curious item appeared in the United States Army newspaper the *Daily Pacifican*, innocuously headlined "86th Infantry Division Is Reorganizing along Battle Lines." The story quoted Colonel Wesley W. Yale, Chief of Staff of the famed 86th, or Black Hawk, Division, as saying the Division was being organized along battle lines and retrained to cope "with possible unrest which may grow out of the political crisis in the Philippines."

"Col. Yale said the Division's mission in the Philippines must be made clear," the story continued. "We are here solely to guard U. S. property. Because of armed raids being made on supply depots, and the unrest expected during the presidential campaign in April, we must be trained and ready."

In Washington, War Department spokesmen were reported "puzzled" by the statement of the 86th's Chief of Staff.

In Manila, Colonel Yale was summoned to a conference with Lieutenant General W. D. Styer, AFWESPAC commander, after which he claimed the army paper's reporters had received "a totally erroneous impression" at a press conference he gave.

Disgruntled GIs pounced on the 86th's reactivation

story to demand a redeployment speed-up. Meeting in
the ruins of Manila's National Library building, twenty
thousand of them voiced protest against what they termed
a slowdown in stateside redeployment and voiced their
disapproval of United States Army intervention in Philippine affairs.

One speaker said:

> The Filipinos are our allies. They fought the Japanese
> while waiting for America to come. We all know that their
> resistance movement saved thousands of lives of American
> GIs for they made it easier for us to liberate the Islands.
> Is this our appreciation for what the Filipinos have done?
> This is a slap on the face of our allies. Let us leave the
> Chinese and Filipinos to take care of their own internal
> affairs.

Thunderous applause greeted the speaker. The GIs
asked questions.

Does the reactivation of the 86th along battle lines bear
any relationship to the attempt of certain interests to
deny independence to the Philippines and to maintain
their prewar economic stranglehold on the Islands?

Is the American flag following the American dollar?

Why do we need 350,000 men to guard surplus property in the Philippines? (General MacArthur considered
200,000 sufficient in Japan.)

The GI demonstration in Manila, which was only one
among many in the Pacific theater, got results. Redeployment of troops for return to the United States was speeded
up. At the same time, however, the *Daily Pacifican* was
gagged. In a signed statement on January 11, thirty-three
members of the staff disclosed "severe editorial restrictions and limitations" had been imposed on the newspaper.

New restrictions on freedom of expression imposed from above [said the statement] no longer enable us to bring the full news and the full truth to our GI readers. To keep faith with our readers we are compelled to announce that our hands are now bound.

We have been denied the right even to print Associated Press and United Press dispatches if they reflect any criticism or dissatisfaction whatsoever with the official policies of the War Department and our theater commanders. In short, we are prohibited from publishing the whole truth.

As soldiers we carry out our orders. As American citizens and as journalists we tell the truth to the entire world.

Against the backdrop of the political developments in the Far East, the presence of British troops in Indonesia to "protect British lives and property" and the presence of American troops in China ostensibly for a similar purpose, the *Pacifican* story on the reactivation of the Black Hawk Division assumed greater import.[1] The implications were disturbing.

Two days before this news item appeared, the Secretary of National Defense, Alfredo Montelibano, boasted that *his* Philippine Army was ready to deal with the "lawless elements" with the acquisition from the United States Army of ten thousand submachine guns and carbines and a small air force.

"The government," announced Montelibano, "declares open war against all lawless elements. I will not tolerate any monkey business."

In thirty-two out of fifty-one provinces, the MP command of the Philippine Army had taken over from the American MPs. This was in January 1946. To keep "peace"

[1] The 86th Division was in February 1946 stationed in Central Luzon, seat of agrarian unrest

and order" in these provinces, Montelibano had 22,235 armed MPs.

Montelibano's statement was a belated, but eloquent, answer to an editorial demand from Roxas' *Daily News* of August 25, 1945, that the government launch an all-out drive against the "lawless elements" and recalled similar statements made by the puppet Laurel when he was the Japs' Commissioner of the Interior in charge of keeping "peace and order."

The *Daily News* editorial said bluntly:

> These lawless elements were most ferocious during the regime of the ferocious Japanese. They thrive under the name of Hukbalahap. According to reliable information, this band of outlaws has been boasting that it is identified with the Osmeña administration, which is said to have recognized it as an armed force.

> The peace-loving Filipinos, therefore, appeal to the United States Army to lend its helping hand to the Filipinos and disarm these lawless elements whose ideals of life are diametrically opposed to ideas sanctioned in a democracy. We appeal to the American Army, for it possesses all the means to undertake the campaign to a successful end without much loss of time.

By a curious coincidence, Laurel made the same appeal to the Japs to help the puppet Philippine constabulary wipe out these same "lawless elements" when they resisted joint efforts of the Japs and the puppet regime to bring much-needed rice and other food products from Central Luzon to Manila. The Japs were stocking up then in preparation for a last-ditch stand against the American liberation forces.

Said Laurel on August 6, 1943: "I am still the Commissioner of the Interior and I am vitally interested in the restoration of peace and order. Peace and order is the starting point, the basic prerequisite for independence. The constabulary will be reorganized and strengthened to compel obedience of unruly elements. If necessary the Nippon forces will be requested to extend assistance."

Substitute "American" for "Nippon" and you have the picture much as it is today. Montelibano talks of "lawless elements." Laurel called them "unruly" and "misguided." On June 16, 1943, Tojo referred to Filipino guerrillas who "voluntarily capitulated" as "bandits."

The "unruly bandit" elements these men referred to are in Luzon, peasant and working-class groups who fought the Japs for three years and never compromised with them and their puppets.

During the Jap occupation the clamor was the same. "Peace and order" had to be preserved. The military police had to be "reorganized and strengthened."

An estimated 70 per cent of these MPs were members of the puppet Philippine constabulary and local police which fought side by side with the Japs in a relentless drive to put down the resistance movement, especially in Central Luzon.

The Philippines became independent on July 4, 1946. "Peace and order is the starting point, the basic prerequisite for independence." How conveniently for the powers to be did Laurel's words fit the situation!

The United States Army reactivated a full infantry division, the battle-seasoned Black Hawk Division which saw twenty-eight days of the most furious fighting in Europe in the closing campaign, and equipped and armed the Philippine Army military-police force of twenty-two thousand men.

The monkey men are gone, but, it would seem, their charming ways must remain with us, for a long time to come.

Had the reorganization of the 86th along battle lines in the Philippines no political implications?

The Yank MPs Return Absentee Landlords to Power

Sometime early in October 1945, Pampanga's provost marshal, an American major, briefed Governor Gerardo Limlingan and, through him, the town mayors, that "any meeting of the Democratic Alliance must be reported immediately" to the military police to enable them to check up on "communistic activities."

The major acted accordingly—and in a manner reminiscent of the Japs.

On Sunday, October 28, the Democratic Alliance committees in Apalit, Lubao, Florida-Blanca, and Magalang, all in the province of Pampanga, organized public meetings. In the first three, permits were issued, but American and Filipino MPs and local police made sure that the meetings would be "peaceful." Pampanga's MP boss threw a cordon sanitaire around the "reds," the simple peasants who had started to reason and to ask questions disquieting to the ruling class, the exploiting cacique class.

Into Apalit came an armored car, two truckloads of Filipino MPs and two jeeps of American MPs. Into Lubao came an armed car, three truckloads of Filipino MPs, three jeeploads of American MPs, and several fifty-caliber machine guns. An equal force, spearheaded by an armored car, came into Florida-Blanca.

The meetings were peaceful.

The Alliance Committee of Magalang was denied a permit for a meeting the same day. The reason, of course, was that the peasant leaders would talk sedition and there would be trouble.

In another Pampanga town the Alliance Committee had a public meeting arranged on October 30. The people gathered, but the speeches were not made. In the meeting were sixteen armed American and Filipino MPs and the local police. In bold tones, the local cops made broad hints that any one who spoke would be arrested and they had their carbines cocked. The meeting dispersed.

At dawn the next day, American and Filipino MPs raided the houses of the scheduled speakers in search of firearms and finding none confiscated GI blankets, clothing, and goods. They were within their rights, too. Only the *ilustrado*, the landed gentry, have a right to such GI luxuries.

Pampanga is the traditional seat of social unrest in the Philippines. This was more so in the light of the explosive political situation, particularly in Central Luzon, where there was a growing feeling that the resistance movement had been sold short.

Let us now take you to a landlord's haven, the town of Concepcion in Tarlac province. This town, which gave to the Philippines Benigno S. Aquino, is the notorious seat of the fascist "experiment" in the liberated Philippines.

Here are the facts.

When the Japs came, the well-heeled took to Manila and engaged in the buy-and-sell. They cashed in on their rice in the black market.

But the peasants stayed behind and fought the Japs. Concepcion became the Hukbalahap nerve center in Tarlac. For about three years it was Huk territory. The peasants, who took to the Huks as they do to their plows, made sure that they got their share of the harvest. They lived well. They ran their own affairs. They had elective town councils and barrio councils.

Then the liberating Yanks came. Now the landlords are back in power and a new story is being written.

Mayor of Concepcion when the Americans came was Dominador R. Santos, thirty-four, a labor leader. He was elected by the peasants in a free election long before MacArthur returned.

An election was held two weeks after the liberation of the town by the Americans and the peasants elected Gregorio Narciso, who served until May 1945.

Late in May, Osmeña returned from Washington. On recommendation of prominent Concepcion residents, he named a new mayor, Alfredo Castro, a wealthy landlord. The Huk was ignored.

In June, soon after taking office, Castro was called to a conference by the big landlords. The meeting was secret. Present among others were Jose and Nicolas Feliciano, who own between them half of Concepcion proper and extensive holdings in other parts of the province. Other landlords represented were Federico Pineda and the Aquinos, first cousins Benigno and Sergio.

The landlords laid down the policy. The peasant organization must be discredited and destroyed.

Then the landlords worked on the MPs, American and Filipino. Most of the Filipino MPs were past masters in Jap ways. They had been members of the puppet constabulary.

Before the war, Concepcion had a police force of fourteen. Shortly before the change-over in command, it had a police force of twenty-eight plus thirty Filipino and twenty American MPs. Part of the salaries were paid by the landlords' private vigilante organization.

Officially, the American MPs relinquished command in Tarlac on January 16, 1946, to the Filipino MPs, but the main American MP depot has not been moved.

The Felicianos, famed for their generosity to the keepers of the peace in prewar days, threw their mansions open to the MPs. Most welcome was Major Devere Woodruff, provost marshal for Tarlac. And, of course, Concepcion's MP chief, Lieutenant William Ramsden.

It was Ramsden who appeared on October 5, 1945, before the congressional committee investigating the "subversive" demonstration of the Democratic Alliance on September 23. Testifying behind closed doors and claiming to be a "Communist," he had said: "To the best of my knowledge and belief, the present activities of the *Hukbalahap* association point to one fact: that there will be armed revolution in the near future."

The MPs started with a big detachment, two to three companies, to win Tarlac back for the absentee landlords.

Men turned informers; labor leaders of Tarlac and Pampanga towns were rounded up. Labor and peasant leaders were jailed, from Porac, Mabalacat, Dau, Angeles, Magalang, and Arayat, in Pampanga (*outside* of the jurisdiction of the Tarlac MP) and from Bamban, Tarlac, Capas, and Concepcion, Tarlac.

In the first batch arrested were from sixty to a hundred labor leaders, most of whom were jailed without charges. Some were held on charges of illegal possession of firearms.

The former Huk-elected mayor was thrown into the Concepcion jail. He was released on bail with two broken ribs. His brother was tortured by MPs, former personal guerrillas of Aquino.

A detainee related how Filipino MPs got two American MPs drunk before they let them into the cell of a partisan. "See this man?" a Filipino MP asked the soused MPs, pointing to a peasant. "He is a Huk. Anti-American." And the drunk MPs loosened up with their fists and boots. The peasant had his hands tied behind his back.

Favorites with the Aquino "gorillas" were such familiar Jap "cures" as the "water cure," the baseball-bat technique (the MPs use the rifle butt instead of a bat), and hog-tying of hands and legs. Playful MPs also like to ram the muzzles of their carbines into the mouths of their victims.

The MPs don't have to bother with filing charges against their "enemies." They round up peasant leaders, all Huk members, from a town or barrio, then lodge them in jail. The charge? The "reds" are taken to a room where the MPs keep a pile of confiscated or surrendered arms. The prisoners *have* to pick *their* arms, any piece, or else. Then it is all legal: illegal possession of firearms.

How are these things possible? Illegal detention for more than six hours without charges.[2] Manhandling. Abuses.

The Concepcion mayor, who takes orders from his masters, the landlords, saw to that. He was not a former justice of the peace for nothing. He knew his law. Here are his choice ordinances, passed and enforced with the co-operation of MPs:

1. Any person in Concepcion, Tarlac, without any reasonable purpose will be apprehended.

2. Any resident who is caught entertaining any of the leaders of the National Peasants' Union will be apprehended.

3. Any prisoner detained who is found to have been visited by anybody, even relatives, shall be punished.

4. The assembly of more than two persons is subversive and will not be tolerated.

5. The town of Concepcion is "off limits" to all "un-recognized" guerrillas. In this resolution, the United States Army was asked to continue maintaining a garrison in the town to keep "peace and order."

That these abuses exist in a "liberated" Philippines is proof that the influence of the puppets remains consid-

---

[2] Under Philippine law, no person may be detained longer than six hours except in serious criminal cases

erable among the landlord class, which rules Tarlac and
the country at large.

Few cases are ever tried in the Concepcion court. When
a case is tried, the landlords appear armed with guns.
In all seriousness, a leading official of Concepcion said
the Hukbalahap was just waiting for help from Russia,
at which time they would "start the revolution."

"The United States and Russia will go to war," the official said, "and the Hukbalahap is waiting for the time to
strike."

"Yes," he said in reply to a question, *"Roxas is for us but
not Osmeña, as he wants the Hukbalahap votes.*[3]

Let's continue with the facts.

Acting on complaints against Concepcion police for
maltreatment of prisoners, Secretary Montelibano sent an
investigator, Emiliano Anonas, to Tarlac on November 2,
1945. Judge Jesús Barrera, Democratic Alliance chairman,
was asked to accompany the prober.

Anonas and Barrera called on the governor, Alejandro
Galang, November 3.

They waited outside the governor's office and after a
while the governor escorted five American officers out
and then called the Manila visitors in. After reading
Montelibano's letter ordering an investigation of the Concepcion police, the governor rushed out of the room and
returned in no time with the American officers.

Then he asked Anonas to explain his mission for the
benefit of the provincial MP top brass.

During the conference, Major Devere Woodruff, excusing himself formally, called the Concepcion MP on the
phone to tip the boys that an investigator from the Department of the Interior was due there at eleven-thirty.
A Concepcion police sergeant who happened to come to
the provincial capital at the time on a motorcycle was

[3] From an investigator's report in December 1945

ordered to hurry back to see that the investigator was
given a proper reception.

When Anonas and Barrera arrived in Concepcion, the
four members of the police force against whom charges
had been filed for abusing prisoners and who were to be
probed by Anonas were, by some curious coincidence,
all out: one had joined the MP, one was being processed,
one was on patrol duty, and one was sick in the hospital.
Or so they were told.

But shortly after lunch, the "sick" one came back on a
stretcher, dead. He and a police informer had been ambushed and killed.

Barrera had a talk with an American MP. When the
MP learned Barrera was Democratic Alliance chairman,
he said curtly: "So it is you who are behind all this
trouble."

Countered Barrera: "If you think I am, why don't you
arrest me?"

The MP piped down. "I would like to get the hell out
of this place."

Montelibano's prober, Anonas, got copies of Concepcion's set of "New Order" ordinances. Another ordinance
had been added, under which any Concepcion resident
who failed to report the presence of a "stranger" in his
house, whether a relative or a friend, to the police was
liable to punishment. This was nothing less than the Jap
Neighborhood Association system at work again.

And the American MPs seemed to enjoy the Jap system
too, and the United States Army used tank destroyers
in Concepcion and in other towns in Tarlac, Pampanga,
and Nueva Ecija when the people were denied the right
to assemble and air their grievances.

In a criminal complaint against two labor leaders of
Concepcion in August, the provincial fiscal charged them
with "inciting" several hundred peasants, "which acts

tended to instigate their followers to meet for unlawful purposes and which tended to stir up the people against the lawful authorities and disturb the safety of the Government, thereby causing a serious disturbance in said town, *which required the intervention of the armed forces,* including tank destroyers, of the United States Army."

In the first week of January 1946 the American MPs of Tarlac stepped aside to give their worthy Filipino brothers full control. Simultaneously, in three places in Central Luzon, battle-happy Filipino MPs struck on January 10.

In barrio San Nicolas, Bongabong, in Nueva Ecija, two truckloads of MPs on patrol duty opened fire on a merry-making group of eighty peasants, killing five, including a twelve-year-old girl, and wounding eleven, most of them women. The vigilant MPs were provoked by a shot which they claimed they heard coming from the group.

In barrio Sierra, La Paz, in Tarlac, trigger-happy MPs swooped down on a group of National Peasants' Union delegates at an informal meeting in a private house and hauled forty-nine "radicals" to the Tarlac provincial jail. The peasants were meeting to select delegates to the Democratic Alliance provincial convention. The MPs clamped the forty-nine in jail, slapped a charge of "illegal association" against them.

In barrio Santo Nino, Concepcion, also in Tarlac, a similar meeting to select delegates to the Alliance provincial convention was raised by an armed posse led by Concepcion's landlord mayor, Alfredo Castro. Shots were fired at the meeting place; one man was seriously wounded. The MPs searched and grilled each one at the meeting and finding nothing released all of them. In the group of about fifty were women and children.

These incidents were not isolated. They came within a week after the announcement by National Defense-

Interior Secretary Montelibano that the Filipino Army
MP command had launched an "open war" to preserve
"peace and order."

The *Daily News* of January 12 came out with an editorial, "Use the Mailed Fist," in which it urged the government to use the "iron hand" in curbing "lawlessness"
in Central Luzon, because "it is important that we demon-
strate before all the world that we can be as determined
to maintain order as we were fierce in our fight for freedom." And the *News* would sanction the use of "even part
of the U. S. Army" to insure "peace and order." Such use,
it added, "would be as honorable as in actual war, only
this time the enemy consists of those who would sabotage
internal peace and the free expression of the people's
mandate."

Nothing was said as to whether the MPs were acting on
their own, or were merely implementing the mailed-fist
policy enunciated by Montelibano to preserve "peace and
order" at any cost.

On what ground could an unprovoked attack with carbines and submachine guns against an unarmed group of
peasants be justified?

Did the killing of five innocent people by trigger-happy
MPs serve the cause of peace and order in Central Luzon?

On January 13, 1946, the elite of Concepcion, Tarlac,
turned out for a farewell party in honor of the man who
brought order to Tarlac, Major Devere Woodruff, Tarlac
provost marshal. Among the organizers of the party was
Mayor Castro. Indeed, the reorganizing of the crack Black
Hawk Division had "no political implications."

The twenty thousand incensed GIs who protested in
peaceful demonstration in Manila against the "deliberate
slowdown" in sending them home "from a peaceful country, the Philippines" had reason to ask:

"There are approximately 350,000 troops in the Philippines now; how many of these troops are really essential?"

As one excited GI from the 86th said: "The Filipinos are our allies. We ain't gonna fight them!"

GI Joe's Postwar Philippine Job

What was the real mission of the American GI in a liberated Philippines?

General Eisenhower explained this at some length on January 22, 1946, in his report-to-the-nation speech on the mission of the American troops overseas:

> There is no effective Philippine agency now in existence to maintain law and order. As a result of the war the Philippines were left without an effective police force and the splendid Philippine scout organizations were practically destroyed. Now armed bands of guerrillas roam the hills, bent on pilferage which only our active presence controls.
>
> We are now engaged in recruiting a force of fifty thousand Filipinos to replace a comparable number of our men in the Philippines and elsewhere in the Pacific, but it will be many months before this force becomes effective enough to accept the responsibility of policing the Islands. It is our clear obligation to assist until the time arrives.
>
> In addition to this activity, American troops have here also the familiar task of liquidating the bases and immense stores of government property which were assembled at a time when these islands were our principal forward base for the planned assault on Japan's home islands. With the exception of air and supply bases on Luzon and Leyte, our Philippine bases and supply points will be progressively reduced and closed out by July 1, 1946.
>
> On the first of January we had approximately 279,000 troops in the Philippines. These will be reduced as rapidly as possible to a garrison of approximately seventy-nine

thousand which will be needed on July 1 to carry out our
continuing responsibilities there.

In an independent Philippines, the United States would
have a modern, fully equipped army of seventy-nine thousand. This was seven times more soldiers than she needed
to keep her sovereignty in the Philippines before Pearl
Harbor. And Japan's war potential has been crushed.

Besides these seventy-nine thousand troops, the United
States will maintain a Philippine scout organization of fifty
thousand troops. Add to these a Philippine Army of a reduced strength, by July 1946, of forty thousand with a
complement of twenty-two thousand of the military-police
command and you have a Fil-American army of 191,000
officers and men to maintain "peace and order" in an independent Philippines, the first member of the United Nations to be so blessed.

The main job of this large standing army, which is
almost as large as MacArthur's army of occupation in
Japan, will be to see that nothing is done to disturb the
quiet and brutal efficiency of the status quo.

"This force [of 79,000 Americans] has a mission," General Eisenhower told a congressional committee on February 14, 1946, "which includes not only dealings with a
large amount of property in the area and assistance to the
Filipinos, but also the support of occupation forces in
Japan."

How does this army of occupation square with America's promise to respect the independence of the Philippines?

How does the presence of British troops in Indonesia and
in other trouble spots in the Orient square with the At-
lantic Charter? With the promise to respect and recognize
the aspirations of subject peoples for self-government, for
independent nationhood?

Roxas knows why the American soldiers are in the Philippines. "Can anyone blame the United States government," his *Daily News* asked on February 20, 1946, "for stationing here forces that would compel respect for law and preserve the democratic processes?"

And the *News* shows where American responsibility lay: "For the United States to stand idly by while the democratic ramparts that she has built are crumbling to pieces, is for her, while the Philippines still owes allegiance to her, to have fought in vain in this part of the Pacific. She would be a renegade to her sacred trust."

Verily the American army of occupation fits into the pattern of Roxas' bid for power.

VIII COLLABORATORS IN UNIFORM

Army Politics and the War Department Directives

PRAISE of the Filipino guerrilla fighter has been lavish. The Jap hated him as much as he feared him. The Jap's fear of him was matched only by the ruthlessness with which he meted out punishment when the guerrilla failed.

Broad as the Filipino resistance movement was, however, it was conspicuous for the absence of top-ranking army officers. These seasoned hands, who could have helped steer the vast underground, preferred the warm comfort of the high-ceilinged office and the cozy chair, supported by lucrative buy-and-sell, to the cold reality of the mountain cave. They shunned the harsh life of the hunted and chose the easy life of the pampered slave.

Contacts with military men were made, but the call of patriotism was unheeded. One name stood out, Vicente Lim, and he is dead, victim of a Jap firing squad. Francisco, Capinpin, Segundo, de los Reyes, de Jesús, Martelino,[1] what big names these could have been, if only the spirit of freedom had been kept alive!

Lim was a military man. He refused to collaborate, because he said he considered himself a prisoner of war and would not be disloyal to his oath to the army. He con-

[1] All brigadier generals in Bataan, except the last-named, who was a colonel

demned his colleagues who collaborated with the Japs.
And he was for "purging" the army after liberation. "Let
the heads roll," he used to tell friends.

The Philippine Army is a collaborationist army in its
essential make-up. There are, of course, noncollaborators
in the upper bracket of the military hierarchy, but it is the
politicos who run the show.

"The army is completely divorced from politics," thirty-
four-year-old Deputy Chief of Staff Brigadier General
Marcario Peralta, Jr., told the press on January 8, 1946.
He added: "I know what course I will follow from the
moment I receive an order that savors of politics."

The facts tell a different story. And it is a story of politics—petty, mendacious, immoral.

Shortly after the re-establishment of the commonwealth
in Manila on February 27, 1945, steps were taken to re-
organize and reactivate the Philippine Army and to raise
it to wartime efficiency. The war against Japan was still to
be won.

The army must be strengthened. The loyalty of its men
must be unquestioned. On March 17, 1945, the Secretary
of National Defense issued General Order No. 20 which
laid down the basic policy regarding military collaboration
with the Japs. The order had the approval of the com-
manding general, USAFFE.

The pertinent section said:

> No officer or enlisted man in the Philippine Army or
> Philippine Constabulary called into the service of the
> United States Forces in the Far East will be retained in
> such service or on active duty in the Philippine Army who
> have accepted appointment or performed service in a mili-
> tary or civil capacity in any activity controlled by the Jap-
> anese or by the so-called puppet "Philippine Republic."

Exceptions were made in two cases: (1) individuals

who ceased such service and joined and participated actively with guerrilla forces or with United States forces prior to September 30, 1944, and (2) officers and enlisted men of the medical service or chaplains' service who performed duties solely pertaining to the medical profession or to religious activities.

General Order No. 20 was intended to purge the Philippine Army of men tainted with collaboration. This was the first forthright stand taken by the returned Osmeña government on the collaboration issue. But it proved unequal to the task of weathering the storm of protest from collaborationist elements that followed in the wake of its publication. Osmeña backed down.

At the end of January 1946, ten months after the promulgation of this order, the Philippine Army had yet to court-martial a man for treason. Only ten cases, an average of one a month, had been decided under General Orders No. 20 and No. 135, and the cases concerned not treason (Article of War 82) but "discredit" to the service (Article of War 97). It was not until February 12, 1946, one year after the liberation of Manila, that the first man was found guilty of treason and sentenced to twenty-five years at hard labor.

The obvious indifference with which the Philippine Army has handled the issue of military collaboration is easily traceable to the really basic policy of whitewashing the collaborators.

High-ranking officers affected by the order opened up a systematic campaign in the press against G.O. 20 as "too harsh." This press drive was implemented by a smear campaign with Tomas Cabili, President Osmeña's first choice as Secretary of National Defense on his return, bearing the brunt of the criticism.

Cabili stood his ground and on January 15, 1945, stoutly defended the order. "It was conceived by the desire that here men who wear the uniform must be willing to pay the price," he declared. "The army is no place for divided loyalty. It is a place for men. If I had collaborated, I would not have the courage now to request reinstatement."

Cabili laid down the policy on military collaboration, but it was sidetracked by Major General Basilio Valdes, Chief of Staff.

As head of the Judge Advocate General's Service, it was the job of Major Rafael Monserrat, a Roxas man, to go after all officers and enlisted men covered by G.O. 20.

He buckled down to the job of whitewashing: "This talk of collaboration bowls me over. There are no so-called collaborators. We all fought. Frankly, I knew early in 1942 we had no chance. On March 15, I wrote in my diary: 'There is no sense in continuing this hopeless fight.'" This he said at a farewell banquet given June 10 in honor of Colonel Orr, AUS, liaison officer at JAGS, Philippine Army.

Cabili implemented General Order No. 20 with an order relegating all affected officers and enlisted men to the "casual camp" at Camp Murphy pending investigation of their cases. This order, however, was never enforced and, in the case of JAGS, deliberately sabotaged.

A verbal order was subsequently issued to key army men that the Cabili order could be "ignored" so that the officers concerned, whose cases were up for decision by the army board of review, should continue to work on their assignments.

In the JAGS, Monserrat's three trusted assistants, previously relieved of their duties because of the Cabili order, were reinstated by Monserrat, with Valdes' approval, and assigned to write out the decisions on the cases of army collaborators covered by G.O. 20. These officers were: Major Mamerto Montemayor, senior assistant to Monserrat, and head of the board of review; Captain Angel S. Salcedo and Captain Fred Ruiz Castro.[2]

Monserrat's unofficial adviser all this time was "Generalissimo" Manuel Roxas, who asked to be reverted to inactive status late in May 1945 to make a determined bid for power. Roxas took this position in a speech at Camp Murphy in June: The question of collaboration (in the army) was up to the United States Army to decide. As long as one was not taken in by the United States Army CIC, he could consider himself free and NOT a collaborator.

In the meantime, while the collaborationists were gunning for Cabili's scalp, President Osmeña continued to hedge. On June 29, he threw in the towel by kicking out Cabili and Confesor.

Cabili had maintained all along that as long as he remained Secretary of National Defense, General Order No. 20 would stay. He told Camp Murphy officers and men on May 3 that he would "not serve one minute longer if this policy is not enforced." In the same speech, he charged high-ranking army officers were sabotaging G.O. 20. "If these officers cannot execute a policy promulgated by the department and approved by both the president and the commander in chief, honor dictates that they should give way to those who faithfully did their duty." In a press statement a few days later, he announced he would "oust" the army collaborators, saying *80 per cent* of the officers "will eventually be dismissed" for disloyalty.

The moment Cabili was out, however, Valdes gave Monserrat the go-ahead signal to revise G.O. No. 20. Putting their heads together, Monserrat and his trusted assist-

[2] These officers were later sent to the United States to take a refresher course, promoted on their return (Montemayor is now lieutenant colonel and Salcedo and Castro are majors), and given choice positions

ants worked on a revised draft. Liable to conviction for
disloyalty were only those who served with the Jap forces
and the puppet Philippine constabulary. No mention was
made of those who held civilian jobs, which meant the
great majority of the ranking officers on the carpet under
G.O. 20 would be given a clean slate. Final decision, which
could not be appealed, was left with the chief of staff,
Valdes.

Clearly the intention was to whitewash the army top
rungers who served in civilian capacity under the Japs.
The small fry were to be sacrificed.

The revised order was forwarded for Osmeña's signature, but the president had sensed the conspiracy and he
advised Valdes to have the order further revised. Monserrat and his lieutenants set to work again. The revised
draft included officers and enlisted men who held civilian
jobs, but this "exception" was inserted: "Officers and enlisted men who can prove by sufficient evidence that they
have used their positions to give aid, comfort and sustenance to guerrilla forces in the Philippines, or participated
actively with guerrilla forces or with United States forces."

This was a made-to-order exception. And in this Roxas
and Valdes can claim credit for affixing their names to a
pile of affidavits attesting to the guerrilla connections of
ranking army collaborators.

The original G.O. 20 had been revised with Osmeña's
approval on the assumption that it denied the constitutional right of the respondent to be given a fair trial, since
it assumed his guilt before he was tried. Malacañan gave
its verbal approval to the revamped G.O. 20 on July 6.

Valdes, however, had the cue and he acted accordingly.
His first step was to recall all papers pertaining to the cases
of officers and men required to resign, or who had been
placed in the casual camp. He gave instructions that
everyone was to be reinstated.

Meanwhile, without any formal orders from the military authorities, officers who had been ordered to the casual camp and those who had been dismissed, or asked to resign, started to report back and take up their duties where they left off.

Cabili was out and an ambitious politico, Alfredo Montelibano, was in. Montelibano asked for time to "feel his way."

On July 19, the first case under G.O. 20 was up for trial, four months after the order went into effect. Major Enrique Sobrepena, of the chaplains' service, was charged under Article of War 97 with discredit to the service. Defended by ex-Justice Mariano Albert and Prospero Sanidad, House Speaker pro tempore, Sobrepena came out of the two weeks' trial a "resistance hero." The prosecution was handled by inexperienced judge trial advocates. G-2 observers at the trial, in an official report, called the choice of prosecutors evident "sabotage" and the trial itself a "travesty of justice."

While the Sobrepena mock trial was going on, a succession of severe shocks sent Philippine Army top brass reeling in confusion. On July 16, General Valdes rushed to AFPAC headquarters on a hurried call. He was confronted with a directive from the War Department. Valdes listened unbelievingly as the order was read and hurried back to his headquarters.

The directive was sent two days later to Valdes, through Montelibano. In his letter of transmittal, General MacArthur expressed the wish to have the instructions in the directive followed.

At the conference, Valdes was told this:

a. Philippine Army personnel in the service of USAFFE must receive the same treatment as to their status during the period of Japanese occupation as we are directed to give scouts and other AUS personnel;

b. AFPAC Headquarters will accept Philippine Army Loyalty Board clearance if that Loyalty Board adheres to the rules which are formulated for the clearance of other United States personnel;

c. The commonwealth government is at liberty to maintain a separate force from its own resources which will not be under USAFFE and which may include such personnel as are ruled out for service in USAFFE;

d. The United States Army will endeavor to absorb as civilian labor Philippine Army personnel dropped as a result of strict rules for all United States military personnel.

e. Back pay may be paid Philippine Army personnel in the service of USAFFE only in accordance with rules and regulations and interpretations of the Missing Persons Act as developed for scouts and other United States military personnel.

The directive means that the Philippine Army was to be purged of collaborators with the United States Army requirements on loyalty as the yardstick and that if the Philippine Government were reluctant to clean house in the Philippine Army, it was "at liberty to maintain a separate force from its own resources."

Valdes got the order. But it was never enforced. The top officers knew such an order existed, but no one, save Valdes, had seen the text. And those who later read the order got copies from an outside source. Valdes had the copy of the War Department directive locked in his desk. The chairman of the loyalty-status board, in charge of processing men for the service, did not know such an order existed then. Neither did the Judge Advocate General, to whom a flood of collaboration cases was being channeled every day.

And yet the machinery of the Philippine Army was supposed to function. Cases were being prepared for court-martial. Claims for three years' back pay, for insurance premiums, and for other collectible "rewards" in cash were being attested. Valdes continued to sign recommendations for the promotion of "friends," who served under the Japs. They were legion.

On July 25, Philippine Army headquarters was in despair. From the AFPAC claims section had come an order suspending payment of salaries. It was only then that collaborationist officers under G.O. 20 were told informally by higher-bracket men that the War Department "had intervened." The United States Army would not pay G.O. 20s. If the commonwealth wanted a separate army, it could have one, at its own expense. No explanation was needed. The implications of the War Department directive were clear.

The collaborationists hoped, however, that commonwealth authorities would save the situation for them. They knew representations were being made with AFPAC for more leniency in the collaboration policy. Osmeña called on MacArthur several times to plead the Philippine Army's case. AFPAC must have wavered for the suspend-pay order was rescinded and there were optimistic speculations at Philippine Army headquarters that the War Department directive was due for a liberal change.

The curtain rang down on the Sobrepena court-martial comedy on August 5, 1945. The verdict was NOT guilty. No one was surprised. It had been taken for granted since the trial started July 19. In fact, the decision whitewashing Sobrepena from the charge of discrediting the service had been prefabricated before the trial opened. The G.O. 20s who ran the JAGS saw to it that the court-martial was made the one-way ticket for all army collaborationists to *vindicate* themselves.

To establish guilt of disservice, three counts had to be proved: (1) the fact of service, (2) the fact of "willing

and voluntary" collaboration, and (3) the motive. Reasonable doubt on any one count could mean a whitewash.

The Sobrepena whitewash was not without its repercussions. A rising feeling of demoralization swept the Philippine Army. Noncollaborationist officers, representing
some 20 per cent, expressed disgust and openly threatened
mass resignation. Besides the whitewash, one other cause
for discontent was Valdes' obvious disregard of G.O. 20
restrictions in the appointment of officers.

Valdes was embarrassed. With unexpected promptness,
he acted to rectify the Sobrepena error. He ordered the
five-man court-martial that tried Sobrepena thrown out
and, later, named a completely new court composed of
noncollaborators. He also announced that the loyalty
status board was due for a revampment.

The harm, however, had been done. A precedent had
been set. Sobrepena's acquittal meant that the issue of
collaboration was, as far as the collaborationist Philippine
Army was concerned, "classified trash." Noteworthy was
the fact that Sobrepena was defended by two collaborators, one of them, Mariano Albert, the chief defense counsel of big-time political collaborators like Teofilo Sison.
(Significantly, Sobrepena's colleague during the Jap occupation, Major Cuadra, was subsequently found guilty and
yet the charges were practically the same as those against
Sobrepena.)

V-J day came to the rescue of collaborators covered by
General Order No. 20. Immediately following the surrender of the Japs, President Osmeña, on prodding from
Montelibano and Philippine Army top brass, pressed for
leniency in the United States Army's policy on collaboration. He saw MacArthur several times to plead his cause.

On August 17, army headquarters was jubilant over the
report that the much-feared General Order No. 20 had
been thrown out. A triumphant lieutenant colonel told his

colleagues: "I was in doubt about collecting. Now I'll get my back pay and quit. To HELL WITH THE ARMY!"

In giving official sanction to General Order No. 135, which was to take the place of General Order No. 20, the War Department reportedly acted on the assumption that the Philippine Army was at liberty to determine the status of its officers and enlisted men so long as it followed a parallel policy as compared with the United States Army in the determination of the loyalty of its men.

This was perfectly all right. But it just happened that in the Philippine Army it was the collaborators who pulled the strings and dictated the policy.

When Rafael Jalandoni was named Deputy Chief of Staff in August 1945, even the top brass were surprised. Behind the appointment was this: On August 1, Valdes hurried to Defense Secretary Montelibano's office to tell him he was up to his neck in work and to ask that a deputy chief of staff be named to assist him. Montelibano asked Valdes for a list of names of prospects and the records of each. Montelibano promised action.

Two days later, Valdes went to see Montelibano again to recommend Jalandoni for the job. Montelibano drew back unbelievingly. "It is Mrs. Quezon's wish," Valdes said firmly. "Oh," said Montelibano. After a pause: "Well, O.K."

Jalandoni was a Montelibano man. A weak, shallow, likable person, Jalandoni is a made-to-order political stooge for a man of Montelibano's ambitions.

Jalandoni was also a Roxas man, through Mrs. Quezon, on whom he was showering his attention, tagging along wherever she went as her self-appointed aide. Before the war, Jalandoni, then a lieutenant colonel, was Mrs. Quezon's official aide.

There was no incompatibility here. Jalandoni was Montelibano's man, also Roxas'. Montelibano was playing an independent game, although he tried to give the impression of backing Osmeña to the hilt. Montelibano was building up his own political machine and he held the two most influential cabinet posts: National Defense, which gave him the Philippine Army; and the Interior, which enabled him to stretch out and place his men in key positions throughout the archipelago.

Jalandoni's cocky deputy, Macario Peralta, was certainly kidding himself when he told the press that the Philippine Army was completely divorced from politics.

IX REACTION BIDS FOR POWER

The Economics of Collaboration

A YOUNG AMERICAN officer told me of his experience upon landing on Luzon early in January 1945. The beach-heads had been secured with little opposition and the boys found time to look around. He and several others strayed into the parochial church of Dagupan, one of the first towns to be liberated. Upon entering the church, they were mildly shocked to see a life-size portrait in full colors of Franco.

"That gave me pause," my friend told me. "I thought we were fighting fascism here too!" He meant, of course, *besides* the Japs.

This was the most distressing aspect of the Philippine scene after liberation. The picture of Franco in the Dagupan church, and this is true in many of the big Catholic churches in the Philippines, is the key to the Philippine feudalistic setup and serves to underscore the basic character of the problem of rehabilitation the Filipinos must face.

My friend was not mistaken in thinking he was fighting fascism in the Philippines too when he saw the picture of Franco in the Dagupan church. Fascism is rooted in the feudal economy of an agriculturally backward Philippines. The war did not destroy the roots of this fascism. It merely accentuated its growth because the forces of liberation unwittingly played into the hands of the forces of reaction and fascism.

The American government was cognizant of these forces. In a memorandum on March 24, 1945, the War Department warned that "there are native fascists in the Philippines" and that "if we want to make certain that fascism does not come to America, we must make certain it does not thrive anywhere in the world."

"All fascism did not die with Mussolini," President Truman warned in his speech June 26, 1945, at the closing session of the United Nations conference at San Francisco. "Hitler is finished, but the seeds sowed by his disordered mind have taken root in too many fanatical brains. It is easier to remove tyrants and destroy concentration camps than it is to kill these ideas which gave them birth. For a good peace, the decent peoples must remain determined to strike down the evil spirit which has hung over the world for the last decade."

In the case of the Filipino people, that "evil spirit" has hung over their heads for centuries. This was probably what High Commissioner McNutt had in mind when he said: "A kind of feudalism has dominated the life of the average Filipino land worker for centuries," and he urged in a speech before the Manila Rotary Club, January 10, 1946: "That feudalism must be progressively eradicated."

Before the war, the Philippines had a full-bloom fascist movement in the Falange. This movement was not eradicated by the war. As a matter of fact, all through the three years of Jap occupation, members of the Spanish community enjoyed privileges reserved only for the puppets and collaborators. For one thing, the Spanish monarchist flag provided ample protection and they carried Franco's colors throughout the occupation. Many a Spanish mestizo made a fortune in the buy-and-sell market dealing in war materials. The Falange was not active as an organization,

but the individual members certainly fared as well if not
better than in prewar days.

The tie-up between the Church and the Falange in the
Philippines is more than spiritual. Both the Church and
the Falange look up to Franco for inspiration. Before the
war, the Falangists paraded their might in the halls of
such popular Catholic schools as San Juan de Letran and
San Beda College in Manila. In the San Beda chapel the
Falange was blessed as an organization devoted to the
Church and Franco and pledged to root out Bolshevism
from the face of the earth.

The Falange demands "blind obedience to all orders of
the chiefs, whatever their category" and metes out "severe
penalty for any infringement on this *virtue.*" The organization, like all fascist groups, is based on iron military dis-
cipline, fanatical religious faith, exaltation of fascist ideals.
The young Falangist must be convinced that he is the
"prototype of the Catholic Spanish knight, intrepid de-
fender of the doctrines of Jesus Christ and soldier of Spain,
the most glorious country in the world."[1]

Three big names loom as the most active supporters of
the Falange in the Philippines, outside of the various religious sects that take direct orders from Spain. A list of
contributors to the Falange fund published on February
29, 1940, included such prominent names as His Excellency Don Andres Soriano, Don Enrique Zobel de Ayala,
Elizalde and Co., Dna. Carmen Vda. de Elizalde, in addition to a number of religious orders.

The Sorianos, the Elizaldes, and the Zobels are three of
the richest families in the Philippines. It is a curious fact
that these three Spanish families have now become Filipino. Soriano put one over and became an American

---

[1] From a booklet on the rules of conduct of "Young Arrows," distributed among members of the Spanish community shortly *after* the liberation of Manila

citizen on October 4, 1945. The decision to become naturalized Filipino citizens came at about the same time,
shortly before the outbreak of the war, when it was believed likely that Franco and his Spain would be em-
broiled in the global conflict on the side of the Axis.

The story of Andreas Soriano is one for the success
books. On October 2, 1945, by order of General Mac-
Arthur, Colonel Andres Soriano, a member of his staff, was
awarded a Silver Star. The decoration was for "gallantry
in action" on Bataan on February 4, 1942. Then a captain
in the Philippine Army, Soriano and two men scouted the
forward area of the 45th Infantry, Philippine Scouts, to
obtain information under constant enemy fire.[2] "Soriano,"
said the citation, "returned the fire until the enemy was
silenced and had his companions withdrawn safely before
withdrawing himself."

The decoration was long in coming, but it was apparently well deserved. A day or so after the award was announced in Tokyo by SCAP, Soriano became an American
citizen on the "recommendation of General MacArthur."[3]
Remarked the then United States Interior Secretary Harold Ickes: "I see where they naturalized a fine upstanding
colonel from the Philippines the other day."

Don Andres Soriano, before the war an open Falangist
and personal representative of Franco as honorary Spanish
consul general in Manila, is one of the big men in the
Philippines today, in business as well as politics.

Soriano enjoyed the confidence of the late Manuel L.
Quezon, and exerted much influence over him. Quezon
held him in esteem; he took Soriano with him to the
United States following the fall of Manila and made him his
Secretary of Finance in the war cabinet.

Soriano has emerged from the war a bigger man of busi-

[2] United Press dispatch, October 3, 1945
[3] United Press dispatch from Washington, October 5, 1945

ness and politics, wielding a tremendous influence over some of the personalities in the political scene. Immediately following the "liberation" of Roxas, he pledged to support him for the presidency against Osmeña. Soriano was careful not to identify himself with Roxas at first, but it was no secret that the attachment between them was very close.

This attachment was personal as well as economic. "I have no political or business connections with Mr. Andres Soriano," claimed Roxas in a press statement in the *Daily News* on August 15, 1945, "much less do I have any business or political connections with *any Jew.*"

Roxas was senior partner of the principal law firm of the vast Soriano interests for years before the war. His partner was Benigno S. Aquino, rabid pro-Jap collaborator who was speaker of the puppet National Assembly. During the civil war in Spain, Soriano contributed handsomely to the fascist cause. In 1939, Franco reciprocated by awarding him the Grand Medal of Naval Merit.

Although he has lived all his life in the Philippines, Soriano retained his Spanish citizenship until late in 1941, when he attempted to obtain Filipino citizenship for fear his assets would be frozen in case of war. He had his business interests in the Philippines and a big brewery in the United States to worry about. The Lichauco, Picazo & Mejia and the Recto law firms pushed the Soriano citizenship deal through the Philippine courts.

The sponsors of Soriano's application for citizenship were Ramon Fernandez, chairman of the board of directors of Soriano's San Miguel Brewery (the biggest in the Far East) and during the Jap occupation a member of the puppet Council of State and Major General Basilio Valdes, Philippine Army Chief of Staff.

At the hearing on the application, an assistant solicitor for the government asked Soriano: "Is it true, Mr. Soriano, that you are a fascist?" Soriano's answer was: "I am accused by some of my friends of *not being one.*" Under Philippine Law, a thirty-day waiting period is required before an applicant for citizenship may be issued his certificate. Soriano did not have to wait. His able legal counsel saw to that.

Behind Soriano's pledge to back Roxas for the Philippine presidency stood the vast resources of the Lord of San Miguel: gold, high finance, banking, insurance, brewery, refrigeration, insurance, import, and export. Soriano is one of the big four of Philippine mining. The others are John Haussermann, Jan Marsman, and J. Mike Elizalde.

Liberation saw Soriano spreading out into other fields of business. With one of America's largest air lines backing him, he inaugurated, early in January 1946, the Philippine Air Lines (PAL). He also went into the construction field with an enterprising American partner, the builder of the famous Boulder Dam. The combine operates under the name Philippine Industrial Equipment Company, or PIECO. This company is the exclusive agent in the Philippines for the following American firms: Westinghouse Electric, International Company, Ingersoll-Rand Company, Taylor Equipment Manufacturing Company, Fulton Iron Works, E. C. Atkins and Company, Western Machinery Corporation, Pacific Wire Rope Company, Pacific Wood Tank Company, Madson Iron Works, the Turl Iron and Car Company, and others.

Soriano also entered the shipping field with an eye on the opening left by shipping tycoons Vicente Madrigal, a collaborator whose assets were frozen, and Esteban de la Rama, who operated with government subsidy before the war. He has organized the only company to exploit the oil resources of the Philippines. He also holds stock in one of the large broadcasting companies established after the liberation. These are only a fraction of his interests, which reach every aspect of Philippine economic life.

On January 15, 1946, a news item from New York monitored by United Press quoted a Washington dispatch by *PM's* Alexander Uhl to the effect that the suggestion that Filipinos might want to reconsider full independence "came *more* from American, Spanish and Filipino interests than from the Filipino people." "Reliable reports from Manila," said the item, "indicate that Presidential Candidate Manuel Roxas privately told some of his friends that he wouldn't oppose the continuing of the status quo for the time being."

Talk of the town was the fact that in the intimate circles of the aristocratic Spanish families of Don Andres Soriano and the Roxases, the presidential candidate Manuel Roxas (no blood relation to the blue-blooded Spanish Roxases) was referred to affectionately as *nuestro pariente* (our relative) Manoling.

The Spanish Roxases, with Soriano and the Elizaldes, were among the heavy donors to the Franco war chest during the civil war. Don Antonio Roxas, Soriano kin (Soriano married into the Roxas family) and partner in Soriano's business, was active in behalf of the Franco cause in the Philippines. His younger brother, Eduardo, fought as a volunteer with Franco's troops in 1939. The Roxases are in the sugar, tobacco, insurance, and engineering lines and in high finance.

The only rival of the Soriano interests is the Elizalde Empire, made up, before the war, of general trade, import and export, shipping, manufacture of rope, paints and oil products, sugar, gold and chromite, insurance, real estate, and distilleries. Elizalde, like Soriano, was in the United States during the war, as Philippine Resident Commissioner until he was "reorganized out" by Osmeña in the middle of 1944 in a purge of the reactionary Spanish advisers of Quezon.

For Don Joaquin Elizalde, as it was for Don Andres Soriano, the Washington "exile" was very profitable. Elizalde returned late in 1945 to announce in an ad in the *Manila Times*, January 21, 1946, the appointment of Elizalde & Co., Inc., as representatives for these American corporations: Westinghouse, De Soto Motors, Sharp & Dohme (drugs), Colonial Dames Co., Ltd., Golden State Company, Ltd., Union Oil Company of California, Joseph E. Seagram & Sons, Ltd., and "other United States industries to be announced later." One of the biggest firms to be organized in Manila after liberation is the Elizalde Trading Corporation, capitalized at five million dollars. Even before the war, Elizalde was pro-Roxas.

An idea of Elizalde's vote-getting technique may be gleaned from the fact that while his big La Carlota Sugar Central in Negros will not be in operation until 1947, he authorized in February 1946 the hiring of two thousand workers. Victory for Roxas meant more jobs for willing hands, the Elizalde strategy implied.

Both Soriano and Elizalde began as big landowners, inheriting through grants originally made by the King of Spain. It was also through such grants that the Catholic Church is today one of the biggest landowners in the Philippines.

These two men and Manuel Roxas are all connected with the landed interests, Soriano and Elizalde through their families, and Roxas through his marriage. Roxas' wife's family, one of the wealthiest in the Philippines, has extensive holdings in Central Luzon.

Almost daily, in June 1945, United States Army trucks unloaded an estimated forty to sixty sacks of rice at a house in Manila occupied by a millionaire landlord of Central Luzon. Don, as he likes to be called, had become the closest friend of General Sato, of the Jap military administration.

For Sato and other Jap officers, Don located fine homes.
He also went into the black market. He had enough rice
to feed a town. The black market enjoyed a long post-
liberation boom and Don was not one to pass up his
opportunities. He had as guests in his house some United
States Army officers [4] who had obliged with a generator,
a refrigerator, and food. He ran around in a big black
Packard.

The Great Liberator as Cat's-paw of Native Francos

The next question is: Where did General MacArthur
come in?

In a speech before the Philippine Congress on July 9,
1945, MacArthur laid stress on the need of preserving
"national unity." This amounted to one thing: Close collaboration between Osmeña and Roxas and their respective factions was to continue with Roxas as a stalking
horse for MacArthur until complete control of the government was won, either by making Osmeña completely
subservient, or by putting Roxas in office as president.

There was little question in the minds of resistance
groups that Roxas is MacArthur's man. Unlike Osmeña,
who was elected vice president in 1941, Roxas owes his
very liberty and his present prestige to MacArthur. He
can be relied upon to do MacArthur's bidding—this thought
preyed on the resistance leaders' minds. Later events served
to strengthen their conviction.

MacArthur's friendship with Soriano and other feudal
lords is a matter of common knowledge. Before the war,
he was associated in some business ventures with Soriano
and a member of his general staff who had wide connec-

[4] In Manila, high-ranking officers preferred to live in private homes,
either independently or as boarders, supplying their own food for themselves and their hosts

tions in Manila.[5] Preoccupied with his military task, Mac-
Arthur leaned heavily on his two experts on Philippine
affairs in running the country after liberation. Our economy was in chaos. People were jubilant, but confused.
Supplies were coming in, and had to be selected and allo-
cated, and priorities given. There was need for action. The
moneyed groups turned to MacArthur's advisers to do an
efficient job.

Manila's commercial press, with a few exceptions, has
from the early days of the liberation toed the collaborationist line. A cursory inquiry into these mushroom publi-
cations reveals a common affinity to opportunism among
the men who run and own them. Roxas was "the strong
man in Philippine politics." Each must hitch his wagon to
the rising star.

Before the war, Manila's press was a publisher's press.
Between the Roces T.V.T. (*Tribune-Vanguardia-Taliba*),
and the Madrigal D.M.H.M. syndicate, and the American-
owned *Manila Daily Bulletin,* public opinion in the Philippines was at best warped, at worst Hearstian.

The war eliminated the D.M.H.M. and the *Bulletin.*[6]
The T.V.T. fared better because Don Alejandro Roces, No.
1 publisher, chose collaboration. The chain became a
medium for Jap propaganda.

In the early days of the liberation, Manila had as many
as fifty-six dailies and weeklies. By December 1945 this
number had dwindled to less than half. Of the twenty-two
dailies listed at the end of the year, only five could claim
a circulation above five thousand daily.

Shortly thereafter the bigger papers, the Roxas syndicate (*Daily News, Balita, Light*), the Ramon Roces chain

[5] MacArthur owns shares of stock in several Soriano mines, including
the Acoje Chromite Co., the Antamok Goldfields, and others. This is true
of Elizalde also

[6] Resumed publication on February 25, 1946

(*Manila Times, Evening News, Liwayway*), the Daily
Standard publishing house (*Daily Standard, Ang Pili-
pino*), and the P.S.P. Publishing firm (*Liberty News, Voz
de Manila, Bagong Buhay*) started to crowd out the
smaller ones, who had no access to newsprint. This fell
into the hands of black marketeers. The biggest paper
dealer before the war in Manila had no paper for the small
independent papers, but its agents did a roaring business
in the black market.

The Ramon Roces syndicate, largest prewar magazine
publisher, has emerged as successor to T.V.T. Ramon is
the son of Don Alejandro, but took an anticollaboration
view under the Japs.

Editorial writer and supervisor of Roxas' papers was
Federico Mangahas, his private secretary and Laurel's No.
1 ghost-writer. Candidate Roxas pursued a foolproof journalistic line. He inquired from hard-pressed editors and
reporters of mushroom papers who came for interviews
how they were getting along and generously offered his
assistance, in newsprint, ads, spot cash. As Roxas' private
secretary, Mangahas became his ghost-writer.

Sample Mangahas line:

> The New Order is a solemn pledge to that end [racial
> dignity and self-respect]. It is more than a pledge. It is a
> definite program of work, and every new day is a witness
> to the determination to leave nothing to chance. The New
> Order allows for no vain speculation. It gives no encour-
> agement to idle day-dreaming. Every second sees the
> forging of tools to implement the construction of a new and
> solid system consecrated to a racial justice.[7]

Into the mouth of Jose Rizal, foremost Filipino hero and
martyr, Mangahas would put these words: "I am with you

[7] Quoted from "Rizal in a Changing Order," *Manila Tribune*, June 27,
1943

in the present emergency. I follow you under the New Order. Your New Philippines is mine. It was part of my dreams. It must be of yours. It is not so much the dawn that is breaking. It is the morning that is here. It is our day!"

It is in "liberal thinkers" like Mangahas and Lopez that Roxas found his apostles. It is from them that he got the inspiration to call his political faction the "Liberal Wing" of the Nacionalista Party.[8]

Manuel Roxas, self-styled Generalissimo of the Philippine underground, ushered himself into the political scene with all the fanfare of a demigod.

He rallied formidable and sinister forces. Formidable, because they include entrenched wealth and privilege and a degenerate bureaucracy loudly resentful of the Osmeña administration's neglect of their interest and welfare in the face of the chaotic situation that followed liberation. Sinister, because these are the forces that make up the backbone of native fascism and reaction.

An enthusiastic Roxas campaigner, a neighbor of ours, left in September 1945 for Leyte to stump for Roxas. "We *have* the money." His eyes glowed. "Do you know [confidingly] that *Roxas is backed by Soriano, Elizalde, MacArthur, and all the rich men?*"

A war was fought to destroy fascism and yet in this democracy, an accredited member of the United Nations, hirelings of fascism are, under the very noses of the liberation forces, busy building where they left off three years ago.

[8] See Chapter XIII

X FREEDOM IN A STRAIT JACKET

Mr. McNutt and Re-examination

As RECENTLY as March 23, 1945, eighteen months after the American landings on Leyte, Paul V. McNutt, speaking "unofficially," told the press in Washington: "If the Philippines step off into an uncharted sea, as some of their leaders seem to be advocating, the islands are clearly destined for trouble. We may have to let the Philippines take their freedom now and learn the hard way."

McNutt also warned that "it is more than possible that if they get their freedom now, they may never again attain their prewar economic stability and may destine themselves to a permanently lower standard of living."

Three months later, he came to Manila to see conditions for himself and in another three months was named by President Truman United States High Commissioner to the Philippines.

It was as High Commissioner that McNutt on March 14, 1938, first broadcast his views on a "realistic re-examination" of the Philippine-American relationship in an address in Washington. Speaking in much the same vein as he did in March 1945, he said: "Politically we brought the islands through progressive steps to the verge of independence. Economically we brought the islands through progressive steps to almost complete dependence upon our markets.

On one hand we sought to sever the ties; on the other we chained them ever closer to us."

McNutt saw the dangers that the Philippines faced. "The Philippines is sparsely populated," he said, "and it is surrounded with nations whose teeming millions are spilling over their natural boundaries. An independent Philippines faces a very real threat of extinction."

But McNutt also saw wherein American responsibility lay: "If we run away our monument will be destroyed. The things we counted on, our aspirations to point the way to a new benign colonialism, our handicraft, will perish. Our grandchildren will read a history which will apply to us the epithet 'quitter.'"

He had a solution:

> With the co-operation of leaders among the Filipinos, we should proceed to a realistic re-examination of the needs of these people and the long-range interests of ourselves. If this study results in a policy favoring a permanent political and economic relationship with the Philippines, it shall be, I trust, because the Filipinos want it and because it is an aid to our national purposes. America will not impose her sovereignty by force upon any people. The enduring welfare and safety of both countries are to be the paramount consideration.

Re-examination stirred Philippine political circles and, for a time, there was a sharp division on the issue, with economic groups, notably the sugar interests, pressing for "realistic re-examination." The Filipino leaders, however, knew the temper of the people. They fought to shelve McNutt's proposal.

With the liberation of the Philippines, however, the question of political status was repeatedly raised in quarters closely identified with American vested interests and economic pressure groups both in America and in the

Philippines. Suggestions came in the form of trial balloons.

One such trial balloon was cut loose when Roy Howard suggested sometime in September 1945 that the United States "annex" the Philippines and make it a state of the union.

"There are many influential Filipinos," Howard wrote in the *New York World Telegram,* "who do not want complete or permanent severance of political relations with the United States." He was, no doubt, speaking in his "unofficial capacity" as a sincere friend of the Filipino people and only incidentally as a Wall Street spokesman. This observation was made following a short visit to the Philippines in August 1945, during which he visited some good friends among "influential Filipinos" who were tainted with collaboration.

The Howard statehood plan caught on. Reactionary sections of the American press toyed with the idea. The *New York Daily News* came out for statehood editorially a month later. Manila newspapers dismissed the suggestion, but one commentator of the *Evening News,* published by the Ramon Roces syndicate, called the proposal "the most practical" since the Leyte landing.

"If for reasons of defense and trade," the *News* remarked, "we are bound to maintain indefinitely some special relations with the United States, why persist in the fiction of independence instead of calling the status self-government. Once the confusion is cleared, the suggestion of statehood is no longer very startling."

In December 1945 High Commissioner McNutt flew to Tokyo to confer with General of the Army MacArthur. On December 20, shortly before leaving for Shanghai, he was quoted as saying: "It is an open secret that *most* Filipinos do not particularly want independence but they may have a try at it." He was also quoted as saying the

United States was committed to go through with independence unless the door "is left open for a change." The initiative, the High Commissioner added, "must come from the Filipinos" and he expressed the belief that if there were "a spontaneous and uninspired request [for the status quo], we probably would grant them the request."

This statement, viewed against the background of Mr. McNutt's previous commitments on the subject, was not surprising, but it gave new cause for alarm among the broad mass of the people to whom the question of independence was a settled issue.

A liberal Manila paper said bluntly:

> We believe that it would be much better if, instead of pontificating on the wisdom of re-examination, Mr. McNutt would cut short his Tokyo sojourn and come right back to his post here to tackle the agrarian unrest, which his boss in Washington has directed him to do. His contacts with the sweating, ill-clad Magbubukid, or peons, who are not ashamed of their brown skin, will no doubt convince him that far from asking for the status quo, these rugged folks would rather have the door permanently closed to Wall Street agents in the guise of re-examinationists.[1]

Meeting in protest in Manila on December 23 some 65,000 people, representing the progressive, peasant, and labor groups who bore the brunt of the resistance, voiced their indignation over the McNutt statement. Asked by the speakers if they wanted independence, the 65,000 roared an emphatic *Yes* and the speakers took Mr. McNutt to task for his attempt to "distort Philippine public opinion."

The High Commissioner returned from Tokyo the same day. He called a press conference to clarify his Tokyo

[1] *Star Reporter*, December 21, 1945

statement on "re-examination." In a written statement, he said:

> I have heard reports that most Filipinos do not desire independence. As far as I am concerned, those are only reports which have no official status. Officially, the policy of the United States is crystal-clear. As requested by the Filipino people, through their leaders, we have promised to grant independence to the Philippines on July 4, 1946. We will carry out that pledge. For my part I shall do my best to make that grant possible and successful.

This statement did not clarify the issue. The average Filipino had always associated McNutt with re-examination.

The independence question came into focus again on January 9, when the Manila press picked up a story monitored by the United Press from London quoting the two Philippine delegates to the United Nations assembly, Pedro Lopez and Manuel Gallego, as saying the Filipinos would consider statehood if it were "offered to them seriously." Said Gallego, who represents the reactionary Filipino landlordism of Central Luzon: "If the offer is seriously made we are only too willing to consider it."

Osmeña promptly issued a statement rebuking the Philippine delegates. The administration paper, *Daily Standard*, on January 11 demanded the recall of Lopez and Gallego who "have proven themselves to be so devoid of honor and self-respect that they could tell the world the brazen lie that the Filipinos would be willing to reconsider their stand on independence."

Their recall, the *Standard* pointed out, would tell the world, and "particularly our great friend and benefactor and liberator, the United States, that we are not a craven race, that regardless of the hardships and difficulties, material and otherwise, that independence might bring,

we would prefer it to any other status however benign."
The *Standard's* position synthesized popular feeling.
The Filipino worker and peasant, who constitute 85 per
cent of the Philippine population, were for independence,
come what might!

On January 15, a news item came from New York quoting an article in the newspaper *PM* by Alexander Uhl to
the effect that suggestions for delay of independence "apparently came *more* from American, Spanish and Filipino
interests than from the Filipino people." The Uhl article
took High Commissioner McNutt to task for allegedly
doing nothing to investigate the agrarian unrest in accordance with the Truman directive of October 26, 1945.[2]

McNutt took exception to the article, saying the original
impression of a "reopening of the independence question"
was based "entirely on a misquotation by one press association" during his press conference in Tokyo on December 15, 1945. In a radiogram to Uhl, McNutt said:

> WHATEVER SINCERE DOUBTS AS TO THE WISDOM OF INDE-
> PENDENCE MAY HAVE BEEN EXPRESSED IN THE PAST BY SOME
> FILIPINOS AND AMERICANS, THERE IS NO LONGER AN INDE-
> PENDENCE ISSUE TODAY. THE ONLY ISSUE IS THE TREMENDOUS
> TASK OF REHABILITATION AND PREPARATIONS FOR INDEPEN-
> DENCE, ON WHICH ALL FILIPINOS AND AMERICANS SHOULD
> CONCENTRATE IN ORDER TO MAKE ECONOMIC DEMOCRACY
> POSSIBLE.

The High Commissioner followed this up with reassuring statements in public speeches that the Philippines had
won its spurs as an independent nation and that the United
States would give every assistance to help them rise
from the ravages of war. Speaking to thousands of GIs in
January 1946 in Manila, Mr. McNutt paid tribute to Filipino loyalty and promised continued American help to

[2] See Chapter XII

the Philippines "based on their willingness to construct
here a free land for free men, free of intolerance, free of
repression, primarily devoted to Philippine interests, but
accepting in full the obligations of the world community."

Two days later, on January 22, the High Commissioner
sent President Truman a statement urging White House
support for the Bell trade measure!

> The situation here is critical. It does not at this moment
> seem possible for the Filipino people, ravaged and de-
> moralized by the cruelest and most destructive of wars,
> politically split between loyalists and enemy collaborators,
> with several sizeable well-armed dissident groups still at
> large, to cope with the coincidence of political indepen-
> dence and the tremendous economic demands of rehabili-
> tation.

"If we understand the temper of the Filipino people
right," the Osmeña administration's *Daily Standard* remarked January 24, 1946, "great as the difficulties of the
situation are, they would rather be independent than be a
Wall Street colony."

At the same time, however, the High Commissioner's
reference to "loyalists" and "enemy collaborators" served
to clarify the political atmosphere. In drawing the line
thus, he in effect put the collaborationists on the spot and
made collaboration a major issue in the presidential election in April 1946. The reaction of Roxas campaign headquarters was typical. Said a spokesman: "We don't feel we
are being alluded to."

In Trial and Disaster the Filipinos Won All

The Filipinos won their freedom in Bataan. If the three
years of epic resistance against the Japanese have any
meaning at all, it is this: that true Filipinos are ready at all

times to suffer and to lose everything, to struggle and to die so that their nation may live; that the present generation of Filipinos is willing to sacrifice for the next; that it is determined to clear away all obstacles to the building up of a national policy dedicated to the freedom and the welfare of the common man.

Franklin D. Roosevelt made a solemn pledge to the people of the Philippines that their freedom would be redeemed. That was only three weeks after Pearl Harbor. He repeated the pledge on August 13, 1943. The Jap timetable had been reversed and the sword pointed irrevocably in the direction of Tokyo. Franklin D. Roosevelt's pledge was clear and strong. The Filipino people heard him make that pledge through the bootleg radio.

> The story of the fighting on Bataan and Corregidor, and indeed everywhere in the Philippines [he said], will be remembered so long as men continue to respect bravery and devotion and determination. When the Filipino people resisted the Japanese invaders with their very lives, they gave final proof that here was a nation fit to be respected as the equal to any on earth, not in size or wealth, but in the stout heart and national dignity which are the true measures of a people.

And that was why the United States, in Roosevelt's words:

> regards your lawful government (in practice) as having the same status as the governments of other independent nations.

> I call upon you heroic people of the Philippines [said Mr. Roosevelt] to stand firm against the false promises of the Japanese as your fighting men and our fighting men stood firm together against their barbaric attacks.

The great day of your liberation will come, as surely as there is a God in heaven.

Franklin D. Roosevelt did not speak for himself. He spoke for the people of America. He spoke for the freedom-loving peoples of the world.

In trial and disaster the Filipinos won all, but retentionists would deprive them of the fruits of their victory.

Free Trade Does Not Mean Freedom

July 4, 1946, marked the auspicious launching of the Philippines as an independent state under the continued tutelage of generous Uncle Sam. For the first eight years, the Philippines can cash in on duty-free trade with America and after this period of free enterprise there will be twenty years of progressively increasing tariffs for most Philippine commodities and declining quotas for the major exports. At the end of the twenty-eight years, conditions being ideal, one may expect the millennium.

By then Philippine productive economy will have been geared so efficiently and effectively as to compensate for every silver dollar America's Wall Street operators have shrewdly invested in shares of Free Philippines, Inc. For free trade with America can only mean dependence on America and not freedom. The history of the Philippine-American free-trade honeymoon dating back to 1909 provides the incontrovertible answer.

Let us consider the facts. During the nearly four hundred years of Spanish rule the Philippines was a source of raw materials and its resources were hardly tapped. American trade with the Philippines had developed during the closing years of Spanish domination, amounting in 1883, for example, to some seven million dollars. After the occupation of 1898, American interests expanded, especially in sugar. Trade developed rapidly and after 1908, when trade

preferences were established under the Payne-Aldrich Act,
the development became more pronounced. Within the
next decade, over 6 per cent of all imports were supplied
by America while 70 per cent of Philippine exports were
sold in the American market. Duty-free trade was provided in 1914 by the Underwood Act.

Further advances were made during the ten-year period
1931–1940 when shipments to the United States accounted
for over 80 per cent of the average total exports. During
the first ten months of 1941 (the latest period available),
exports reached 88 per cent, an all-time high being registered in October when 94 per cent of Philippine exports
were destined for the American market.

The result of this lopsided trade relationship between
the Philippines and the United States was the development, on one hand, of an artificial prosperity with vested
interests reaping all the profits and the disruption, on the
other hand, of old Philippine home industries with the
subsequent reduction of the great masses of Filipinos to a
condition of near peonage and dependence on a feudal
autocracy of big landlords and politicians.

Some labor statistics in 1939 bear out this development.
Out of a prewar population of sixteen million, men and
women above the age of ten in gainful occupations totaled
8,466,493; the men numbered 4,219,278 or 49.8 per cent
and the women, 4,257,215 or 50.2 per cent. Of the total
employed, 3,456,270 worked in agricultural pursuits, the
ratio of men to women being 6 to 1; while 3,478,084 were
employed in domestic and personal service with the
women outnumbering the men 26 to 1.

In all industries where they were employed, women
averaged *less* than one peso, or fifty cents, a day, while the
bulk who were employed as domestic and personal help
received as low as four pesos, or two dollars, a month.
Wages in *gainful* occupations ranged from forty-four cen-

tavos, or twenty-two cents, in agriculture to the equivalent of seventy-two cents in public service.

Salaried employees were listed as 824,115, with 303,952 or 36.9 per cent receiving less than five dollars a month and a fortunate 889, or .11 per cent, with $350 or more a month. Philippine industrial "prosperity" showed 601,335 employed in manufacturing and mechanical industries with an average daily wage of sixty-one centavos, or thirty cents, or $7.25 a month.

This situation was inevitable. Free trade made the Philippines too dependent upon the United States and our country became in fact a mere agricultural appendage.

The Filipino middle class shared in some small way in the economic prosperity of the country. The peasants and the working classes, backbone of an agricultural economy, not only did not share in this so-called prosperity but they were in fact harnessed under the double burden of native and foreign exploitation. What actually happened was the superimposition upon the old feudal economy of the most extreme feature of capitalism: monopoly.

The system of free trade developed, after the passage of the Tydings-McDuffie Independence Law in 1935, into one of special privilege for the few who captured exclusive control of the export trade under a system of quotas.

The extent of this monopolistic control and the relative curtailment of the rights and liberties of the millions of Filipinos dependent on export industries may be gleaned from more statistics. In 1940, investment in sugar mills was distributed as follows: 55 per cent Filipino, 32 per cent American, 12 per cent Spanish, and 1 per cent other foreigners. This compares with 45 per cent Filipino, 30 per cent American, 25 per cent Spanish in 1933 before the quota system went into effect.

In coconut oil, of the eight large plants engaged in the

export trade before the war, only one was owned by Philippine capital and this single Filipino factory obtained only 7065 tons of the total of 200,000 long tons. Thus 96.5 per cent of the quota went neither to Filipino producers of the raw material nor to Filipino processors. Non-Filipinos also controlled cigars and other tobacco products, with Spanish interests owning 60 per cent of total investment in factories and the remaining 40 per cent divided among American, Swiss, Chinese, and Filipino investors. Of the cordage (Manila hemp) quota, only four manufacturers were entitled to allotments and none of these was a strictly Filipino enterprise. Pearl buttons, also on the quota list, were produced exclusively by non-Filipino entities.

Base metals do not come under the quota system, but the same quota-monopolists who enjoy the export-trade privileges control the rich mining industry. The big four of Philippine mining are John Haussermann, Andreas Soriano, Jan Marsman, and J. Miguel Elizalde. Mines operated by these four accounted easily for 60 to 70 per cent of the annual gold production of over ₱78,000,000, or $39,000,000.[3]

These statistics show that the authority to control foreign trade lies in the realm of private privilege. The establishment of quota monopolies, to quote economist Dr. Jose S. Reyes,

> is clearly a step in the direction of a static economy; it has created a group vitally interested in maintaining the status quo in the present organization of Philippine industries, including the disjunction of producer and processor; it has, to the extent that these monopolies of exportation constitute a necessary part in the production and marketing

[3] In 1940, production totaled ₱78,375,384, seven per cent over the 1939 figure, an all-time high

of the country's export commodities, placed the industries concerned in a strait jacket.

The creation of such vested interests in the Philippines economic framework was an obstacle to Philippine independence. Quota-monopolists have consistently opposed independence for selfish motives; resisted all attempts to change the status quo.

When it became clear, following the passage of the Tydings-McDuffie Act, that vested interests would suffer from the granting of independence to the Philippines, many anti-independence moves were undertaken. The most significant of these was the "re-examination" movement which McNutt launched in 1938. The movement found enthusiastic support in the Philippine Civic League, an organization of quota-monopolists pledged to give active assistance to any group or movement for postponement or re-examination of Philippine independence. Closely associated with this league were the Spanish interests led by Soriano, Elizalde, and the Tabacalera,[4] and big Filipino sugar Bourbons.

The continuation of free trade after Philippine independence will place the Philippines in the anomalous position wherein her political independence will be nullified by her economic dependence upon the United States. To the average Filipino, free trade had been a noose around his neck. The export industries paid handsome dividends to the quota-monopolists, but the improvement in the living standards of the Filipino worker was negligible.

In mining, which paid the highest wages in the Philippines, the average daily wage in 1939 was sixty-nine cents; 11 per cent of the workers earned less than one peso, or fifty cents. In sugar centrals, the daily wage averaged 1.13

[4] Compania General de Tabacos de Filipinas, oldest and most powerful Spanish firm in the Philippines, which enjoyed tobacco monopoly for years

188

Betrayal in the Philippines

pesos (sixty-one cents), with 30 per cent receiving less than one peso per day. Common laborers averaged sixty-four centavos (thirty-two cents) daily. In tobacco factories, workers averaged 1.10 pesos for men and 81 centavos for women. In cordage, the average was 1.71 pesos, with 58 per cent receiving less than one peso daily. In the coconut industry, workers received as low as fifty-four centavos; the average for the industry was ninety-seven centavos. In lumber mills and logging, 64.4 per cent of the workers received less than one peso daily. Philippine industrial resources were little developed and, in most cases, hardly tapped, and the country remained mainly agricultural with relatively minor service and consumer-goods industries.

At the time of the Pearl Harbor attack, light industry was just beginning to appear. It consisted of a few cement plants, coconut-oil mills, one cotton mill, edible-oil-products factories, shoe factories, candy and shirt factories. This reduced the market a more highly industrialized Philippines would have afforded to other sections of American industry and finance. The American taxpayer footed the bill for what was in essence a subsidy for a few sugar and other quota-monopoly industries. The American taxpayer also was denied the benefits of an expanding market for American products. Trade has not only been limited but the balance of trade has been unfavorable for America with the Philippines buying less than it sells.

The Philippine economic setup before the war was underscored by these features: [5]

1. The Philippines were engaged almost wholly in agricultural and extractive industries. The entire economy rested on the production of foodstuffs and of agricultural,

[5] Sixth annual report of the United States High Commissioner to the Philippines

forestal, and mineral raw materials the bulk of which are exported to distant countries.

2. By value over 80 per cent of Philippine exports were marketed in the United States, largely under the protection of nearly duty-free entry and high prices resulting from the application in the United States of high tariffs against competing goods from other countries.

3. The forty years of political connection between the Philippine Islands and the United States resulted in an unvarying relation of currencies, sound financial and commercial connections, and marked similarities in consumer habits.

4. Banking, manufacture, foreign trade, domestic wholesale and retail trading, public utilities including transportation and communication services, mineral production, offshore fishing, and lumbering were principally in the hands of American, British, Chinese, and Japanese minorities who have no direct voice in local government. Except insofar as the local government subsidized or capitalized banking, manufacturing, and trading, the mass of the population confined its energies mainly to agriculture.

5. While nearly three fourths of the area of the Philippines was suitable for agriculture less than half had been brought into cultivation or pasturage; settlement of new land had been painfully slow; the population piled up in extraordinary density along the coasts with continued reparcelment of two to five hectare freeholds and tenancies; and the number of landless increased annually.

This is an eloquent summation of the result of America's half-a-century-old misadventure in free enterprise under the guise of free institutions in the Philippines. Paradoxically, it is the same magic formula that is being offered as the over-all solution, the protecting climate, to the task of building a new and independent Philippines on the ruins of the old, as a reward for Filipino heroism and loyalty in war.

This is the meaning of the Bell Bill,[6] which the American Congress roused from its winter hibernation in mid-February 1946, a trade-preference bill made into a trade-rehabilitation bill retaining all its original features and looking more, in its finished form, like the 1946 edition of the Tydings-McDuffie Independence Act of 1935. With this difference: the Philippines becomes independent *first* this time, before she actually has to undergo a period of 28 years of economic strangulation in a brand-new strait jacket, tailored by Wall Street.

The Bell Act is intended to effect a gradual adjustment of Philippine trade economy from a condition of almost complete dependence on United States markets to normal competitive trade between the sovereign nations. Eight years of free trade is the initial step, to be followed by twenty years of progressively increasing tariffs for most commodities and declining quotas for exports.

In effect, however, as it has been pointed out in this chapter, this would freeze the economic status quo in the Philippines so that the quota-monopolists who controlled the economic life of the country before the war would be assured of a continued monopoly for the next quarter of a century. Newcomers, including independent Filipino business enterprises released by liberation, and struggling to get on their feet, would have no chance.

Under "Miscellaneous" provisions in the Bell Bill appears this section on "Rights of United States citizens and business enterprises in natural resources." It reads:

> The disposition, exploitation, development, and utilization of all agricultural, timber, and mineral lands of the public domain, waters, minerals, coal, petroleum, and

[6] Filed by Representative Jasper Bell in November 1945

other mineral oils, all forces and sources of potential energy, and other natural resources of the Philippines, and the operation of public utilities, shall, if open to any person, be open to citizens of the United States and to all forms of business enterprise owned and controlled, directly or indirectly, by United States citizens.

The intention of the bill is to give reciprocal rights to Americans and Filipinos. On the question of immigration, however, while the Filipinos are limited to a yearly quota of one hundred, the Americans are to be allowed one thousand. This is only one instance of nonreciprocal rights embodied in the bill.

Will Clayton, assistant Secretary of State, told the Senate Finance Committee April 5, 1946: "Those provisions [on equal rights and others] are not reciprocal. We cannot give the same rights to the Filipinos. The Bell Bill would require that the Philippines permit Americans free access to enterprises. It would permit them to engage in many activities in the Philippine Islands from which Filipinos, as aliens, would be barred in the United States."

When the Bell Bill was first introduced in Congress in September 1945, it included the "equal rights" proviso in these words:

> Notwithstanding any existing provision of the constitution and statutes of the Philippine Government, citizens and corporations of the United States shall enjoy in the Philippine Islands during the period of the validity of this Act, or any extension thereof by statute or treaty, the same rights as to property, residence, and occupation as citizens of the Philippine Islands. Such rights shall include rights to acquire land of the public domain, to acquire grazing, forestry, fishing, and mineral rights, and to engage in the ownership and operation of public utilities, and all such rights shall be acknowledged, respected, and safeguarded

to the same extent as the same rights of citizens of the Philippine Islands.

Philippine officials were furnished copies of the Bell Bill and Osmeña, who was in Washington in the fall of 1945 to work for Philippine relief, had expressed his approval of the bill as drafted.

Action on the bill and on the companion Tydings War Damage Bill, which was filed at about the same time, dragged until McNutt flew to Washington in February 1946 and personally plugged for the two measures. It was in the closing stages of his fight for approval of these bills that a monkey wrench was thrown into the picture and this resulted in the most bitter outburst of anti-American feeling in the Philippines in the half century of American rule.

What touched off this nationalistic blast was the filing in both houses of the United States Congress on March 24, 1946, of identical bills by Senator Tydings and Congressman Bell to amend the Philippine Constitution and enable the United States Government to acquire real and personal properties even after independence. Section 10 of the Tydings-McDuffie Independence Act provides that on July 4, 1946,

the President of the United States shall by proclamation withdraw and surrender all right of possession, supervision, jurisdiction, control, and sovereignty then existing and exercised by the United States in and over the territory and people of the Philippine Islands, including all military and other reservations of the Government of the United States in the Philippines (except such naval reservations and fueling stations as are reserved under section 5), and, on behalf of the United States, shall recognize the independence of the Philippine Islands as a separate and self-governing nation and acknowledge the authority and control over the same of the government instituted by the people thereof, under the constitution then in force.

The Tydings-Bell amendment sought to keep for the United States, notwithstanding the covenant under the Independence Act,

all the right, title, and interest of the said government or its agencies or instrumentalities to all such real and personal property as may on the date of independence be vested in, or later be acquired by, the government of the United States for use in the performance of the functions of the army, the navy, the United States coast guard, the United States merchant marine, the War Shipping Administration, the United States Maritime Commission, the Commodity Credit Corporation, the War Damage Commission, the Alien Property Custodian, the Veterans Administration, the Foreign Funds Control and disbursing agent of the Treasury Department, the American Consulate, the United States Information Service, and the Foreign Liquidation Commission of the State Department, the Office of International Trade of the Commerce Department, the Federal Bureau of Investigation of the Justice Department, the United States Commercial Company of the Reconstruction Finance Corporation and the Public Health Service of the Federal Security Agency, and of any other agency or instrumentality of the United States Government.

From Manila came a big howl. Government officials, business elements, the press, progressive and liberal groups, labor and civic organizations, and student and university associations burned the wires to Washington in unified protest. A Malacañan spokesman said: "These bills constitute an expression of suspicion and doubt on the part of certain American interests in the good faith and ability of the Filipino people. But the true intent of these bills is to make Philippine independence a farce, to keep the Filipino permanently under American control."

A leading Manila daily said:

> The strategy adopted by the re-examinationists and their congressional allies has all the earmarks of years of planning and bidding for time. The softening operations had been directed only against economic targets. But on D-Day, the shape of things to come could no longer be concealed. Independence was to be by-passed, just as Truk had been by-passed in the great offensive to Tokyo, but it was also to be rendered equally untenable and impotent.[7]

One liberal paper branded it "an unholy scheme to plunder the Philippines and convert it into a happy hunting ground for American businessmen" which is being carried out "with a mixture of American ingenuity and Japanese rapacity." And it concluded with this analogy: "When the stag, fatally wounded, staggers to some hidden spot to die, the vultures, we are told, start gathering for the feast. Mortally stricken by this war which has taxed its resources to the limit and sacrificed the flower of its youth, the Philippines today stands at bay, and the vultures are gathering."[8]

Sergio Osmeña defined the Philippine position in a strongly worded cable on April 4, 1946, to Washington. The Tydings-Bell identical bills, Osmeña asserted, "are tantamount to a repudiation of an agreement entered into between the American people and the Filipino people when the Independence Law was accepted by the Philippine Legislature and ratified by the Filipino people in the

[7] *Evening News*, April 11, 1946
[8] *Philippine Press*, April 5, 1946

plebiscite approving the Constitution of the Philippines."
They were, he said,

A CURTAILMENT OF PHILIPPINE SOVEREIGNTY AND A VIRTUAL
NULLIFICATION OF PHILIPPINE INDEPENDENCE. THE ACT IS
UNFAIR AND UN-AMERICAN, AND FINDS NO PRECEDENT IN THE
ANNALS OF AMERICAN RELATIONS WITH SOVEREIGN STATES.
IT VIOLATES THE SPIRIT AND LETTER OF THE CHARTER OF THE
UNITED NATIONS WHICH CATEGORICALLY RECOGNIZES THE
EQUAL RIGHTS OF ALL NATIONS WHICH ARE MEMBERS OF
THAT GREAT ASSOCIATION OF FREE PEOPLES. NEITHER THE
PAST NOR THE PRESENT CONDUCT OF THE PHILIPPINE GOVERN-
MENT AND THE FILIPINO PEOPLE MERITS THESE PROPOSED
MEASURES WHICH, IF ADOPTED,WILL REFLECT AGAINST THE
GOOD FAITH, ALTRUISM, AND SINCERITY OF THE UNITED
STATES ALL OVER THE WORLD. CONSISTENT WITH OUR RIGHTS
AND OBLIGATIONS AS AN INDEPENDENT NATION, THE PHILIP-
PINE GOVERNMENT IS ALWAYS READY TO CREATE OPPORTUNI-
TIES FOR AMERICANS, NOW AND IN THE FUTURE, TO PRESERVE
THE TIES OF FRIENDSHIP BETWEEN THE PEOPLE OF THIS COUN-
TRY AND THE UNITED STATES.

Even Candidate Roxas felt compelled, in the face of
strong public opposition to the proposed legislation, to
issue a statement endorsing Osmeña's position.

McNutt came in for a barrage of critical fire from the
Philippine press and from progressive and liberal groups
for his active sponsorship of the two bills on Capitol Hill.
The militant Civil Liberties Union, which counts on its
roster leading Filipino liberals who occupy high posts in
the government, demanded in a press statement the recall
of the High Commissioner:

The Civil Liberties Union cannot believe that the
Tydings and Bell bills reflect the opinion of the American
people, whose sense of fairness is well-known. Rather, the

CLU believes that these measures are inspired by American imperialists who intend to make the Philippines their exclusive hunting preserve.

Mr. McNutt, by his blanket endorsement of the Bell Trade relations bill, his ominous silence on the Tydings and Bell bills and his efforts to make the Filipino people believe that these bills are for their benefit—when, in fact, they would benefit American vested interests—has identified himself with them, thus belying his professions of friendship for the Filipino people. The CLU believes, therefore, that Mr. McNutt's continuance in office is prejudicial to Philippine-American relations.[9]

Before returning to Manila for the April 23 election, McNutt made sure the Bell and Tydings Bills were given the right of way. They were approved by both houses of Congress on the eve of his departure and sent to the White House for signature.[10] The Tydings War Damage Bill voted the sum of $625,000,000 for Philippine rehabilitation, classified as follows: $400,000,000 for individual war-damage claims, on the basis of five hundred dollars each individual claim; $120,000,000 for financing highways, docks, and other public facilities; $5,000,000 for repair of government buildings; and $100,000,000 worth of surplus property such as trucks and other equipment in the Philippines, which were to be turned over to the young republic.

Little was said about the Tydings-Bell amendment or "Property Act," as it came to be known later. In the fury of Philippine reaction against it, the authors evidently withdrew quietly. In Washington, McNutt stated it was "important for the Philippine people to understand that the so-called Property Act is only in form an amendment

9 *Manila Daily Bulletin,* April 6, 1946
10 Signed by President Truman, May 1, 1946

to the Independence Act but does not act as part of the Philippine Constitution." In Manila, a spokesman for McNutt explained: "Nothing in this purely formal and unimportant amendment gives any new authority to any agency of the United States to operate in the Philippines except as agreed upon between the United States government and the Philippine government when it becomes independent." [11]

But McNutt promised rectification. "If experience indicates the desirability of improvement," he declared on April 21, 1946, "the American people will be or are ready to take measures to improve the bill."

What the fuss was over this "purely formal and unimportant amendment" the half-confused little Filipino perhaps does not know. But he may well ask himself: "Is this perhaps what is meant by economic democracy in action?"

Certainly, he did not bargain for this when he fought three years in a thousand and one Bataans against the Jap imperialist!

The quota-monopolists are to be rehabilitated *first* in the Philippines. Our people, as always, will take everything in their stride, but this blow hits far below the belt.

The American FEA Plugs for Big Business

Early in June 1945, the Foreign Economic Administration was set up in war-torn Manila to begin the work of making a prostrate Philippines attractive to American capital. Van Lear Woodward, director of the mission, told Philippine businessmen, for the most part American old-timers:

> The basic policy of the United States Government is to encourage private trade, and *no* government agent, either

[11] *Manila Times,* April 14, 1946

United States or Commonwealth, should go into business. *The vitality of private trade is far superior to that of any government.* Of course, we all realize more and more the need of government aid, but there is a big difference between aid and co-operation. We face facts. The good old days will never come back.[12]

In a war-torn Philippines, Woodward saw his job: "the restoration of private trade as soon as possible." To this end, he would block off government agencies, either United States or Commonwealth, from putting their finger in the business pie, which is, or should be, exclusively "private." Woodward urged Philippine businessmen to do their utmost in taking care of the incoming goods, that is, civilian relief, and not to rely on the United States Army. "We have *terrific* pressure by the Commonwealth in their desire to go into certain types of business, if WE don't see to it that all are supplied to the fullest extent possible."

In this same conference, Woodward promised to give American importers and exporters of Manila the "right connections" in the States. While "assuming all of you have your connections in the States and know whom you are going to do business with," Woodward nevertheless had prepared "for anybody who may want it" a list of "what I call responsible exporters and importers in the United States."

The list included: American Steel Exports Company, New York; American Trading Company, New York; Atkins, Kroll and Company, San Francisco; Balfour, Guthrie and Company, San Francisco and New York; W. D. Blood, Inc., New York; T. R. Boody and Company, New York; Connell Bros. Company, Ltd., San Francisco; N. L. Davies Company, Seattle; Dodge and Seymour Company, New

[12] Italics supplied

York; Dodewell and Company, Ltd., New York; Fidelity Trading Company, San Francisco; Frazer and Hanson, Ltd., San Francisco; W. R. Grace and Company, New York; George Jensen and Company, Seattle; Muller and Phipps, Ltd., New York; Oties McAlister Company, San Francisco; Login Corporation, San Francisco; Pullock and Company, San Francisco; L. D. Seymour and Company, New York; Smith, Kirkpatrick and Company, New York; Frazer and Company, San Francisco; Getz Bros. and Company, San Francisco; Sunset Produce Company, San Francisco; and Wessell Duval and Company, New York.

Ewald E. Selph, general counsel of the American Chamber of Commerce in Manila before the war, was the FEA mission's general counsel and also acting director of the mission in charge of hemp procurement.[13] Charles A. Gwin, Woodward consultant, "is primarily a lumber expert." James Scott "is our sugar expert and is known to many of you," according to Woodward, who hastened to explain that sugar "is getting into the wrong channels."

Cordage interests were heavily represented. Sugar and coconut oil were in equally competent hands. The 1941 export industries were to enjoy top priority. The quota-monopolists had not been sleeping.

Under Woodward, the FEA started out to reclaim for American monopolists their privileged position before Pearl Harbor, temporarily relinquished during the war, but now open again for exploitation.

The FEA published a "watched list" which black-listed top Filipino importers and exporters who remained in business during the war and foreign business concerns, including Chinese and others. At the same time, it prepared a top priority list of business firms, in this case all American firms, which were to get the lion's share in

[13] Selph is also a counsel for the Manila Electric and Railway Company (Meralco), biggest American utility firm in the Philippines

the first shipments from the United States of food products and other essential commodities, the first items in the Philippine relief bill. These companies included: Connell Bros. Company, Ltd.; Atkins, Kroll and Company, Inc.; Libby, McNeil and Libby (Philippines, Inc.); Getz Bros. and Company; Ligget and Myers Company; Kuenzle and Streiff, Inc.; and J. P. Heilbronn and Company, paper dealers.

Favored from the start, these companies had the say-so on the shipments of food products, textiles, and clothing articles to Manila following liberation. Between them, the incoming shipments were prorated months in advance, to the exclusion of Filipino businessmen and others. They had shipping priority; their control was virtually complete. Because they did not have facilities for distribution, these American firms passed the job to the well-established Chinese wholesalers and retailers. The shipments flowed in and the American merchants funneled these to the Chinese and through the Chinese to the black market.

Many Filipino merchants placed orders directly with American exporters in the United States, but they could get shipping priority only through a "favored" American firm and this meant an importer had to pay a fee. The shipping priority continued for an indefinite period following the liberation of Manila.

The Foreign Economic Administration pursued a clearcut policy of giving big business its due first. Two instances best illustrate the point.

In August 1945, the commonwealth government created the Petroleum Products Control Administration, or PEPCA, to supervise the distribution of rationed gasoline and other commodities. Shortly afterwards, the prewar Big Three in gasoline, Shell, Socony, and Texaco, organized a parallel association, the Petrol Distribution Association of the Philippines, or PDAP. The FEA officially advised the

commonwealth that henceforth the government had to
deal with the PDAP for the distribution of petroleum
products. Before the PDAP was created, the commonwealth, through the PEPCA, dealt directly with the United
States Army. The FEA changed this. Petroleum products
had to be distributed by the Shell-Socony-Texaco combine at a fee of ten cents or twenty centavos extra per
liter distributed to the public. Some $350,000 to $400,000
worth of gasoline was distributed monthly for civilian
use in Manila. On this, the Shell-Socony-Texaco combine
got its ten-cent a liter cut, just because these trusts were
in business in 1941. And the public paid the extra bill.

The other case was this. During the same month, the
United States Army advised the commonwealth it had
received fifty thousand dollars worth of Chevrolet spare
parts for METRAN (Metropolitan Transportation agency
under the government's Civilian Emergency Administration) trucks. Before the commonwealth could take over
the shipment, the FEA politely stepped in to say that 60
per cent of these spare parts had to go to Yutivo and Sons,
a large Chinese-owned hardware company. By *right,* the
FEA said with authority, Yutivo, prewar Chevrolet agents
in Manila, should get the entire shipment. The commonwealth got only 40 per cent directly and the 60 per cent
through Yutivo, at the agent's "marginal" price. These
were not isolated cases.

In some places, the FEA handled the distribution of
American Red Cross relief. Consider the FEA in Albay,
one of the hemp-producing provinces on Luzon.

The FEA's provincial office in Tabaco was organized
in August 1945. Immediately upon its establishment,
FEA "agents" started to buy Manila hemp and to pay for
it in used clothing from ARC shipments, which were intended as relief, or gifts to Filipino war sufferers. The
FEA office, with a local expert in hemp as manager, paid

for hemp either in cash or in used clothing. He kept no price list, but made his own evaluation of used clothing. The clothing eventually found its way to the black market, where the great bulk of the population, who have no hemp to sell, had to pay fantastic prices.

The Union Obrera de Tabaco (Tabaco Labor Union) filed a complaint with the FEA office in Manila protesting against this practice. But the FEA continued to buy hemp. In no time the FEA had a monopoly on the hemp supply. The control extends today to other hemp-producing regions of the Philippines.

Van Lear Woodward stayed in Manila hardly three months. In August 1945 he was recalled by Washington and replaced. But his basic policy enunciated before the American businessmen of Manila remained and was implemented by the FEA.

Late in 1945, the FEA was dissolved, but its main functions were absorbed by another agency, the United States Commercial Company. Without much loss of time, the USCC became a full-fledged business concern.

The rise of the mighty USCC from January 1946 on is something over which the Filipino people will never cease to marvel. One often wondered whether it was the United States or the USCC that was really running the country.

United States Army surplus commodities in the Pacific were figured at billions. The war ended abruptly. Part of these surplus supplies eventually found their way to civilian use. The bulk, consisting principally of machinery and equipment, was, of course, left to chance and the elements.

Through the Foreign Liquidation Commission, sales of surplus goods in the Western Pacific Theater, the Philippines, and Okinawa, netted the United States Treasury on the average some seven million dollars a month. For instance, the three months' total from November 1945 to January 1946 was twenty million dollars.

This helped, claimed the FLC, to take the bottom out of many flourishing black markets in Manila and the provinces. The black markets flourished nevertheless, because the people who have to pay the price and never earn enough to meet the price never benefited directly from these army "liquidation" sales.

Such army surpluses were disposed of in bulk. That was the efficient way. That was the army way. It was wasteful to sell directly to the people. Let big business handle the distribution the efficient way. The established importers and exporters, the wholesalers, get the consignments. From wholesalers to retailers through their middlemen, and through the black market to the people. It is little wonder that in Manila, one year after liberation, native chicken eggs still cost twenty to twenty-five cents apiece. In prewar years, a dozen cost fifteen cents. A sixty cents' daily wage was a living wage. In battle-scarred Manila today, a decent meal cannot be had for less than two dollars.

But all the hemp and the coconut oil that our liberated country could produce were being bought at controlled prices by the trusted minions of big business and being shipped to the American market where the quota-monopolists were making a killing at *their* price.

Surely, a people who have fought as valiantly for their country as the Filipinos did deserve to own it.

The black market in Manila had the American GI coming and going. This was true everywhere in the liberated world. But some well-meaning GIs felt the Filipinos, whom they liberated, had it over the rest. Griped one to his congressman: "The American people are being asked to give a windfall [$100,000,000 as an outright gift proposed by

Senator Tydings after his Manila visit in May 1945] to a thief that is robbing us."

Editorially a liberation daily took issue with GI Joe:

DEAR JOE

You are probably eating better than most Filipinos. You have meat, vegetables, bread, butter, milk, candies, soft drinks, and a lot of other good things Filipinos had not seen, until you came, for three long years. You always had these, more or less regularly. You got them as a matter of course.

You get tired of these and go to restaurants for something fresh, not out of a can. It seems inconceivable to Filipinos that anyone should get tired of such rare and wonderful stuff, but you do. Most Filipinos consider themselves fortunate if they are able to eat rice regularly, and a little fish. Anything in addition, like a bit of meat, he looks on as a luxury, a special dispensation, an occasion for celebration. You have things most Filipinos only dream about, and you get tired of them. That is a matter of note and surprise to Filipinos. They wish they were in your place.

You go to restaurants and they charge you prices that are undoubtedly exorbitant and you call Filipinos a nation of thieves. You are a fair-minded guy. Is that being fair? These restaurants rob you when you get your extras, your good time, your fun. They rob us when we get our daily meals. They condemn our housewives to be satisfied with the scraps they leave in the black markets, to pay terrible prices for them, so that we may eat. You understand why we have to pay these prices. *We* have to. *We* cannot understand why you do, when you don't have to. You have plenty. You have enough.

Without these restaurants, which thrive on your patronage, which are maintained, in effect, by you, we would not have to pay so high in the market for the food we need. These restaurants would not be there to compete with us to get the best for you, and leave the rest to us. You would not be robbed. We would not be crucified.

Be fair, Joe. *We* are being hit more than you are, and you are partly the cause. Do not confuse us with the thieves, we are their victims more than you are. You don't have to be. *We* have no choice. Think this over before you write that letter to your Congressman.[14]

[14] Editorial in *Philippine Press,* August 1, 1945

XI BEHIND THE AGRARIAN UNREST

The Feudal Economy of the Haciendas

PHILIPPINE ECONOMY is rooted in the feudal economy of sixteenth-century Spain, which the conquistadores implanted on Philippine soil. The land and the people were divided among certain Spanish grandees whose duty it was to protect and to govern and to provide opportunity for the practice of the Catholic religion. In return for this service, onerous tributes were exacted from their people, who were kept in rank ignorance, the better to be exploited. Under Spain, the Filipino was a serf.

The half century of American occupation brought about a substantial advancement in education, public health, self-government, and an increasing national income. Literacy rose from 18 per cent in 1903 to over 48 per cent in 1938. In spite of these accomplishments, however, neither a sizeable independent middle class nor an influential public opinion has developed. The bulk of the newly created income went to the government, to the landlords, and to urban areas, and served but little to ameliorate living conditions among the feudal peasantry.[1]

This condition was the result of America's experiment in free enterprise which created an artificial prosperity for

[1] Fifth Annual Report of United States High Commissioner to the Philippines

the major Philippine export industries and committed 85 per cent of the Filipino population to a backward agricultural economy in which ownership was concentrated in the hands of a few.

Such uneven development served to widen the chasm between the feudal aristocracy, less than 5 per cent of the population, which controlled wealth and political power, and the broad common mass of the landless rural class, dispossessed tenants, peasants, and workers. During the transition years, following the passage of the Tydings-McDuffie Act, this gap between the small ruling class and the mass population was considerably broadened, with subsequent deterioration in the relations between them and the rise of class antagonism.

Organized as a political democracy with no legally constituted privileged classes, Philippine society is nevertheless sharply divided, because the system engendered by a monopolist economy necessarily becomes one in which the privileged rule. The creatures of American-export control monopoly: the sugar and tobacco barons, the hemp producers, and the business tycoons, are the modern prototypes of the Spanish *encomenderos* and caciques of yesterday.

The social chasm is such that even where the aristocracy is native in stock, its relation to the masses is that of master rather than brother. Of the Filipino worker, Quezon said in 1938:

> As he works from sunrise to sundown, his employer gets richer while he remains poor. He has to drink the same polluted water his ancestors drank for ages. Malaria, dysentery, and tuberculosis still threaten him and his family at every turn. His children cannot all go to school, or if they do, they cannot finish the whole primary instruction.

Statistics eloquently bear out what President Quezon

meant. As late as 1940, the majority of the Filipinos lived under an agricultural system based upon feudal practices. Millions of peasants were bound, and still are, to the soil in a state no better than peonage.

"A kind of feudalism," McNutt told Manila Rotarians in January 1946, "has dominated the life of the average Filipino land worker for centuries. That feudalism must be eradicated." 3

In 1939, the average daily wage of the agricultural worker was twenty-two cents while the average monthly salary was seven dollars (American money). The women workers, whose number in all occupations exceeded that of the men, received the lowest average daily wage, sixteen cents. The lowest average monthly salary, three dollars, also went to the women.

A comparative study made of the average daily wage of agricultural and industrial workers for the ten-year period from 1932 to 1941 shows no improvement. In some cases there was actual deterioration in the wage status.

With these meager daily earnings, the living cost for agricultural workers averaged 18.41 pesos or $9.20 and for industrial workers 22.02 pesos, or $11.01, a month. These figures cover the barest necessities of the family. Expenses for taxes, medicines, and household necessities are not included. The question is not whether these laboring masses can live on what they earn, but how they live on their wages.

It is not surprising that, although the Philippines is an overwhelmingly agricultural country, the proportion of the landless is shockingly high. According to a study made in 1940, less than 40 per cent of the 3,143,886 families comprising the Philippine population own both house and land.[2] A little over 40 per cent own houses which stand

[2] Statistics from 1939 Philippine census

on rented sites, the terms of the leases in most instances being brief.

The percentage of the landless is particularly high in the Central Luzon provinces of Nueva Ecija, Pampanga, Tarlac, and Bulacab, which constitute the rice bowl of the Philippines, with a population of close to 1,390,000, or about 8.7 per cent of the total population, today estimated at between seventeen and eighteen million. In Nueva Ecija, for instance, less than 30 per cent of the 81,215 families own both house and land. Of this number, says the late J. Ralston Hayden in his book, *The Philippines*, 50,563 families "own cottages on other persons' lands and comprise the peasantry that brings off the generous annual paddy crops, associated with them being 7,340 families owning neither house or land."

"Small wonder," continues Dr. Hayden, "that there is serious agrarian discontent in these two provinces, especially in Nueva Ecija, where many of the landless are former homesteaders who have lost their holdings through the operation of an ancient politico-socio-legal system which often makes it possible for the rich to dispossess and exploit the poor."

The agrarian problem is basic because it is geared to the whole agricultural economy, under which 75 per cent of the population are dependent on rice as their staple diet. Half of the farms under cultivation in the Philippines are devoted to the production of this cereal. In 1938, only 14.1 per cent of the total land area was under cultivation, but agricultural activity accounted for 80 per cent of the national income.

Some idea of the farm holdings and ownership may be gleaned from the fact that of the 1,634,736 farms in 1939, only 22.6 per cent contain less than one hectare, or about 2.6 acres. On the average, at 1938 prices, each farm could

earn 120 pesos or sixty dollars a year. Farmers with less
than one hectare cannot maintain a normal, much less a
decent, standard of living. The fact that about one fourth
of all farms have less than one hectare indicates the magni-
tude of the problem of improving the lot of the small
Filipino farmer.

The 1939 census also showed that only 1.3 per cent of
the Philippine population own the large farms with an
area of twenty hectares or more, that is, over fifty acres.
Significantly, according to this census study, "actually,
the concentration of land holdings is far greater than is
shown by these data as many of the small farms operated
by tenants [sharecroppers] are owned by farmers having
large farms. One-half of the farmers (those having less
than 2 hectares of cultivable land) control less than one-
fifth of the total farm area."

No less significant is the concentration of idle land in
large farms. Almost 80 per cent of all idle land is in farms
having an area of five or more hectares. Of the total land
area of cultivable farms, 1,675,000 hectares are cultivated
and 865,000 are idle, a ratio of 2 to 1. This disproves the
claim of Filipino landlords that there are not enough
farms to give to sharecroppers.

The social unrest in our big haciendas (estates) is
caused by a system which "often makes it possible for the
rich to dispossess and exploit the poor." Under this system,
the rice crop was split fifty-fifty between landlord and
tenant. On the average, this leaves 60 *cavans* (1 *cavan*
weighs about 120 pounds) to the tenant each year. In prewar years, a *cavan* of palay (unhusked rice) cost 2.50
pesos so that a tenant's share amounted to 150 pesos, or
seventy-five dollars a year. The tenant has to set aside part
of his share, about half the amount, to meet the food
requirements of his family for a year. The rest gives him
some eighty to ninety pesos, or forty to forty-five dollars,

from which he has to deduct his half of the cost of seed-
lings, harvesting, and threshing. He lives on the balance,
if any is left. In general, this amount varies from 50 to 75
pesos a year.

No one can subsist on twenty-five dollars a year. And
yet this is the position of the Filipino peasant today in a
liberated Philippines. One would say that a fifty-fifty sharing formula is equitable. It is, on paper. Under the peculiar
conditions of exploitation of tenants by landlords in Central Luzon, however, the system works one-sidedly in
favor of the exploiters.

Take only one aspect of the problem: the loans advanced by the landlords to tenants. In pre-war years, legal
interest was 12 per cent. It was common practice to increase this interest rate by requiring the tenant to sign a
receipt for a larger amount than he received. Under this
system, not even death could wipe out a tenant's debts.
It has always been thus in a feudal Philippines.

Quezon, landlord in his own right, sought remedial
legislation, but little was accomplished because he failed
to recognize that the tenant could not make anything
approaching a decent living under a fifty-fifty crop division.

Osmeña tried to meet this problem after the liberation.
In September 1945, he named a cabinet committee which
brought together landlords and tenants. A sixty-forty crop
division was adopted.

The Quezon administration hit upon one practical solution of the tenancy problem: the purchase of big landed
estates and their resale to the tenants on an installment
basis. They also undertook a program of land resettlement
projects in Mindanao. The most successful of these was
the Koronadal Valley Project.

The government "transplanted" about two thousand
peasants and their families to Koronadal in 1931. After

a year, settlers had transformed what had been wild
grassland into a self-sufficient agricultural colony. In the
summer of 1940, I visited this colony. The "indolent"
landless tenant whom a feudal aristocracy had kept in
bondage for generations had turned into an energetic,
prodigious farmer.

A Koronadal overseer explained the experiment to me.
"Our problem is not so much how to produce for profit, for
that we can very well do, but how to rehabilitate unfor-
tunate people who have come here in search of a little
security and happiness. Many of these poor people could
not even look others in the face when they arrived. Our
task is to help make them self-respecting men and women."

*The Jap invasion, however, threw out this experiment
in human rehabilitation.*

The Rise of the Hukbalahap

Paradoxically, the Jap invasion was a blessing to the
peasant. The landlord left his hacienda in the hands of his
overseer and stayed in Manila where there was "peace
and order" under the Jap bayonet. The peasant stayed
behind and worked the fields. He fought the Jap, who
tried to grab his produce.

The peasant took the occupation in his stride. "As the
enemy attacked and invaded Luzon," said the United
States High Commissioner in his 1942 report, "the mass
population exhibited a calmness and stout-hearted serenity
that were quite striking. The people realized that their
arms were being defeated, but they faced the situation
without recriminations and with the typical self-confidence
of an agricultural community reliant on the family and
village system. They adopted their own simple and effective decisions and maintained an admirable solidarity."

In Central Luzon, the peasant fought. During the day,

he took up his plow. During the night, he struck. Central Luzon became a no-man's land for the Japs. During the three years of resistance, they rarely ventured out there in groups smaller than ten. In this struggle, the Japs found active support from the puppet Philippine constabulary which the landlords, acting through their spokesmen in the government, the puppets, helped to organize and which the Japs equipped.

The Japs had their own Fort Santiago in San Fernando, capital of Pampanga Province. When the Americans came, they found in the yard and under this torture house more than two thousand skulls and skeletons of victims of Nippon "justice." Thousands more were killed in Jap and puppet constabulary garrisons not only in Pampanga but in other provinces. What did this mean?

When the Japs came, they instituted a reign of terror. The landlords and their hirelings brought out the names of labor "agitators," peasant leaders, and union organizers, and gave them to the Jap military police, the dreaded Kempei-tai. With the help of the puppet constabulary men, the Japs liquidated the "bad elements." Here was a chance to eliminate the "breeders of discontent" in the big haciendas and the landlords found the brutally efficient methods of the Kempei-tai most gratifying.

Out of this struggle was born the Hukbalahap, the militant peasant army of the resistance movement. The name is from the Tagalog, Hukbo ng Bayan Laban sa Hapon, or People's Anti-Japanese Army. The organization became the chief concern of the Jap military authorities and the puppet government.

The minutes of a meeting of the Laurel cabinet in January 1944 reveal that "the most serious concern is the Hukbalahap." At the same meeting, the puppet minister of justice, Teofilo Sison, reported that "in Pampanga, guerrilla bands are actually helping the authorities in getting

rid of the Hukbalahap." Reference is made to the so-called
"guerrilla" groups which were subsidized by the feudal
landlords, who hated and feared the peasant turned
guerrilla fighter.

The Hukbalahap was conceived in December 1941 and
formally organized on March 29, 1942, while Bataan was
standing up gallantly. Its record shows a continuous growth
through a determined struggle in co-ordination with the
common people. It was born from the masses of Central
Luzon, was fed and cared for by them, fought for and
with them, stayed and grew with them. It united Filipinos without regard to political, religious, or social differences for resistance against the Japs and for the day
when America's liberating forces would return. The Hukbalahap did not follow a lie-low policy, a policy of waiting. They fought throughout the three years.

By February 1945, when Manila was liberated, the
Hukbalahap had killed some twenty-five thousand Japs,
spies, and collaborators. It had fought over twelve hundred engagements with the enemy and the puppet constabulary, during which the Japs often used planes, tanks,
and trench mortars, and attempted encirclement of Hukbalahap forces by surrounding large areas. The enemy
knew no peace and rest in Central Luzon in those bitter
three years.

Central Luzon was vital to the rice-eating Japs. It was
even more vital to the people. The flat terrain gave the
enemy all the advantages in a fight, but the peasant was
equal to the struggle. The Hukbalahap co-ordinated their
efforts with the labor groups in the production of rice
and other crops and what was more important, in pre-
venting the harvest from going to the Japs. At the same
time, they instituted rigid price-control regulations in the
towns and barrios throughout Central Luzon and reduced
profiteering to a minimum. They moved and lived mainly

on the plains and used the mountains only as bases for temporary retreat. The peasants served, even while they plowed the fields, as part of an endless relay of signal, courier, and sabotage corps.

The puppet government named provincial and municipal officials, but these kept to the larger towns where the Japs had garrisons. In the absence of legally constituted governments, the peasant army helped the people to establish local councils to unite them in the struggle. The people recognized and supported these councils and not the governments set up by the puppets and the caciques, and maintained under the protection of Jap and puppet constabulary soldiers.

After the landing of the American liberation forces on Luzon Island, the Hukbalahap were prepared to take over the government of the liberated areas. In most of these places, the Americans found the armed peasants had cleaned out opposition and were in control of local governments and had installed their own officers. The Army's Philippine Civil Affairs Unit replaced most of the men and these in turn gave way later to political henchmen of the ruling Nacionalista Party, many of whom were of dubious reputation and whose loyalty was under question.

This was a disappointment to the Hukbalahap and the nonrecognition of their fighting forces and later the unveiled hostility of army authorities toward their organization, because of their known leftist sympathies and the Marxist leanings of some of their leaders, gave rise to a bitter feeling of resentment and contributed immeasurably to the confusion in the handling of these "misguided elements." The arrest of their top commanders, Luis Taruc and Casto Alejandrino, and their subsequent confinement for seven months as "security risks" by the United States Army CIC merely fanned this resentment and served to becloud the whole question of the Hukbalahap and at the same time to expose the political implications of the army policy.

A few facts will throw light on this question. The Hukbalahap had worked in close co-operation with other guerrilla forces in Central Luzon commanded by American officers from Bataan. On May 21, 1942, Taruc, Huk commander in chief, effected liaison with Lieutenant Colonel Claude Thorpe, who was placed in command of guerrilla activities in Central Luzon.

With the Hukbalahap, Thorpe drew up a plan of resistance to harass the enemy rear and "make this island uninhabitable for the enemy even if we have no help from the south." In a letter to Taruc, on June 22, 1942, Thorpe said assistance from army officers who had escaped from Bataan was "increasing every day" and he expressed confidence the resistance would "continue to grow." Thorpe outlined what the Hukbalahap forces were to do: to gain all possible accurate information of enemy troop concentrations, establish communications, seek support and continue to increase guerrilla forces, and concentrate and co-ordinate attacks on enemy concentrations.

"From this," Thorpe wrote, "will grow our forces to maximum effective strength for our big finale. The rainy season is our friend and their enemy."

Efforts at co-ordination of forces were pressed and on July 7, 1942, Thorpe's staff, headed by Captain Joseph Baker and Captain (now Colonel) Bernard L. Anderson, entered into an agreement with the Hukbalahap military committee, of which Taruc was chairman, to form a joint guerrilla command in Central Luzon. Main points of the accord were: mutual collaboration on all necessary actions with the establishment of a central headquarters of the Central Luzon Command, "independent action" of the Hukbalahap on organizational and political matters, and mutual assistance between the guerrilla units of the commonwealth and the Hukbalahap on military supplies and equipment.

This agreement was subject to final approval by Colonel Thorpe, who was immobilized at the time by sickness, but the pact did not materialize because Thorpe and his deputy Baker were captured by the Japs and executed.

Thorpe's successor, Colonel G. Merrill, kept in touch with Taruc and his Hukbalahap, because he recognized the fighting quality of the Hukbalahap and he was anxious to co-ordinate guerrilla activities. A deputy he sent to the Hukbalahap reported on March 26, 1944, that the Huk "numbers among its members an estimated 30 per cent of properly inducted USAFFE men and some Philippine Scouts and Philippine Army men." He recommended to Merrill "that the Colonel authorize someone to make an effort to put the Huk organization on a status that would enable us to aid them legally with arms and ammunitions if and when we may secure some from outside."

The relations between the USPIF (United States Philippine Islands Forces) under Merrill and the Hukbalahap deteriorated, however, despite the efforts of Merrill and the Huk leaders to come to a common understanding. This was due in large measure to the tactlessness of officers under Merrill's command, whose air of superiority was resented by the Huk leaders. The basic issue, of course, was political.

Roy C. Tuggle,[3] who signed himself assistant to the executive officer of the USPIF, wrote the Hukbalahap a few days before the Leyte landing that "any organization which fails to co-operate will be regarded by incoming troops as unlawful armed bands" and pointed out, on his own responsibility, that the "United States Army does not recognize any political aims or ambitions, and it is the position that in time of war, the only political activity

[3] Before the war, a mining broker in Manila

which is *legal*, is political activity aimed at the maintenance of the loyalty of the masses to the established and
legal existing government."

The efforts at reconciling the conflicting claims of the
USPIF and the Hukbalahap continued until the American
landing on Luzon in January, but deep-rooted political
differences had already placed the question under a cloud
of mutual suspicion. Tuggle wrote Taruc on January 16,
1944:

> I am instructed to also issue warning to all guerrilla
> units, that the killing of any person or the taking prisoner
> of any Filipino, except in case that person may be proved
> beyond all question of doubt to have attacked with armed
> force, or to have actually betrayed the guerrilla cause to
> the enemy, will be considered *murder* or kidnapping with
> threat to murder.

Significantly, it was on charges of murder, kidnaping,
rape, looting, and sedition that the United States Army
CIC arrested Huk commanders Taruc and Alejandrino
and kept them in jail for over seven months. Alejandrino
was released first and was turned over to the commonwealth government with an oblique hint from certain high
army authorities that vigorous action be taken to prosecute
him.

Solicitor General Lorenzo Tanada, however, found no
case against Alejandrino and ordered his release without
bail. Seeing Alejandrino cleared, the army authorities released Taruc directly, instead of turning him over to the
commonwealth.

Taruc was bitter at his detention as a "security risk."
"We fought the Japs for three long years," he declared.
"We fought them when our so-called leaders betrayed
the people to the enemy. Throwing me and some of my
companions in jail was certainly a poor reward for our
services."

Taruc complained of the "shabby" treatment he and his companions received. "We did not expect this treatment from Americans who are pledged to fight fascism and who have assured us Filipinos that they are our allies. They certainly did not treat us as allies."

The Huk commander revealed that many of his men were maltreated by American MPs and that he himself was confined in a dark cell for three weeks in Pampanga. "But," he added, "despite the series of provocations, indignities and humiliation to which we have been subjected, we still have faith in the great mass of the American people, especially the progressive and liberal elements to whom Democracy is not a mere word." [4]

The Hukbalahap, which highly placed United States Army authorities considered the most effective guerrilla organization in Central Luzon, had a fighting strength of five thousand armed men, ten thousand lightly armed first reserves, and some thirty-five thousand unarmed reserves. Most of their original arms were obtained from Bataan and captured from Japs.

Of the total Huk fighting force, only three hundred officers and men have been recognized by the United States Army, while at the same time the Philippine Army has absorbed thousands of post-Leyte guerrillas belonging to small opportunistic groups which sprung into existence following General MacArthur's promise, shortly after his return, of "rewards" to guerrillas. The Hukbalahap had requested that in the matter of recognition of their fighting men their organization be incorporated as a unit. When plans were announced for the Philippine Division for the invasion of the Japanese mainland, the Hukbalahap offered a full division. The authorities, however, showed little interest in recognizing Huk units and the peasants themselves lost all interest when they saw opportunistic groups and even collaborationist elements being recognized and

[4] From an interview in the *Philippine Press*, October 3, 1945

rewarded with back salaries by the United States Army. (The Huk military committee renounced all "rewards" in a meeting early in November 1944, saying that a people fighting for its freedom does not think of rewards.)

It is not surprising that the Hukbalahap today remain in possession of their arms and that they have no intention of turning them in. "Of course we have arms in Central Luzon," Luis Taruc told the Manila Rotary Club in February 1946, "arms wrested from the enemy during the occupation. But these arms are of little importance. What we value most are our lives, our honor and our principles. But as long as the people see sinister fascist threats to their security, they will not give up their arms."

The peasants see plainly that the routing of the hated invaders still left in their midst an enemy to be wiped out. Their hatred for the Japs differs little from that they bear the feudal landlords who today seek to impose the old slavery. They naturally want to retain their arms until they can be certain that the foundation for a real democracy is securely laid and that the betrayers of the people's trust are punished.

The leader and spokesman of the peasants in this struggle for better living conditions and the correction of agrarian injustices is the unassuming thirty-two-year-old partisan commander Luis Taruc. A product of the soil, born of peasant stock, Taruc found his thirst for an education hampered at every turn. He managed to go through high school and two years at college as prelaw student, but he found odd jobs could not take him through to a college degree. He returned to the farm. The rank injustices, the oppression, around him fired his inquiring mind to make a study of the agrarian problem in an effort to find a permanent solution. His search led him to Pedro Abad Santos, most influential of Filipino prewar labor leaders, a practical socialist. Abad Santos gave Taruc every

opportunity for self-study and Taruc developed into an
effective union leader and organizer. He proved his mettle
under fire.

What do the Hukbalahap want? "We do not and never
will advocate armed revolt," Taruc says, "but will pursue
our aims within the framework of the duly constituted
government." These aims include the elimination of collaborators from positions of power and the broadening of
democracy in the Philippines by the increased participation of the workers in the government.

The peasants wanted independence. "Only as free citizens of a free nation," Taruc declares, "can the Filipinos
individually and collectively develop their capacities to
the fullest. The fact that the Filipino people's resistance
was spontaneous, without any previous planning by the
United States Army or the Commonwealth authorities, is
an eloquent testimony to the love of freedom of the Filipino masses, to their capacity for organization."

The peasants want the base of democracy broadened.

Democracy-in-action in the Philippines [says McNutt]
means encouragement of efforts here to solve the cen-
turies-old problem of economic serfdom in the Philippines.
The simple land worker here, who is the vast majority of
the population, neither owns the land he cultivates nor
does he share in the benefits of the modern age. Yet these
were the very people who stood by us most unflinchingly
during the war. Simple and unlettered as they are, they
still understood the word democracy. They struggled for
it, starved for it, died for it.[5]

Today, the Jap is gone and the cacique is back in his
hacienda and the peasant who fought off the Jap and won
his freedom in the struggle finds that he is back where he

[5] Speech in Manila beamed to the United States in February 1946

was before the Jap came. He cannot understand why this
has to be. He knows only that he sacrificed, that he fought
for *his* land, and he feels that he deserves to own it. He
cannot understand why he has to be chained again to the
old system.

And so there is unrest in the great haciendas of a liberated Philippines. At the root of this unrest is the fundamental fact that the autocracy as a class wants to impose
its own solution to the problems of another class, the
peasants.

In such a situation, should the United States Army try
to disarm the Filipino peasants as the reactionary landlords openly advocate?

The answer is obviously no. First, because by taking this
action the Americans will promptly find themselves in
armed conflict with the very Filipinos who offered the
most effective and sustained resistance to the Japs in Central Luzon and who have taken and are taking the most
uncompromising stand against collaborators. Second, because the Americans would be suppressing a movement
that is not only legitimate in its essential aspects but
merits their active support since it is aimed at broadening
the base of democracy in the Philippines.

The problem undoubtedly has a boundless potential for
revolt. On the one hand, one finds a state controlled for
generations by a reactionary landlord class. On the other,
one sees a depressed class of people with well-founded
grievances who have come in possession of arms through
struggle against a savage enemy and are unwilling to surrender these arms unless their grievances are redressed.

What is to be done? The landlord-controlled state must
initiate reforms sufficiently broad to give the peasant a
purchasing power commensurate with his status in a progressive community. This he can expect only from an expanding industrial economy aimed at the development of

new industries and the progressive eradication of our
feudalistic setup. A return to the prewar economy is not
only a step backward but a deliberate reversal of America's pledge to prepare the Philippines for independent
nationhood.

The war has opened possibilities for a permanent solution of the agrarian problem. The Osmeña government
had discarded the old practice of dividing the crop fifty-
fifty between landlord and tenant and had instituted a
sixty-forty division. This is a mere palliative, but a good
beginning for a program of progressively increasing the
tenant's share to enable him to live decently.

The big landed estates should be broken up if the peasant is to be given a chance to own a farm. Lands and other
properties of puppets and collaborators who are proved
guilty by the People's Court should likewise be confiscated and given to tenants. Many collaborators acquired
extensive properties in which they invested their ill-gotten
gains from the sales of war materials to the Japs.

The liberated tenants must be given a real start in life.
They must be given every opportunity to acquire a farm
they can call their own, which they can work so they can
become independent farmers and not enslaved peons.

XII THE DIRECTIVES OF MR. TRUMAN

An Illegal Congress Pockets Three Years' Back Pay

PRESIDENT OSMEÑA arrived in Washington on September 29, 1945, to be accorded full military honors including a nineteen-gun salute and to receive a warm welcome from high-ranking administration officials.

The Philippines was in the limelight again. Osmeña's visit, the third since liberation, could not have been better timed. There was talk of reparations for war damages in the Philippines. Washington was responsive. The Big Four were shaping Allied policy on Japan then and Secretary of State Byrnes announced that Pacific nations, including the Philippines, would be invited to sit in.

Osmeña was getting the breaks. Washington pledged rehabilitation money. Two days after his arrival, Osmeña conferred with President Truman. To the press, Mr. Truman announced:

> It would be neither just nor fair to the loyal people of the Philippines who have been our brothers in war as well as in peace to proclaim their independence until the necessary program of rehabilitation has been worked out and until there has been a determination of the fundamental problems involved in our mutual relationship after independence.

More conferences were to follow. Osmeña was elated.

He told the press the United States "is approaching our problems as it always has during our many years of fruitful association, sympathetically and constructively" and expressed his confidence that Philippine rehabilitation problems would be solved.

In Manila, meanwhile, things were happening:

The Roxas camp was becoming bolder in its methods, reminiscent of fascism. There were floods of "hush money." Gangs of tough *hombres* were making the rounds of newspaper stands buying out all copies of the liberal *Philippine Press*, run by resistance fighters, and tearing them while awed news venders looked on.

On October 10, Osmeña saw the then Secretary of the Interior Harold L. Ickes. Mr. Ickes told his friend to "do something about the collaborationists in the Philippines."[1] Asked by the press what Osmeña replied, Ickes declined to say anything, but he reiterated his unequivocal stand that the Philippines must clean house before it could expect aid.

In Manila, however, the Osmeña administration was doing precisely what Mr. Ickes had hoped Mr. Osmeña would not do. Collaborationists were being eased into high-paying jobs by the administration.

No act of any Philippine legislative body has provoked more public indignation than the appropriation by the Philippine Congress of three full years' back pay for its members.

When Congress was called to its first special session in June 1945, Osmeña submitted a limited budget for the fiscal year covering only the most essential activities of the government. No provision was made for the payment of back salaries. On September 4, however, during the second special session, he recommended an appropriation of ten million pesos for partial payment of back compensa-

[1] *Manila Times*, October 13, 1945

tion to "loyal and deserving" government employees and the sum of three million pesos as an additional fund for contingent expenses.

In the provision for back pay for government employees, no mention was made of members of Congress. They however managed not only to include themselves among the "loyal and deserving" that must be compensated but to appropriate to themselves three years' full pay, amounting to ₱31,600 for each member.

When the rider was first exposed by the newspapers, spokesmen for Congress made indignant denials. Speaker Zulueta defended the constitutionality of the act, saying: "We are paid an emolument by virtue of a provision of the constitution. We are entitled to that the moment we are elected and qualified."

As public indignation over the outrageous congressional self-donation continued to mount, however, Zulueta and other Congress spokesmen tried to laugh the whole thing off. Said Zulueta to the press, without revealing his identity: "All right. We do not collect the three years' back pay but extend our term for another four years without any further election. We are willing."

Bluntly, the *Philippine Press,* a liberal daily, charged in an editorial (October 9) titled "Theft":

"Anyone in the government service who appropriates to himself any sum from the public fund without first and previously rendering some service for it is robbing the people of their money."

On October 10, the Democratic Alliance wired a vigorous protest to President Truman, impugning not only the validity but the moral propriety of the payment of three years' back salaries to Congress and seeking the President's direct intervention to the end that congressmen whose loyalty is under question be denied the right to any payment and that the collaboration question be settled resolutely.

On October 12, university and college students and labor groups and government employees staged a mass rally and demonstration at Plaza Guipit, Sampalec, and voiced their condemnation of "congressional venality and greed."

TRY THE COLLABORATOR-CONGRESSMEN TOGETHER WITH YAMASHITA, one placard said. DOWN WITH THE JAP-MINDED CONGRESS, cried another. The rally was conspicuous for the presence of Provost Marshal J. P. Holland's armed MPs.

Zulueta sent informers to the meeting to check up on the speakers and what they had to say. Told that government employees were among the audience, Zulueta called up the presidential secretary and demanded that an investigation be made.

To newspapermen, Zulueta cried in exasperation: "What if it is immoral? Everything is immoral nowadays."

The back pay rider was passed by both houses of Congress in the closing hours of the special session early in October. Contrary to previous practice, newspapermen were kept out of the deliberations of the senate and appropriations committees on the budget.

The moment the salary vouchers were ready, there was a general stampede of jubilant congressmen in the direction of the disbursing office.

Too Hot to Handle; Roxas Shouts Interference

Washington took positive steps to solve the Philippine muddle on October 26, 1945, when President Truman issued a series of directives in which he recommended specific steps to carry out the United States' program of assistance to the Philippines.

Two of these directives were especially significant, one on the solution of the agrarian unrest, addressed to United States High Commissioner Paul V. McNutt, and the other on the issue of collaboration, addressed to Attorney General Tom Clark.

"During the war," the directive to Mr. McNutt said, "the tenants organized a guerrilla army which reportedly did good work against the enemy. After the enemy was defeated in their localities, they did not disband and today constitute a special problem which threatens the stability of government.[2]

"On the other hand," the directive continued, "their legitimate claim to fair treatment and the assistance they rendered in the resistance to the enemy require that they be not dealt with in a ruthless manner." Mr. Truman therefore urged McNutt "to order a prompt investigation of agrarian unrest and to recommend remedies or reforms which ought to be taken by the Commonwealth Government and by the United States Government."

In his directive to Attorney General Clark, Truman said in part:

Regrettably, a number of persons prominent in the political life of the country assisted the enemy in the formulation and enforcement of his political policies and the spread of his propaganda.

Others in the field of trade and finance seized upon the occasion to enrich themselves in property and money at the expense of their countrymen.

Reports have appeared in the press which indicate that a number of persons who gave aid and comfort to the enemy are now holding important offices in the Commonwealth. Reports further indicate that the Commonwealth Government is only beginning to investigate, charge and try the offenders. It is essential that this task be completed before the holding of the next Commonwealth general election.

[2] Reference is made to the Hukbalahap

The Truman directives caught the collaborationist clique in the Philippine Congress in the midst of a witch hunt. Roxas' *Daily News* found them too hot to handle. It failed to publish the one on collaboration.

But Roxas took the directives in his stride. In a press statement, he turned them around as "conclusive proof of the utter incapacity" of the Osmeña government to cope with problems, some of which, he claimed, were of "purely domestic concern" (collaboration).

Roxas' private secretary and ghost writer, Federico Mangahas, called the directives "authoritarian," saying: "This is a hangover of totalitarian and total war." The *Manila Post*, an "independent" paper run by post-liberation guerrillas, made the fine distinction that the Truman directive on collaboration was "substantially identical" to the "oft-repeated stand" of Roxas and in "bold contrast" to the sweeping Ickes blast.[3] (On September 6, 1945, Roxas' *Daily News* had defined its stand in an editorial titled "Collaboration Is Nothing but a Myth in the Philippines.")

In Washington, meanwhile, Osmeña very modestly claimed credit for all the Truman directives except the two on collaboration and agrarian unrest. Collaboration meant Roxas and agrarian unrest meant the Huks and Osmeña did not want to antagonize either.

Indeed, from that time on, it became more and more apparent that Osmeña's strategy envisaged a double-edged appeasement of the powerful economic forces represented by the Roxas clique and the "subversive" and "radical" elements, the peasants, workers, and liberals, represented by the Democratic Alliance.

Roxas claimed collaboration to be mere fiction, which made his position rather vulnerable, but, significantly, Osmeña himself had abetted such "fiction" by continuing

[3] October 31, 1945

to restore to their prewar jobs, despite the Truman directives, key men in the civil service who served under the
puppet regime. In the majority of cases, promotions in
salary were thrown in.

Sometime before this, a curious news item was played
up by the Manila press. On November 11, newspapers carried a story to the effect that leading members of Congress
were working on a plan to convert the Philippine Congress, minus members tainted with collaboration, into a
national advisory or consultative body which would assist
Osmeña in formulating policies.

The plan was not original. In fact, the idea came from
Osmeña himself when he flew for an urgent conference
with the late President Roosevelt in February 1945. Osmeña knew then that Congress was heavily tainted with
collaboration and that, if these members were to be
weeded out, there would be no senate and the House
could hardly make up a quorum. He therefore cabled
Congress leaders in Manila for their opinion. Osmeña was
under a cloud at the time and practically begging for support. Congress leaders simply would not hear of the suggestion.

In the face of the Truman directives, the situation was
changed. Osmeña admittedly had a strong hand and Congress was for baiting him to see whether he would bite.
What was significant was that behind the plan to convert
Congress into an advisory body was Roxas himself. Roxas
saw in the plan an opportunity to remain on the administration band wagon and run things *his* way.

On November 21, the administration's *Daily Standard*
featured a story on the findings of Osmeña's campaign
manager, Jose O. Vera, following an island-wide survey of
the political situation. More than 85 per cent of the electorate, said Vera, are for Osmeña-Roxas unity. He put the

issue of a party schism up to Roxas squarely: "It is Mr. Roxas who can make unity a tremendous asset of the Nacionalista Party, since he is the one who seems to be giving the impression that he is ready to bolt the party."

Osmeña Defines a Collaborator

Osmeña returned from Washington on November 21, 1945.

"I bring no magic formula for the solution of our postwar problems," he told a cheering crowd, "but I bring the full backing of the American people."

He ended his report-to-the-nation speech with his old battle cry of national unity. "We must bury our rivalries, our jealousies, in the common cause," he said.

Three days later, he met the press. He was asked what he planned to do about collaboration. He hedged, but left no doubt what he meant when he said Washington's view as he understood it was that "all those who occupied important positions and who had taken part in the formulation of policies and decisions, *willingly or not,* and who by their acts placed themselves in positions of responsibility in the government, are considered collaborators." In this, Osmeña merely paraphrased Franklin D. Roosevelt's definition of collaboration.

One thought was in the newspapermen's minds: Roxas. According to this definition, Roxas was a collaborator because, *willingly or not,* he occupied an important position in Laurel's puppet republic.

Osmeña's appeal for unity was addressed to the people. Obviously, the appeal was meant for Roxas' followers.

Osmeña was asked by newspapermen who his running mate would be. He answered: "Frankly, gentlemen, I have not given that a thought. All my interest and attention has been directed to rehabilitation. Once I have accomplished

that, I would feel satisfied. If the people should want a
change in the government, I am willing to step out."

On another occasion, he told Zulueta (November 25):
"We must have unity. I am willing to step out to achieve
it. If Manoling [Roxas] is willing, both of us should step
out and give way to a compromise candidate, like Yulo!"
(Yulo had been released and cleared.)

What was Osmeña's position? This may be summed up
in what his trusted envoy Alfredo Montelibano told a
member of the Democratic Alliance executive council in
an off-the-record conference on September 24, 1945:

From the Nacionalista standpoint, an Osmeña-Roxas
ticket was logical. It was a "foregone conclusion." Three
things were to be considered: Osmeña, Roxas, and the
Democratic Alliance.

> Osmeña [said Montelibano] is sure of re-election, and
> he feels he can, and expects to, remain in office for one
> term, four years.

> Roxas has given no hint, unless one takes the changed
> *Daily News* line on Osmeña as an indication, that he
> would be willing to play second fiddle to Osmeña.

> Osmeña knows the Democratic Alliance is the emerging
> opposition party, and is the party that will not compromise
> on principles. While he feels that he can count on the
> DA's backing in the elections, however, he has made no
> move or given any hint that he wants the DA's support in
> his re-election.

> If Roxas should decide to fight Osmeña, the Old Man
> will have to make overtures (which he is *now* doing) either
> to the DA or to Roxas. If the DA decides to support him,
> well and good. But if the DA should run an independent
> candidate, then the Old Man must look to his own chances
> because he knows the DA votes, for the most part peasant
> and labor votes, are potentially his votes.

The Old Man will not take any chances of losing.

It was this outside chance that Nacionalista bigwigs, Montelibano concluded, were capitalizing on to convince Osmeña to take the slightly tainted Roxas into his bosom again, even if that should mean risking another slap from Washington and the American people. And, of course, the ire of the literate Filipino mass.

It boiled down to this: To the Nacionalista oligarchs, the Democratic Alliance and other progressive organizations represented the most serious threat to the ruling party. And the threat must be crushed. That was why Montelibano said an Osmeña-Roxas *rapprochement* was a "foregone conclusion."

XIII THE STRUGGLE FOR POWER

Amnesty for the Quislings?

THEORETICALLY, Sergio Osmeña inherited from Manuel L. Quezon the feudal-landlord and vested interests that supported and controlled the Nacionalista Party. These interests, however, were more concerned with the preservation and possible extension of what they had. During this post-liberation period of stress, they knew that a Roxas, cocky and aggressive, was a surer bet than an Osmeña, a seasoned leader, but in the twilight of his political career.

In actual fact, Manuel Roxas had become, through his "liberation" by General MacArthur, the spokesman of the collaborators and the most reactionary section of our feudal aristocracy. And Filipino liberals and progressives and the common mass who resisted the Japs believed with reason that, if Roxas could compromise with Jap fascist-imperialists and become a collaborator, he could also compromise with American imperialists and allow a "re-examination" of the Philippine independence question after the election.

The political struggle that followed in the wake of Philippine liberation was fundamentally a struggle against the very forces that the war was fought to destroy. The war has been won, it is true; but remnants of fascism continue to thrive in many parts of the world. This is true in the Philippines, where a nascent fascism has been strengthened as a result of the war, where a handful of men have maneuvered themselves into a position to control the economic and political life of the country.

The split in the Nacionalista Party,[1] which has dominated the Philippine political scene for forty years, is only an outward manifestation of the struggle. Twice before the Nacionalistas split. In both instances, the clash was over personal leadership; no principals were involved.

The first indication that a break was impending in Nacionalista ranks came during a special three-day session of the Philippine Congress, called to pass an election law.[2] A senate-House impasse developed over the question of poll inspectors. The senate, led by Roxas, passed a bill permitting the Philippine Army and guerrilla fighters and enlisted men to vote and splitting election inspectors between the Nacionalista wings. The House blocked the senate bill, insisting that army regulars be excluded from voting and that no provision be made for an election inspector for a seceding wing.

The impasse continued and Osmeña had to extend the session twice while the senate and the House bickered. Osmeña himself, always the appeaser, paved the way for the final passage of the election bill by advising the House speaker in a personal note that Roxas could have his poll inspector.

On December 22, 1945, Roxas opened his campaign headquarters and told his awe-struck sympathizers he had decided to run for the presidency "to give the little man a new deal."

The "little man" met the next day at Plaza Guipit, Manila's Hyde Park, to denounce Roxas and his reactionary backers. Under the banner of the Democratic Alliance, some sixty-five thousand peasants, workers, and progres-

[1] January 1946
[2] December 8, 1945

sive and resistance groups reiterated their stand on the
independence and collaboration issues and promised to
support Osmeña only "if and when" he "determinedly
fights against such fascist onslaughts and determinedly
takes care of the needs of the people" and "categorically
severs relations with the vested interests and the puppet
and collaborator agents represented by Roxas." The demonstration was peaceful and orderly. The rally clearly
demonstrated the Democratic Alliance strength and gave
Nacionalista leaders pause. One direct result was the renewed efforts of Nacionalista appeasers to bring Osmeña
and Roxas together.

From the Roxas camp came a proffer of the olive
branch. On December 29, Roxas canceled a scheduled
flight to Panay Island to start his presidential stump and
had a conference with Osmeña. He demanded nothing less
than Osmeña's surrender of the prerogatives of office and
control of Congress, the cabinet, and the Nacionalista
Party.

Osmeña was unsure of himself and was considering one
of two possibilities: to withdraw from the presidential race
in the interest of party unity, or to fuse with Roxas on
Roxas' terms. The Manila press played up the Osmeña-
Roxas bickering, but the real issue escaped it. All the pro-
posals and counterproposals boiled down to the issue of
collaboration.

Press talk was that Osmeña was being pressed to grant
a general amnesty to all puppets and collaborators after
he assumed office.

Into the office of Solicitor General Tanada on January 1,
1946, popped the president's erstwhile favorite son, Sergio,
Jr. He was in his usual talkative mood. What he had to
say was plenty and disquieting.

Sergio, Jr., himself under the collaboration cloud, had
been talking with his father about the touchy issue.

"Why don't you forget all about collaboration?" Sergio, Jr. asked Sergio, Sr.

"I can't do that." Sergio, Sr. was grave. The words were significant, but the aging face told much more. Don Sergio was laboring under a tremendous inner struggle.

After a long pause, the Old Man told his son: "That is the work of Tanada."

That was why, on New Year's Day, Sergio, Jr. paid the hard-working chief prosecutor a visit at his office.

Unwittingly, in this interview, the president's son revealed the rottenness and the bankruptcy of the ruling Nacionalista Party, the party that sold out to the Japs and that is today determinedly, without scruples and in complete disregard of common decency, applying the squeeze to re-establish its strangle hold on the national life of the country.

From the president's son came this revelation: The main issue facing the Nacionalista Party was collaboration. Osmeña, pessimistic about his own chances of re-election, was debating whether to withdraw from the presidential race, or to submit to Roxas' demands for a fusion. If Don Sergio had been less scrupulous, the coalition would by that time have been a fact.

Roxas had made no bones about his intention, if elected, to issue a general amnesty to all collaborators after independence. Significantly, the Old Man himself had told intimates it was also his intention, if he should continue in office, to grant such amnesty to the "small fry." He revealed this to his son when Sergio, Jr. asked him what he intended to do with the collaborators.

Roxas was willing to forego all his other demands, such as control of the cabinet, Congress, and the party convention, but would press for all his worth for one condition: a general amnesty to all collaborators.

If Roxas were elected, the puppets would go scot free.

That was a sure thing. Osmeña was not certain of his re-election. If he decided to withdraw, he would leave the field to Roxas. Should he take Roxas as his running mate, it would mean the loss of self-respect. And Osmeña was too big for that.

The chief prosecutor of the collaborators had this to ponder: "Why should I waste my time prosecuting these collaborators when they will be pardoned anyway?"

What of collaboration? As far as the Nacionalista Party oligarchs were concerned, it would be for the best interests of the nation and the party to forget it.

And what of Tanada and his job of bringing the collaborators before the bar of justice and vindicating the people's name? Must this also be forgotten?

Their leaders were plotting a second betrayal of the Filipino people.

Roxas Talks of His "Redemption"

Roxas applied relentless pressure on Osmeña to make him withdraw from the presidential race. He fired the opening gun in the presidential campaign with a denunciation of the "impotent" Osmeña administration the first week of January 1946, only to resume amity talks with Osmeña the day he returned to Manila. These parleys were really aimed, more than anything else, at breaking Osmeña's resistance.

Roxas demanded in his conference with Osmeña that the president withdraw from the race for the "sake of the country." He had boasted of the "overwhelming" support he would get from the Luzon provinces and of his popularity everywhere. In his attempt to wear down Osmeña's resolve to run, he had the assistance not only of Montelibano, Osmeña's emissary in the amity talks with Roxas, but also of Zulueta. The defection of Montelibano and

Zulueta was a blow to Osmeña. This was the reason why he announced to a surprised cabinet at a special meeting on January 8 that he had decided to withdraw. The cabinet persuaded him to change his decision. Osmeña diehards had seen through Montelibano's and Zulueta's maneuvers. The president realized that two of his "apostles" had betrayed him and that convinced him he had to go out and fight.

In this political war of nerves, Osmeña found a restraining and reassuring hand in the Democratic Alliance. All the time that the amity talks with Roxas were continuing, he and his men had been conferring with the executive council of the Alliance for a possible coalition to check Roxas. The coalition of the Osmeña wing and the Democratic Alliance appeared only logical. On January 9, 1946, his *Daily Standard* quoted an Osmeña cabinet man as saying that "the candidate that gets the vote of the Hukbalahap and the other factions under the Democratic Alliance will surely win victory." This was clearly where the Alliance fitted into the political equation. The Central Luzon vote, for the most part peasant, labor, and progressive, represents the strength of the Alliance. In the 1940 elections, this area accounted for more than 200,000 votes.

On January 11, the *Standard* announced in a banner headline: OSMEÑA LAUNCHES CAMPAIGN. In the evening of that day, Osmeña had a long huddle with Democratic Alliance leaders. The conference was spirited and cordial. The president's grip was firm and warm at parting. Tears welled in his eyes as a DA executive told him emphatically: "You've got to fight, Mr. President. Your whole brilliant career as a public man is at stake. The people need your unselfish leadership now more than ever."

The coalition was sealed. Osmeña announced that the Nacionalista schism was definite and that he was out to win.

While Osmeña and the Alliance were talking of a coalition, Candidate Roxas was stepping up his presidential drive with a four-day stump of Panay Island. "The present administration," he charged, "either through design or through ignorance, is trying to establish a political philosophy similar to Japan" and added: "We are fighting against fascism and for democracy, justice, constitutional government, and the interest of the masses."

The Osmeña faction, through the *Daily Standard*, flung the charge back in Roxas' face:

> Mr. Roxas cannot even dare to face the fact that there is great social unrest precisely because he and his backers and supporters are suspected by the masses of trying to plot against their freedom, against the establishment of progressive democratic institutions, in order to pave the way for an authoritarian regime under Manuel Acuna Roxas. It is Mr. Roxas and what he stands for that have aroused the masses to unremitting vigilance, to the demands for greater and greater economic relief and concessions in order for them to be able to fight harder *when and if the armed attack from the Right materializes.*

The break in Nacionalista ranks was precipitated by two fundamental issues, the issue of collaboration with the enemy and the question of independence. Nacionalista diehards fought a stubborn, losing battle to hold the party ranks at all cost, but in the end had to give up. They had thought all along that as in the past only the question of leadership was involved in the Osmeña-Roxas rivalry.

The issue, however, transcended all personal considerations. The war released two forces which are in sharp conflict in the Philippines today. One is a powerful reactionary minority thirsting and straining to strangle the Philippine national economy and the other is a resurgent democratic citizenry, hardened and steeled in the resistance, fighting to keep and extend the democratic peace gained at the cost of so much suffering and blood under the most trying three years in Philippine history.

The war saw the betrayal of the Filipino people by their chosen national leaders. It exposed the moral bankruptcy and corruption among these men who collaborated with the enemy. Their collaboration was the natural outgrowth of an opportunist and weak character which they had already developed in the prewar years.

In the vanguard of this reaction is the "strongly pro-American" Manuel Roxas, its "fiery, smart, flashy" spokesman.[3]

The rebel wing of the Nacionalista Party met in convention on January 19, 1946, in Manila to nominate Roxas and Elpidio Quirino, senate president pro tempore.

The faction retained the Nacionalista name and called itself "The Liberal Wing." This was not only misleading but dishonest because the Roxas "liberals" included well-known collaborators, in addition to big landlords, businessmen, and politicians. Of the sixteen official candidates for senator on the Roxas ticket, ten had accepted high positions under the puppet regime, while half of the remaining six engaged in buy-and-sell.

The convention was striking for two things: the composition of the delegates, which was easily 80 per cent collaborationist, with buy-and-sell men in the majority; and the pro-collaboration speeches.

On that issue, the plank said: "We promise to prosecute mercilessly those guilty of collaboration. Nothing shall make us swerve from this purpose. We shall demand the severest punishment for the guilty." It maintained, however, that the "mere fact that a man held an office during the Japanese occupation does not *per se* constitute collaboration."

[3] *Time*, February 4, 1946

In the opinion of the convention, Laurel was not a collaborator. One speaker, Mrs. Cristina Suntay Aguinaldo, daughter of the revolutionary general Emilio Aguinaldo, himself accused of collaboration, praised Laurel, who, she said, did everything to promote the welfare of the people. She expressed hope that he would be "spared." The convention cheered!

Another speaker, Virginia Oteyza, prewar councilor of Baguio City, who herself engaged in buy-and-sell, said: "If we are to condemn as collaborators those who worked for the people's welfare then I would rather die as a collaborator than live as a super-isolationist hero [Osmeña]."

Most revealing was the speech of a Chinese-baiter, Jose Tapacio Nueno. "We don't like a president who is a *mandarin*." (Enthusiastic cheers. Osmeña has Chinese blood.)

Roxas, the star performer of the convention, acclaimed as "savior," "redeemer," "*the* Leader," harangued the crowd for an hour, denouncing Osmeña for every possible ill he could think of.

"I greet you as a soldier in a new crusade," was his opening remark, "a crusade for democracy, for justice, to lift our prostrate country and bestow on her the blessings of democracy and peace."

In this crusade, Roxas was "first, for constitutional government; second, for restoration of democratic processes; third, for honesty in the government; and fourth, for peace and order."

Speaking of his "Liberal Wing" as the "people's party," he appealed to his followers to "forget personal preferences," and to "sacrifice all" for the benefit of the party. The ideal of one party, one leader, one nation.

He reserved the final word for himself. "I took my risks [his voice vibrant with emotion]. GOD SAVED MY LIFE! GOD WILL SPARE ME THESE DAYS!"

The ovation was wild as the Redeemer finished his message.

The time was January 19, 1946, and the place, Manila, the Philippine Islands.

But it could have been Nuremberg, 1933.

The Progressives Join Forces with Osmeña

It was inevitable that Osmeña, a consistent nationalist, and the Democratic Alliance, which represents elements in the vanguard of the resistance against the enemy, would be drawn together in the struggle against the powerful forces of reaction supporting Roxas.

The Democratic Alliance fought the proposed fusion of the Osmeña and Roxas factions and when the split became an accomplished fact joined forces with Osmeña because it realized that a victory for Roxas would mean the end of concessions won and a return to the status quo with entrenched wealth in the saddle.

The Osmeña faction and the Alliance held separate conventions in Manila and adopted their respective platforms. Meeting on January 21 the "Loyalist" Nacionalistas proclaimed Sergio Osmeña and Eulogio Rodriguez Sr. as the official candidates for president and vice president on a platform that condemned the "bastard applications of Japanese ideology" and the *Fuehrerprinzip* so evident in Roxas' bid for power.

Jose Romero, a senatorial candidate, keynoted the convention's sentiments: "Men with this messiah complex have ever been the bane of their country and of the world. This is the mentality that produces Hitlers and Mussolinis."

His acceptance speech followed closely the party platform. He pledged a new deal for the masses by casting aside "the backward economic practices which make the

rich richer and poor poorer" and bringing about "a more
equitable sharing of the crop between tenant and landlord." He pointed out that the Philippines would have to
lean heavily on the United States for its rehabilitation, but
added: "Fortunately, the help which the Philippines will
receive from the United States will be considerable." He
reiterated his stand for independence, pointing out that
even before the actual grant of independence the Philippines as a member of the United Nations had been
"launched in the field of foreign relations."

The convention authorized the Nacionalista Party di-
rectorate to continue negotiations with the Democratic
Alliance for a "tactical" coalition.

The Alliance's five-point platform consisted of (1) independence without re-examination at any time, (2) democracy against fascism, (3) anti-collaboration, (4) social
security and agrarian reforms, and (5) industrialization.

The Alliance met on January 27, to ratify the coalition.
Unexpected opposition developed because of a strong feeling among the peasant delegates from Central Luzon
against the Osmeña administration's vacillating stand on
collaboration. A resolution was introduced demanding that
the Osmeña administration adhere to the Roosevelt policy
on collaboration by purging the cabinet, the Philippine
Army, and other government agencies of the disloyal. This
was proposed as a condition for the coalition.

The formal coalition was effected February 1 when
representatives of the Osmeña faction, the Democratic Alliance, and the Popular Front signed a resolution to join
forces in the election to combat "the sinister forces of reaction, including re-examinationists, collaborators, vested
interests, and imperialist agents."

The joint program was highlighted by seven points:

1. Independence on July 4, 1946. No re-examination at
any time.

2. Anti-collaboration. Removal of all collaborators from

positions of power and influence: political, economic, and otherwise, and punishment of those guilty of treasonable collaboration.

Acceleration of demobilization of the Philippine Army before elections with a view to having an army of patriots, purged of all collaborators, *willing* or *unwilling*.

3. Development of democracy in the political, economic, social, military, and cultural fields. Democracy should be in substance and not merely in form, in practice and not merely in theory. Development of local autonomy. Extirpation of fascism, especially the *Fuehrerprinzip*, the idea of an indispensable and infallible leader. Orientation of the Philippine Army, especially the MP, in democratic, anti-fascist ideas and procedure.

4. Promotion of the economic security and independence of the common citizen. Establishment of a Bill of Economic Rights for individuals.

5. Promotion of social security and agrarian reforms. Social security shall include at least measures providing for collective bargaining, the right of self-organization, and the outlawing of company unions.

6. Maintenance of equality for the Filipinos as a nation and as citizens in our international relations.

7. Formation of a coalition government upon the defeat of the party of fascist reaction at the polls, in order to insure complete victory over fascism.

For the first time in the political history of the Philippines, the lines were clearly drawn to focus attention on the basic issue of democracy and progress versus fascism and reaction.

The Masses Find Their Voice

The progressive movement in the Philippines is centered in the Democratic Alliance, originally integrated from resistance groups which fought the enemy during the

occupation and during the liberation campaign. These
groups include the Hukbalahap; the Free Philippines unit
organized by liberal journalists and professional men identified with the Civil Liberties Union and other progressive
groups before the war; the Blue Eagle guerrillas, led by
business and professional men; the Fil-American Cavite
guerrillas; the Fil-American Batangas guerrillas, and units
of the USPIF (USAFFE) guerrillas, organized by Bataan
veterans.

The Alliance was formally launched as a political party
in July 1945. Plans for its organization, however, dated
back to September 1944, before the American landing in
Leyte. The progressive resistance groups never discounted
the possibility that the puppets would make a determined
bid for power after liberation. A political alliance of guerrilla groups was therefore conceived and sometime in
September 1944 a party of four made a risky trip on a
batel (small sailboat) to contact active guerrilla forces in
the Visayas, particularly Montelibano's group in Negros
and the Confesor-Peralta guerrillas on Panay.

Contacts were made with Montelibano and the initial
plans for a People's Alliance were drawn up. The four-man
contact mission was still in Negros when the American
forces of liberation hit the Leyte beaches. There was no
chance of making the Panay trip.

The People's Alliance developed into the Democratic
Alliance. Since its organization, the Alliance has been re-
inforced by other resistance and noncollaborator groups
and individual citizens. The Alliance is in actual fact the
extension of the resistance: the military, political, and
economic struggle against the Japs, to preserve the democratic peace won in that struggle and assure for the heroic
mass which propelled it a real measure of security and
freedom. By December 1945 the Alliance had on its roster
other progressive and labor groups.

In its declaration of principles, the Alliance asserted that it was

keenly aware of the existence in our midst of a powerful, organized reactionary minority which, in its desire to protect its selfish special interests, is boring into our government to impede, if not altogether prevent, the progress and the spirit of self-determination that is now sweeping the whole world, and to curtail the democratic achievements already won through political struggle during the period of American domination, and through revolutionary struggle against the Japanese fascist-militarists.

President of the Democratic Alliance is Judge Jesús Barrera, former president of the Civil Liberties Union and an organizer of the Free Philippines resistance. In the executive council with him are Dr. Vicente Lava, advisor of the Hukbalahap, a former professor at the state university and a top-flight Filipino scientist; Jose Hilario, an organizer of the Blue Eagle guerrillas and Undersecretary of Finance in the Osmeña government; Rafael Ledesma, Manuel Crudo, and J. Antonio Araneta, all active in the resistance, and J. B. L. Reyes, Assistant Solicitor General and an organizer of the Free Philippines.

Membership of the council was increased by four early in 1946 with the inclusion of Luis Taruc, commander in chief of Hukbalahap, Juan Feleo, vice president of the National Peasants' Union, and Mariano Balgos and Pedro Castro, of the Committee on Labor Organization.

Organized Filipino labor has the militant CLO for its spokesman. The CLO is the labor arm of the Democratic Alliance. Under its wings are some ten thousand skilled workers in Manila, connected with the Manila Railroad Company, the RCA, the Manila Trading (Ford) Company, the International Harvester Company, printing presses, shoe factories, dockyards, waterworks, and United

States Army and Navy projects. Its national chairman is
Cipriano Cid, president of the Philippines Newspapermen's Guild.

In the first six months of its organization, after the
liberation of Manila, the CLO called eleven strikes, in
eight of which the workers gained full victory. Strikes
settled under CLO leadership resulted in an aggregated
daily wage increase of one million dollars for city workers,
a record unprecedented in the Philippines. Biggest of
these strikes was the walkout of the five thousand workers
of the government-owned Manila Railroad Company
(then under United States Army control) in January. The
workers won collective-bargaining rights and a 100 per
cent wage boost.

By the end of March 1946 the CLO had increased its
membership eightfold, with thirty-five thousand full-
fledged members in Manila and forty-five thousand in the
provinces. It could claim a record of more than twenty-
four strikes won.

Significant is the fact that the CLO for the first time
succeeded in organizing laborers in government-controlled
enterprises, including the National Development Company, the Manila Railroad Company, the Metropolitan
Transportation Company, the Philippine Relief and Rehabilitation Agency, the Metropolitan Water District, and
workers of the City of Manila, and obtaining collective-
bargaining rights and substantial wage boosts for them.
In the case of the Metropolitan Water District, the
workers won a seat in the management. Noteworthy also
is the fact that these CLO-sponsored strikes had been
won through arbitration, with the Court of Industrial Relations mediating for the government, and in no instance
had violence been resorted to.

In these strikes, two precedents were established: the
government committed itself to recognize the right to

strike and the right to organize and the government was compelled to enter into collective bargaining with labor and to recognize labor's right to be represented in management.

The Democratic Alliance has given voice to the demands of the "inarticulate" broad mass of the Philippine population. These are the people most affected by the war. The specter of insecurity has cast a darkening shadow over them. All the hopes that welled in their hearts, that fired them to heroic action and sacrifice for the past three years —the hope of a tomorrow that would give them freedom and a little security—are today slowly turning to bitterness and angry despair. And it does not take a charlatan to fan the flames of this bitterness over shattered hopes into open hostility toward the powers that be.

XIV Footnote to Freedom: The Fallacy of a Hands-off Policy

MANY thinking Filipinos have been disturbed by America's split personality on collaboration. In Europe, she has uncompromisingly pressed for the prosecution of quislings. She has taken strong measures against Franco. She has given no comfort to the other breast-beating little Hitlers, like Argentina's Peron, and has consistently pursued a policy of uprooting the vestiges of fascism everywhere.

In the Philippines, America's policy is equally clear-cut. Franklin D. Roosevelt had said that those who collaborated with the enemy should be removed from authority over the economic and political life of the country. When he landed on Philippine soil, MacArthur swore "to bring to justice every disloyal Filipino who has debased his country's cause." In September 1945, Harold L. Ickes warned Osmeña of the "probable reluctance" with which America would release funds for rehabilitation "if it becomes generally believed that that government has failed diligently and firmly to convict and punish those guilty of collaboration." In October 1945 Truman implemented the Ickes directive with instructions to the United States Attorney General to see that the task of investigating, charging, and trying Philippine collaborators be "completed before the holding of the next Commonwealth general election."

There could be no question in the minds of the Filipinos as to what America's policy was with respect to collaboration. The people applauded when McNutt drew the line, in January 1946, between "loyalists" and "enemy collaborators."

Collaboration became logically the major issue in the presidential election of April 1946. On this issue hinged the entire question of American assistance in the big task of Philippine rehabilitation. Harold L. Ickes reflected Washington's feelings on the matter in his directive to Osmeña. Roxas realized this and he did the politically wise thing by not accepting Osmeña's invitation to accompany him to Washington. He felt reasonably sure he would have received a "rough" reception.

It was comforting for Roxas, therefore, to read in the newspapers on February 15, 1946, that President Truman had approved High Commissioner McNutt's hands-off policy in the Philippine presidential election. At least he was in the clear until April.

The Osmeña campaign strategy had stressed one particular aspect of collaboration: That if Roxas were elected, the Philippines could not hope to secure any assistance from the United States for rehabilitation. "Americans have sacrificed much in this war and they are not going to help a man who actively aided the Japs," said Tomas Confesor, Philippine member of the Far Eastern Advisory Council.[1] "The American people have only genuine admiration for the Filipino people because they believe that we have set a high standard of courage and patriotism," declared Tomas Cabili, Philippine delegate to the UNO conference in London. "The American mentality will not understand and will never sympathize with those who worked with the Japanese during the occupation."[2]

[1] From the *Manila Post*, February 20, 1946
[2] From the *Daily Standard*, February 22, 1946

It would seem, however, that the Osmeña campaigners had reckoned wrongly. On February 26, 1946, McNutt issued a matter-of-fact statement:

> We neither support, directly or indirectly, any candidate, nor do we look with disfavor, directly or indirectly, on any candidate. The U. S. Government will carry out its promised aid to the Philippine people regardless of whom they choose for their next president.

The statement was made apparently to dispel any doubts as to the United States Government's hands-off policy.

The statement produced unexpected results. It caught the Osmeña camp out on a limb. It was as much of a shock to them as it was a source of jubilation to Roxas. It cracked wide open the claim of Osmeña supporters that the election of Roxas would jeopardize Philippine efforts to secure American aid. "It should blast for all time," Roxas' *Daily News* whooped editorially, "the asinine charge from Cabili, Confesor and their notorious company of slanderers that General Roxas was *persona non grata* to the U. S. Government and that President Osmeña was the only Filipino leader who could ever get rehabilitation from that government."

"Mr. McNutt's pronouncement should put an end to all attempts by those men to terrorize the Filipinos into electing the Malacañan candidate," Roxas said triumphantly. "It also implies that the efforts of Malacañan, Confesor, Cabili, and others to brand me as a collaborator in the United States have utterly failed."

The situation produced by the hands-off policy in the Philippines is no different in its larger implications from that resulting from the nonintervention policy in the Spanish Civil War. It is working against the interests of the common people. It is helping a post-liberation native

Franco, who has taken up the cudgels for reaction and the forces of empire and is out to give his country back to its prewar exploiters.

America pledged her word to redeem our freedom. She kept her word. MacArthur returned to liberate us. But he also liberated Manuel Roxas and there the vicious cycle began. We have our quislings and our Lavals. We know who they are and what they did. That was why we cheered when our liberator clamped them in jail. But MacArthur made an exception. He liberated one of them.

As in Spain in 1936, so now ten years later, America has fallen in with the rightists and the collaborators. She has given Roxas and his rightist backers the necessary weapon to hoodwink the Filipino people into accepting an onerous status quo, which can only mean the reimposition of the rule of a reactionary minority and the loss of the democratic peace and freedom won in the heroic struggle against Japanese fascism. This means victory for the Spanish fascist interests, for Soriano and Elizalde. It means victory for Wall Street vested groups. It means victory for the collaborators and lackeys of the Jap military fascists, for the betrayers of the people's trust and honor.

The Filipino people fought and suffered and sacrificed for three bitter years. They emerged from that struggle a free people, "a nation fit to be respected as the equal of any on earth, not in size or wealth, but in the stout heart and national dignity which are the true measures of a people." [3] For them the dawn of real freedom has come. But Manuel Roxas and the rightist clique whose interests he represents hold back that dawn. They are trying desperately to stem the surging tide of nationalism that is today sweeping the liberated Philippines along with the rest of the colonial world.

[3] Message of Franklin D. Roosevelt, August 13, 1943

Roxas doles out promises of agrarian reforms to the peasant, of giving him a bigger share in the harvest. But he would sanction resort to a mailed-fist policy to muzzle the common man, whose champion he claims to be, in the name of "peace and order." While men taking orders from him sabotage efforts to give the peasant a larger share, he promises jobs for all. He would not lift a finger to help Philippine labor press its demands for higher wages and an economic bill of rights. He talks of building a new nation, free, democratic, strong, self-sufficient, but he would open the floodgates of the Philippines to the forces of empire and give Wall Street every advantage the better to exploit our untapped wealth.

XV THE FILIPINOS TURN TO A STRONG MAN

... And Drift toward Civil Strife

WHEN ON MARCH 14, 1946, two days before the deadline set by law, Chief Prosecutor Tanada indicted the top Filipino collaborators for treason, the name of Manuel Roxas was not on the list. Over fifty-five hundred cases were filed against political, economic, and military collaborators. At the head of the list was Laurel; next, Vargas. All members of their cabinets and the men who held key positions under them were indicted. Roxas, Laurel's closest adviser, was not touched.

The same day, a delegation of peasants and workers led by Luis Taruc called on Tanada to demand that Roxas be indicted for treason. Tanada told them: "Roxas is a collaborator, but under our laws of treason, he cannot be charged with the capital offense."

Under Philippine law, which is closely patterned after American law, two witnesses are required to the same overt act, or a confession of guilt in open court. To bring about conviction, treasonable adherence to the enemy must be proved and that the commission of an overt act gave, or tended to give, aid and comfort to the enemy. In recent pronouncements of the United States Supreme Court, still another count must be proved to convict a man for treason: treasonable intent.

What are the facts behind Tanada's position? In November 1946 he flew to Tokyo at the invitation of the Chief Counter-intelligence Officer of the United States Army, Brigadier General E. R. Thorpe. Tanada asked him about Roxas. "What about him?" the general countered. "If you think you have a case against him, young man, go ahead and prosecute him."

Tanada had been shown, before he left Manila for the Tokyo visit, the papers on Roxas from the CIC files. Each thread of evidence against him for alleged collaboration had ended in a whitewash by some officer, or official investigator. The case was not only weak, but Tanada saw he had no case against Roxas based on CIC findings.

Nevertheless, Tanada continued to work on the Roxas case. On his return to Manila from Tokyo, he was able to gather additional evidence that would throw light on the case. His main drawback, however, was the two-witness requirement for every overt act to prove treasonable intent.

Up to the last few days before the deadline for the filing of treason cases, Tanada hoped that he would have more tangible evidence on which to prosecute Roxas, but his hopes were unrewarded. On the other hand, circumstances worked adversely to undermine his own resolve to prosecute all the top puppets without exception. Roxas maintained that he had been "cleared" by General MacArthur, who not only "liberated" him, but lost no time in reinstating him to his old rank as one-star general and assigning him to his general headquarters. MacArthur's silence was taken to mean tacit affirmation of Roxas' claim. In Tanada's mind, there was no doubt that the general meant to clear Roxas when he liberated him. And in weighing the possibilities of prosecuting Roxas, Tanada never discounted the possibility that the general himself, or a spokesman, might sustain Roxas' contention were he to be indicted. Such a possibility might appear farfetched; nevertheless, it could not be discounted in a case in which an element of "reasonable doubt" was strong.

That doubt, Tanada believed, was also manifest in Washington's own undecided attitude on collaborationism. In his directive to the Attorney General on October 26, 1946, President Truman stressed the need of completing the trial of collaborators "before the holding of the next Commonwealth general election." Early in January 1946 a special assistant of the Attorney General arrived in Manila as the vanguard of a fact-finding mission to make a study of collaborationism. "We hope to do a fast job," the special investigator told the press, "but not a hasty job. Our objective is to get at the facts as President Truman directed us to do." [1]

The special investigator worked closely with Tanada, conferred with the judges of the People's Court, and observed the court in action. The high caliber of the prosecutors and the judges impressed him. He studied all phases of the question, poring over the records. In a report to the Attorney General in February, the investigator criticized Osmeña's vacillating policy on collaboration and, at the same time, pointed to Roxas as a collaborator. He commended the prosecutors and judges of the People's Court and urged that Washington extend facilities to the court to expedite the trials.

Washington's answer was to issue its hands-off policy in the presidential campaign.[2] What were the Filipino people to think when Washington failed to define its position in a decisive campaign between a noncollaborator and a collaborator?

[1] *Manila Times*, January 3, 1946
[2] Chapter XIV, The Fallacy of a Hands-off Policy

The case of Roxas was clouded in doubt and confusion because of his "liberation." Washington's hands-off policy made the issue even more confusing and the heat of the election campaign left the people in a state of unimaginable confusion.

Tanada fidgeted on the horns of the dilemma: to prosecute or not to prosecute Roxas. Two paths were open to him: first, to prosecute Roxas and risk his acquittal on "reasonable doubt" before the election on April 23 and, second, not to press charges against Roxas and leave the judgment to the electorate.

In either case, Roxas stood to gain and Tanada was convinced that the second alternative, all things considered, was the less objectionable. If charges were filed against him, Roxas would have demanded an immediate trial and a verdict before the election. If he were acquitted and Tanada was convinced that, with all the facts on hand, he had a weak case against him, this would have paved the way for certain victory at the polls. He would be hailed as a hero. On the other hand, Tanada knew that if he did not file charges against Roxas, this would be used as one more proof of Roxas' "vindication."

The Roxas *Daily News* blared: TANADA CLEARS ROXAS. The Philippine electorate, groping for enlightenment and confused by the weak official policy on the matter, believed the *Daily News*.

There was only one issue in the election, collaboration. Osmeña allowed the question to take its "natural course," permitting political exigency to be his guide. The people looked to him for guidance, but he refused to campaign in his own behalf, trusting to his forty-year record of unbroken and unselfish service to his people and to his unfailing trust in their sense of justice.

The campaign, the bitterest in Philippine history, was one of distortion and vilification and rank demagoguery.

The issues were ignored, or sidetracked. Up and down
the country, Roxas and his troupe of top-flight trum-
peteers pleaded, gloated, begged, cajoled, promised,
threatened, and promised some more. The Osmeña government was "weak, impotent, corrupt, and inefficient,"
Roxas told enthralled crowds. The people were being
"oppressed, suppressed, and tyrannized" by this *weak* and
fascistic government. Osmeña was "sick, impotent, senile,
decrepit, old" and a "fascist" and he should be defeated.
Osmeña refused to go out and see his people and be seen
by them. He carried on with his duties in Malacañan,
worked longer than usual.

"This government is committing highway robbery
against the people," Roxas ranted.[3] "High officials and
friends of Malacañan have become millionaires overnight.
I promise you a living wage, no matter what happens."
The people believed him.

The commonwealth was in the red by over forty-five
million dollars. The expected income by June 1946 was
less than fifteen million dollars. The last reserve in the
Philippine treasury would be wiped out by the thirty
million dollars deficit. The Philippine republic would start
with empty coffers. The guerrillas clamored for the redemption of guerrilla currency, more than sixty million
dollars' worth, issued during the occupation. Depositors
urged the redemption of Philippine National Bank notes.
The people clamored for relief, for back pay for loyal
government employees, for higher wages and cost-of-liv-
ing bonuses, for full compensation for war widows and
orphans, and for properties and work animals lost. Osmeña would promise nothing. Roxas promised everything.
The people believed him.

Roxas warned that, if Osmeña won, revolution would
break loose. In Manila, the representative-elect, a Roxas

[3] United Press dispatch, March 29, 1946

man, warned that, if Roxas lost, he would "rise" at the head of "my thousand guerrillas with machine guns and mortars."

Malacañan said: "The utterance of such a thought by such a personage cannot but fail to encourage in some minds, especially those partial to fascism and the rule by 'Strong Men,' theories and beliefs destructive of democracy." The Democratic Alliance warned: "The threat of revolution issued by Mr. Roxas should not be taken lightly, considering his character and fascist association. Fascist *coups d'état* have been staged before in other countries under circumstances very similar to those now obtaining in the Philippines."

Roxas denied that he threatened the people with revolution, but the people *believed* the threat.

At a rally in Manila in February, Roxas quoted the hanged Jap General, Yamashita, conqueror of Singapore and butcher of Manila, as having told the United States Army CIC that "had Roxas co-operated with me the Americans could not have landed so quickly." [4] In an article in the *New York Daily News* in April 1946 an American correspondent, Lowell Limpus, revealed an interview he had with Yamashita in his death cell. Limpus said Yamashita and two other Jap generals "laughed loudly when they were asked about the guerrilla status of Roxas." Limpus quoted the Tiger as saying: "I never heard of him [Roxas] as a guerrilla."

At the same Manila rally, Roxas made the specious claim that it was on *his* tip five days before the Leyte landings "warning him [MacArthur] that the Japanese Empire would use its entire resources to stop the Americans" that MacArthur destroyed the major portion of the Jap Imperial Navy in the great naval battle in Philippine waters. General MacArthur certainly did not have to rely

[4] *Manila Times,* February 25, 1946. Yamashita was hanged February 23

on Roxas' word. But Roxas made the people believe it
was on his "timely" warning that MacArthur delivered the
coup de grâce to the Jap navy.

He waxed virulent as the election day drew nearer.
Two weeks before the poll, he took up the familiar fascist
technique of raising the Communist bogey. "I am fighting
in this election," he told big meetings on Luzon Island,
"not because I want to be president, but because we must
save this country from chaos, corruption and Commu-
nism."[5] And yet in Pampanga, a "communist-infested"
province, Roxas henchmen and military-police units flooded
the towns and barrios with leaflets appealing to the Hukbalahap and peasants to vote for Taruc as representative
and for himself, because with him as president and Taruc
as leader in Central Luzon peace and prosperity were
assured!

Certain articulate British nationals plugged for Roxas
among American business circles and among the younger
officer class of the United States Army. There was danger
to Philippine democracy, *specifically* to British colonial
policy in the Far East. That danger must be removed at
all cost.

To McNutt in Washington, Roxas wired a complaint
against "terroristic practices" in Central Luzon, alleging
the people would not be able to vote freely and that election lists had been "padded" and demanding a probe. Mr.
McNutt indorsed the Roxas charges to Osmeña in a radio
letter April 11, with the suggestion that Osmeña investigate the matter. Osmeña made no comment, but Malacañan spokesmen termed the charges "unfounded." What
the Philippine electorate did not know was the fact that
Roxas' native province, Capiz, was the only one among
the fifty provinces where the number of registered voters,
69,281, exceeded the number of eligible voters, 66,594.

[5] United Press dispatch, April 9, 1946

Pampanga, according to the same statistical data, had 91,751 registered voters out of 109,320 eligible voters.

It was a serene and dignified Osmeña who spoke before the Manila electorate in his first and only public appearance in the campaign, three days before the election. In measured tone, heavy with emotion, the president delivered a subtle blast at Roxas: "It goes without saying that there still is much trouble and suffering in the land, but to systematically find fault, to invent grievances, to foment discontent—that is the work not of true leadership but of demagoguery."

He denied that chaos threatened the country, but warned that the country's welfare was "rashly imperiled by the big ambitions of little men." He revealed he "early decided not to attempt to wage a personal campaign for my election," because to have done so

> during the past critical months, I would have had to give second place to my duties as President of the Philippines in the all-important task of laying the foundations of rehabilitation.
>
> I have not come to you to promise you the moon, the sun, and the stars. It would be childish of you to believe me if I made such promises. I stand on the oath I took as President of the Commonwealth of the Philippines, the oath which, God willing, I shall take again as President-elect of the Republic: that I will faithfully and conscientiously fulfill my duties, preserve and defend the Constitution, do justice to every man.
>
> I promise this, and also that we shall remain the friends and allies of America, that great and most enlightened nation of all time, to which we owe our liberties, our very lives.
>
> I promise to stand by the common man of the land, so

that he may enjoy that other freedom the great President
Roosevelt called the freedom from want.
God guide you all. God preserve our nation.[6]

The Filipino people went to the polls. When the votes
were counted, Sergio Osmeña had lost.

Roxas promised the people everything; Osmeña nothing,
because he had not the means. But the people took the
promise for the substance. Because they were anxious for
a change and Roxas promised change, they elected him
with a clear majority. Of the 2,300,000 votes cast, Roxas
carried a 200,000 majority.

Roxas carried the majority of his sixteen senatorial candidates with him to victory on the crest of the overwhelming demand for change. His hold on the Philippine Congress, however, is precarious, because the Osmeña faction
and the Democratic Alliance won enough seats to place
his leadership in the balance. In the senate, seven of the
sixteen senators-elect are Osmeña men, including Tomas
Confesor and Tomas Cabili. Of the eight hold-over senators, whose term expires in 1947, four are for Osmeña and
four for Roxas, but one Osmeña man and two Roxas men
are indicted for treason before the People's Court and
presumably cannot assume office. The Osmeña faction is
assured ten votes against Roxas' eleven, which leaves him
without a sure majority.

In the lower house, Roxas must reckon with the Democratic Alliance, which elected seven out of the eight representatives from Central Luzon. With the election over,
the Osmeña-Democratic Alliance coalition ceases to be
a political group, but opposition forces are now rallying
around the Democratic Alliance. In the vanguard of this
opposition are the seven Alliance representatives, all well-

[6] *Manila Times,* April 21, 1946

known resistance leaders, including Luis Taruc. With the
seven DA representatives, the Osmeña faction in the
house counts with thirty-six seats. This leaves Roxas with
sixty-two seats, which is short of the two thirds majority required in all important voting such as the approval of the
Bell Trade Relations and Tydings War Damage Acts.

The defeat of Osmeña was the victory of the collaborators. The town of Santa Rosa, hotbed of the Makapili, the
pro-Jap organization whose members fought against the
liberating forces, gave Roxas a fifteen-to-one majority.
Popular feeling is that Roxas will grant a general amnesty
to political prisoners. In fact, a month before his inauguration as president, Roxas had "assigned" his trusted men,
collaborators all, to key posts in the commonwealth so
that they might be "consulted" by the outgoing Osmeña
appointees on what the Roxas administration intended to
do. Men who remained at high posts in the government
under the puppets Laurel and Vargas and who were not
reinstated by Osmeña, because they were held by the
United States Army CIC, have been recalled.[7]

In an exclusive interview with the Manila correspondent
of Hearst's International News Service, on April 27, 1946,
Manuel Roxas declared his administration would take
steps to "set the Philippine house in order, restore domestic tranquillity, re-establish the democratic rights of the
people, and safeguard the welfare of the common masses."

Roxas laid to rest, said the I.N.S. correspondent, rumors
that he would throttle the activities of the People's Court,
or grant amnesty to alleged collaborators under indict-
ment. "Those who are guilty," Roxas was quoted as saying, "will be punished."

The same day this interview was published, two Roxas

[7] Pio Joven, technical adviser who accompanied Roxas in his trip to
Washington with McNutt in May 1946, was deputy auditor general under
Laurel. He was not reinstated by Osmeña, because he held a high policy-
determining position under the Japanese

henchmen let the cat out of the bag. Vicente Francisco, counsel for certain collaborators, revealed he was drafting legislation to abolish the People's Court.[8] His colleague, Prospero Sanidad, one of the Laurel "special representatives" in the pacification drive under the Japs, told enthusiastic Roxists at their party headquarters: "If I were a member of the lower house of the new Congress, I would see to it that the Huks, or Communist members, will be deprived of their seats. Communists should have no place in our scheme of government, especially in the independent government we are soon to set up."[9]

(NOTE: The Roxas majority refused to seat three Osmeña-DA senators and the seven Democratic Alliance representatives on the ground that their election did not reflect the popular will. Under the Philippine constitution, no member of Congress may be denied a seat without a formal hearing by the Electoral Tribunal of each house. When I left Manila in September, these opposition legislators had not yet been seated.)

In the same press interview with I.N.S., Roxas declared that he "would move with finesse" in handling the "lawless elements," so that there would be "a minimum of incidents in connection with peace and order."

This brought to the mind of Manila residents the familiar sight of the stern-faced Generalissimo making a round of city precincts on Election Day in his car, escorted by two jeeploads of bodyguards armed with carbines and submachine guns. For the first time in Manila politics, city thugs, armed with .45s and carbines, "patrolled" the polling places in Manila's labor districts, riding in jeeps plastered with Roxas posters. Roxas may have had no knowledge of this, but in the public mind the mere association of his name with the underworld is

[8] *Manila Chronicle*, April 28, 1946
[9] *Manila Post*, April 28, 1946

viewed with no little alarm. There were shooting incidents. In the province of Camarines Sur, the governor,
an Osmeña man, was ambushed and seriously wounded.
A seven-year-old boy was killed by a stray bullet. In
Bacolor, Pampanga, at midnight on Election Day, Edil-
berto Joven, sixty-two, president of the Democratic Alliance provincial chapter and a former provincial governor,
was machine-gunned in cold blood. His brother, who was
with him, survived with serious wounds. Roxas partisans
figured in both cases.

In Sulu, in the Moro country, Osmeña received a big
majority. "But the victors," reported the Manila correspondent of the *Chicago Sun*, "were not happy. The majority should have been greater." And the reason was
given: military police stationed in Sulu had thrown in their
lot with Roxas and Osmeña voters were scared away from
many precincts.[10] In Manila, Osmeña was blanked in several precincts, despite the fact that out of four inspectors
in each precinct two were supposed to be his own appointees.

The enthusiasm for Roxas was really tremendous. Six
weeks before the election, the G-2 section of AFWESPAC
made a forecast of the election, giving the Central Luzon
provinces of Pampanga, Nueva Ecija, and Tarlac to Osmeña 100 per cent. Two weeks before the election, the
same source forecast for Roxas victory in Tarlac and 45
per cent of the Nueva Ecija vote. United States Army CIC
men reported that Roxas was a good bet to win in Nueva
Ecija. "Incidents" between MPs and Huk partisans were
reported. On Election Day, planes of the military-police
command flew low full throttle out over Nueva Ecija
towns and barrios while tanks, with trigger-happy MPs
squatting on top, "patrolled" the precincts to see that the
voting was "orderly and efficient." In the days immediately

[10] *Manila Times*, April 26, 1946

preceding the election, these same MPs rolled through Nueva Ecija and some Pampanga towns distributing Roxas campaign literature.

With the rise of Manual Roxas to power, the Philippines return to the Quezon political philosophy of an autocratic one-party rule. A "strong man" has come upon the scene of a war-ravished Philippines, a "dynamic leader," "the Savior," "the idol of the common masses." The same vested groups that supported the autocratic Quezon and kept him in power backed Roxas to the hilt in the presidential election and will keep him at the helm. The big moneyed groups, the sugar and tobacco barons, the Soriano and Elizalde interests, the economic collaborators, the native and foreign retentionists will see to it that their vested rights are protected.[11] Labor will have its hands full holding fast to its newly won rights under the short-lived Osmeña regime.

Roxas professes loyalty to the two-party system and he has expressed his desire to see a "strong opposition" led by Osmeña.[12] The Osmeña Nacionalistas cannot long remain in the opposition. Because of his defeat, Osmeña is retiring. Osmeña had trusted his men, but many of them let him down. When the going got tough, they switched their support to Roxas, swapping votes to insure their own election. This sell-out was manifest in the election returns. Osmeña lost badly in many districts where his men won handily. It was only in his native Cebu and in Central Luzon that he won a clear-cut victory. Most of

[11] Roxas' two most trusted advisers today are Joaquin M. (Mike) Elizalde and Jose Yulo, puppet Chief Justice. Elizalde was Roxas' biggest single backer in the election outside of Andres Soriano, while Yulo is now on the board of directors of the Elizalde interests and is their legal counsel, getting a fat retainer's fee. These are two of the men on whose "wise counsel" the new Philippine executive must depend to formulate a program in which the much maligned "little man" will be given his just share of democratic freedom

[12] *Manila Times,* April 30, 1946

the Nacionalistas behaved in true yes-man fashion. They split over personal issues in the election, but with the election over they will fuse again, with the acclaimed new Quezon cracking the whip.

The strong opposition that Roxas talks so glibly about will be handled with a real Quezonian technique, with the big stick and the mailed fist. Roxas made a campaign boast that reveals his political philosophy nakedly: that he would restore "peace and order" within sixty days after he was elected. In his first interview after his election, he asserted he would "move with finesse" in curbing the "lawless elements," which to him are synonymous with the Hukbalahap, spearhead of the resistance movement in Central Luzon. This is the trouble spot in the Philippines today and Roxas expects to "restore domestic tranquillity" with the full support of the twenty-three thousand MPs that were partial to him in the election and the forty thousand regulars of the Philippine Army, armed with tanks, planes, mortars, and machine guns supplied by the United States Army.

It is easy to see in which direction the liberated Philippines under the risen leader Roxas are headed. The letter of an American GI to a Manila friend underscores the situation rather pointedly. The letter, written in March 1946, concerned Brigadier General Macario Peralta, cocky guerrilla leader whom Osmeña relieved as Deputy Chief of Staff of the Philippine Army and sent to Washington to work for war-benefit payments to widows and orphans, because of his pro-Roxas activities. Aboard the S.S. *Sea Cat* going over, Peralta made a hit with GIs. One of them wrote to a friend in Manila:

But M—— and I ran into General Peralta who was coming to the U.S. on the same ship. He's the Filipino brigadier-general with the big veterans organization and the reactionary reputation. He had been the leader of a big guerrilla group on Panay and is quite a powerful man in the Roxas camp. We talked with him for about two hours —found him young, sharp, personable. But he was extremely emotional, imbued with the spirit of *his own* military importance and completely aware of what he could do with his military machine. He claims to control 100,000 or more men, many more votes in Panay, and we were distinctly impressed by his attitude that if called upon (and he considered the possibility not unlikely) he would *have to get Taruc.* He evidenced the most complete confusion as to the real problems in the P.I., and contradicted himself every time he mentioned the word democracy, for the words power and army were always involved in his definition.

On April 27, 1946, the chairman of the committee in charge of the May Day celebration in Manila called at the office of the Chief of Police to get a permit. The permit was ready, but the Chief of Police refused to deliver it unless the applicant agreed to these five conditions:

1. No arms are to be carried in the demonstration.
2. No speeches attacking the United States Government.
3. No speeches attacking President-elect Roxas.
4. No subversive and/or pro-Russian speeches.
5. No hammer-and-sickle flags are to be displayed.

The Chief of Police merely acted under instructions from a higher authority. The implications of these conditions were clear. Under the New Order with the ex-collaborator Manuel Roxas at the helm, the democratic rights of the people will be "re-established," but criticism of the powers that be will not be tolerated. For the Philippine Republic must have "domestic tranquillity" if the country is to be saved—for its masters.

One month before his inauguration as President of the Philippines, Roxas, "moving with finesse," had clamped down on free assembly and free speech. What will it be like after he has consolidated his control over Philippine political life?

The Philippines are headed toward internal strife.

Postscript

"Now that Roxas has been elected president, I'm going straight. I'm going to give up crime and serve my sentence and become a law-abiding citizen. All I wanted was to do my bit in helping Roxas get some votes in Nueva Ecija."

The statement was from Nicasio Salonga y Rodriguez, twenty-five, No. 1 Manila gangster, in an interview at police headquarters in Manila on May 1, 1946, following his surrender to the authorities. Salonga "escaped" from the government penitentiary, twelve miles from Manila, a few days before the election with three companions and once outside were joined by their buddies to "do their bit" for Roxas in Nueva Ecija. "Inside job," said the press.

Immediately after his election had been conceded by Malacañan, President-elect Roxas asked High Commissioner McNutt to "sponsor" him in Washington. On May 8, he flew to Washington in McNutt's C-54 to present the Philippine case to the American people.

The plane stopped at Atsugi Airfield near Tokyo, where it was met by General MacArthur, who had an intimate chat with Roxas for ten minutes before the plane took off again.

The next day, MacArthur's headquarters released a long official statement clearing Roxas of all collaboration charges. "Roxas is no collaborationist," MacArthur said. "I have known him intimately for a quarter of a century and his views have been consistently anti-Japanese." And he added: "After General Wainwright's surrender, I eventually established contact with Roxas from Australia and thereafter he not only was instrumental in providing me with vital intelligence about the enemy but was one of the prime factors of the guerrilla movement."

Against this statement of the great Liberator, of course, are the facts. If Roxas is not a collaborationist, he certainly believes in giving collaborators first choice in the distribution of the spoils of office. He has surrounded himself with the same men who ran the government for Laurel and Vargas.

"The government has acted positively and decisively on the problem [of collaboration]," MacArthur further said in his statement. "Under the leadership of Roxas, then senate president, legislation was passed setting up the People's Court for such a purpose."

It was under Roxas' leadership that the People's Court bill was sabotaged in the Philippine Congress and every attempt made to emasculate the tribunal and to make the collaboration trials a mockery. Here again MacArthur knew the facts, but chose to indulge in rhetoric.

"The recent election," MacArthur concluded, "which selected Roxas for the presidency, reflected the repudiation by the Filipino people of irresponsible charges of collaboration made in foreign countries by those who lack adequate knowledge of the circumstances."

But Douglas MacArthur must have known that the Filipino people were not sufficiently informed of the real facts.